MW01195037

The I.W.W.:

Its First One Hundred Years

1905 – 2005

The history of an effort
to organize the working class

A corrected edition of the 1955 volume, *The I.W.W.: Its First Fifty Years* by Fred Thompson, with new chapters by Jon Bekken on the history of the Industrial Workers of the World from 1955 to 2005, and bibliographic notes providing sources for further exploration of IWW history.

Published by the
Industrial Workers of the World
Cincinnati, Ohio
www.iww.org

Photo Credits:
all photos from Industrial Workers of the World collection, Archives of Labor
History and Urban Affairs, Wayne State University; except for photos pages
43, 115, and 130 from Labadie Collection, University of Michigan; photo
page 201 by Frank Callahan; photos pages 211, 226, 230, 235, and 237 from
Industrial Worker files; photo page 214 by Bob Helms; photo page 220 © by
David Bacon/dbacon@igc.org.

About the Cover:
The black cat first became a prominent IWW icon in connection with the
harvest drives, symbolizing direct action on the job – sometimes rendered as
"bad luck to the boss." It has been adopted by syndicalist unions around the
world. Design by Alexis Buss.

ISBN: 978-0-917124-02-0

Approved for publication as official union literature by the General
Executive Board of the Industrial Workers of the World, February
2006.

Printed by union labor by Red Sun Press, Boston, Mass.

Contents

Preamble to the Constitution of the Industrial Workers of the World

(As Amended 1908 & 1999)

The working class and the employing class have nothing in common. There can be no peace so long as hunger and want are found among millions of working people and the few, who make up the employing class, have all the good things of life.

Between these two classes a struggle must go on until the workers of the world organize as a class, take possession of the means of production, abolish the wage system, and live in harmony with the earth.

We find that the centering of the management of industries into fewer and fewer hands makes the trade unions unable to cope with the ever-growing power of the employing class. The trade unions foster a state of affairs which allows one set of workers to be pitted against another set of workers in the same industry, thereby helping defeat one another in wage wars. Moreover, the trade unions aid the employing class to mislead the workers into the belief that the working class have interests in common with their employers.

These conditions can be changed and the interest of the working class upheld only by an organization formed in such a way that all its members in any one industry, or all industries if necessary, cease work whenever a strike or lockout is on in any department thereof, thus making an injury to one an injury to all.

Instead of the conservative motto, "A fair day's wage for a fair day's work," we must inscribe on our banner the revolutionary watchword, "Abolition of the wage system."

It is the historic mission of the working class to do away with capitalism. The army of production must be organized, not only for the everyday struggle with capitalists, but also to carry on production when capitalism shall have been overthrown. By organizing industrially we are forming the structure of the new society within the shell of the old.

Forward: The Long Memory

This is the story of the IWW's first 100 years. I have been a member of this union for over 50 of those years, during which I have seen it grow, fade, surge, drift, bottom out, and revel in victory. I have watched in dismay as again and again it consumed itself from within, wrangling over what ultimately amounted to nothing. I have seen it rise up in astonishing fits of solidarity. But through all the ups and downs, the vagaries of running an organization on a shoestring, the consistent attacks of pie cards and labor fakirs, and (since we never turn anyone away) the confusion generated by our share of self-righteous lunatics, there remains one thing I have never seen: I never saw us disappear. We just don't go away! We're still here in fair or windy weather, waving the red flag of solidarity, pricking the bubble of craft unionism, asserting the essential solidarity of all labor.

This union is amazingly powerful not because of our numbers, but because of our ideas. Good ideas don't go away.

I have often said that the long memory is the most radical idea in the world. We Wobblies have that long memory, carried forward year after year by the elders in our union. It has been my joy and perhaps my salvation over the years to seek out and learn from fellow workers like Fred Thompson, Jack Miller, Herb Edwards, Minnie Corder, and so many more. When I was a young Wobbly with no clear vision of my own class identity, they shared with me the substance of their lives, and in that sharing gave me a vision of who I am and where I came from that's more powerful, more exciting, and ultimately more useful than the best book I ever read.

I will never forget Fellow Worker Jack Miller, after describing working conditions in the forest in 1916, saying, "My union was my family, my religion, my only reason to go on living and struggling."

The long memory; the power of ideas; direct action; building economic democracy where we live and work, because we know if we can't build it there, the biggest ballot box in the world won't give it to us – that's us. And we're not going away. Ever.

Last year we celebrated our centenary in Chicago at a gala concert where I was invited to speak. I thought back over the years when I soapboxed with San Francisco's Phil Melman, or sat enthralled by the oratory of Frank Cedervall. I was holding within myself a vision of their eloquent courage, their raw persistence, and the stark simplicity of their sublime rants as I rose and said:

"Fellow workers! The Industrial Workers of the World is going to organize the entire working class. What is the working class, fellow workers? The working class is anyone who has a boss and works for wages. Always remember, class is not defined by income level but by your relationship to the means of production. If you don't own the tools of your production, if you don't own your workplace, if all you're doing is selling your labor energy to get a paycheck, it doesn't matter if you're a college professor or a ditch digger – you're in the working class and better be proud of it. Why, the middle class is just a joke made up by the bosses to keep us fighting against each other.

"Now, the Industrial Workers of the World is going to organize the working class into one big union of all skilled, semi-skilled, and unskilled workers, organized by industry instead of by craft. Look, I was walking out of an airport in Portland when I ran straight into a picket line. The flight attendants from Eastern Airlines were on strike. I said, 'Give me a picket sign!' As we circled around the sidewalk, I said to the workers around me, 'Look up there, you can see flight attendants in your union walking into work up at United and over there at Northwest. What do you think about that? Isn't that union scabbing? What would it be like if every wage worker on every airline, from the pilots to the janitors, belonged to one international airline workers' industrial union – would you be out here picketing? No! You might even wind up owning an airline!'

"That's the idea: industrial unions joining together in one big union – the O.B.U. – and then, fellow workers, the general strike. When the clock strikes and the signal is heard, millions of workers put their hands in their pockets and everything stops. Then we find out at last who has the real power.

"Is it the boss? [Shout "No!"]

"Is it the Congress? [Louder "No!"]

"Is it the President? [The "No!" heard round the world]

"Who has the power? ["We Do!"]

"Who has the power? ["WE DO!!"]

"Power in the union!

"Thank you!"

So there you have it. Read this book. Study it. It tells the story of where we've been. Then take what you've learned and use it to take us where we need to be.

Yours for the O.B.U.,
Utah Phillips, X342908

About the Authors

When the first part of this volume was published in 1955, several reviews expressed surprise that an "official history" should be so candid. Fred Thompson, who wrote it, liked to quote what Lissagary wrote in his participant history of the Paris Commune: that to glamorize such events and omit what may embarrass is like giving sailors a chart that leaves out the reefs and shoals. That spirit has animated successive editions of this history.

Both writers have been active participants in many of the events about which they write, and have talked with participants (and reviewed contemporary and historical accounts) in events they missed.

Fred Thompson was born in St. John, Canada, in 1900, and became a member of the Socialist Party of Canada in his youth. As secretary of his local he was in correspondence with radicals on both sides of the border. He worked in a paperbox factory, a sugar refinery, and the Halifax shipyards where he was involved in his first strike, went west in 1920, and joined the One Big Union of Canada. He came to the United States in 1922, worked in a Hoquiam sawmill and on various construction projects along the west coast, joining the IWW in San Francisco in September. The following April he was arrested in Marysville and after two trials was convicted as an IWW organizer under the California Criminal Syndicalist law.

After his release in 1927 from San Quentin, where he had the company of over 100 other victims of the same law, Thompson was active in efforts to repair the 1924 split in the IWW. He was also elected to the General Executive Board representing Construction Workers Industrial Union 310. At various times he edited IWW newspapers, and was an instructor at the union's Work Peoples College, an organizer in Detroit and Cleveland in the mid-1930s, secretary of the Cleveland Metal and Machinery Workers Industrial Union 440 from 1943-1946, and author of several IWW pamphlets. He died in Chicago in 1990.

Jon Bekken was born in Chicago in 1960, and grew up in San Diego, California, where he joined the IWW in 1978. He has worked as a typesetter, office worker, recycler, and teacher. He has served as IWW General Secretary-Treasurer, on its General Executive Board and International Solidarity Commission, and as coordinator of the Education Workers Industrial Union 620 Organizing Committee. He is presently editor of the *Industrial Worker*, and associate professor of communication at Albright College.

This is the third edition of this work, which has been out of print for many years. The second edition appeared in 1976 as *The IWW: Its First 70 Years*, with a chapter by then-*Industrial Worker* editor Patrick Murfin on the 1955-1975 period. That material has been extensively revised for this volume, but Murfin's chapter remains an important source for discussion of those years.

This work is drawn from first-hand accounts of IWW campaigns, many published in the *Industrial Worker* and the *General Organization Bulletin*, as well as from IWW archives and other sources. As such, even more than other histories, it is a collective product. Drafts of the 1955-2005 chapters were circulated to participants in many of the events it chronicles, as well as to other IWW activists. Among the many who helped out with their recollections, corrections, and challenges to the way particular events were interpreted, we owe particular thanks to: Alexis Buss, Robert Helms, Arthur J. Miller, Steve Ongerth, Robert Rush, and Evan Wolfson. Three *Industrial Worker* interns helped with research and related tasks: Wesley Enzinna, Keith King, and Andrew Linke. William McLaughlin did the final proof-reading on the book.

May 1, 2006

A Note on the Text:

The text of *The IWW: Its First 50 Years* (chapters 1-13) is reproduced here as originally published, except that punctuation and typographical errors have been corrected and some archaic language updated. In two places, updated information included in the 1976 edition as asterisked footnotes has been interpolated into the text in brackets. The original numbered notes are reproduced at the end of each chapter, followed by new notes on sources for further research that incorporate material from the 1976 edition and subsequent scholarship.

1. Why the IWW Was Started

The IWW was started in 1905 by "seasoned old unionists," as Gene Debs called them,[1] who realized that American labor could not win with the sort of labor movement it had. There was too much "organized scabbery" of one union on another, too much jurisdictional squabbling, too much autocracy, and too much hobnobbing between prosperous labor leaders and the millionaires in the National Civic Federation. There was too little solidarity, too little straight labor education, and consequently too little vision of what could be won, and too little will to win it.

Building a new labor movement was not a project to be undertaken lightly. Even to build a new craft union was something then to undertake with great caution and secrecy, but the six men whose meeting in the fall of 1904 gave eventual birth to the IWW aimed at one organization of all labor to replace the existing labor movement. When they met it was only 18 years since the AFL had been set up to rout the Knights of Labor and to protect the craft unions from the inroads that its greater vision of solidarity was making on their vested interests. The Knights had been rendered impotent only ten years earlier, and labor leaders still watched vigilantly lest any similar movement break out. Those who could be counted upon to help were few and were already active in the existing labor movement, its socially minded or radical minority, and were engaged in vigorous disputes among themselves over theory and policy. To identify themselves with this new effort might mean the loss of their union positions, and worse yet, turning over those positions to reactionaries who wanted not only the job, but the opportunity to make the unions more acceptable to the plutocrats on the Civic Federation.

The six men who met in Chicago in November of 1904 to consider what might be done to correct the inadequacies of the labor movement did so secretly. These six were Clarence Smith, secretary of the American Labor Union; Thomas Haggerty, editor of that union's paper, *The Voice of Labor*; George Estes and W. L. Hall, president and secretary of the United Brotherhood of Railway Employees; Isaac Cowan, American representative of the Amalgamated Society of Engineers; and William E. Trautmann, editor of the *Brauer-Zeitung*, official organ of the United Brewery Workmen. Involved, but unable to attend, were Gene

Debs, long interested in industrial unionism especially for the railroad workers, and Charles O. Sherman, secretary of the United Metal Workers. The common interests of these men perhaps best explain why the IWW was born; and their discordant interests, the troubles of the labor movement that the IWW was to inherit.

The United Brotherhood of Railway Employees consisted of men mostly in the Chicago and nearby Indiana yards, and some in Kansas, who had been with Debs' American Railway Union in 1894, and who resented the action whereby he "had left them without a fighting industrial union and forced them to enter the scab craft movements after he changed the ARU to a political movement," as one of them described their situation.[2] Estes had helped organize the Order of Railroad Telegraphers and, when given the job of revising its constitution, had urged a federation of all railroad brotherhoods, and the dropping of the phrase in its statement of purpose, "no quarrel with capital." When the ORT joined the AFL, Estes and those supporting his program withdrew and with members from other railroad crafts started the UBRE. However, it felt too isolated and that year, 1904, it had applied to the AFL for a charter. This was refused, as the Scranton Declaration of 1901 restricted industrial unionism to the coal mines, and to avoid antagonizing the railroad brotherhoods that the AFL hoped might join it.[3]

The United Metal Workers had dropped out of the AFL that year. In 1900 Charles Sherman, with Gompers' approval, had gotten the three Chicago locals of metal workers, which were affiliated directly with the AFL, to call a convention to launch their own international. Their originally extensive jurisdiction had been steadily eaten away. After organizing the coppersmiths 95 percent throughout the United States, these men were surrendered, against their own wishes, to the Sheet Metal Workers. A special charter issued in 1902 lopped off the bridge and structural iron workers. The expense of efforts to adjust jurisdictional claims had exceeded $4,000, and the 1904 convention of the AFL ordered the union broken up into further pieces. On referendum the United Metal Workers voted 92 percent to disaffiliate and to adopt an industrial structure. Though this had meant more opposition and raids, it grew more rapidly, according to Sherman, after its separation from the AFL.[4]

The Amalgamated Society of Engineers had been brought here by skilled machinists coming from Britain with a strong attachment for the semi-industrial structure of their union that had been the model of progressivism from 1851 until the "new unionism" was born on the docks of Britain in the 1890s.[5] Its American section had just been thrown out of the AFL on jurisdictional grounds in 1904.

The United Brewery Workmen was fighting for preservation of its industry-wide jurisdiction. Inside it a schism had been developing between the previously dominant socialistic old-timers and the rising crop of "major party" labor politicians. It had been born of America's first "stay-in" strike, in the Jackson Brewery in Cincinnati in 1884. In those days to keep the brauerei-knechte or "brewery peons" at beck and call, management housed them on the property in a "schalander." They were still mostly German-speaking in 1904. In this first stay-in strike, the workers sent management out, barricaded themselves with barrels of beer against the state troopers, and had a food supply to last them for weeks. Every shot at the barricade poured precious amber fluid down the streets, unstained by blood. The employers gave in, and the union was founded. It declared it would be industrial, and among its purposes was one of educating its members to make good beer to add to the joy of the Cooperative Commonwealth.[6]

The Brewery Workmen grew to a national organization, affiliating with the AFL in 1887. Many of its locals were affiliated with the Knights of Labor. This was encouraged because of the extra boycott power it gave, for the union relied heavily upon this weapon and was engaged for fourteen years (1888-1902) in a boycott against the National Brewery Owners Association. As a national body it joined the Knights in 1893; then, under penalty of losing its AFL charter, withdrew in 1896, still urging its individual members to stay with the badly routed Knights to build the greater solidarity. That same year the coopers' union demanded it get the brewery coopers. Then in 1898 came a demand to surrender the engineers. In 1902 the AFL ordered the firemen and engineers out of it. At the 1904 AFL convention the teamsters demanded 10,000 beer truck drivers. The brewery workers voted on referendum 34,612 to 367 not to surrender to these claims.

At the Brewery Workmen's convention in September 1904 there had been some talk of leaving the AFL and joining with the American Labor Union, the other major participant in this November conference; but it was plain that the ALU must become a bigger union to make such a switch possible, and enable the Brewery Workmen, if so affiliated, to enforce boycotts and resist jurisdictional raids. The brewery workers were also held back by an internal "right-left" schism, born of the political policy of "reward your friends," and the need of city central labor bodies for ties with whichever party got in, ties that were indispensable in the racketeering in which central labor bodies, especially through their building trades, were at the time heavily involved. Trautmann, representing the progressive brewery forces, attended both this and the January conference without notifying his union.[7]

The American Labor Union had been founded by the Western Federation of Miners in 1902 because these metal miners wanted a class-wide labor body with which to affiliate. It had not flourished, and a chief reason for this November conference and eventually for the determination to launch the IWW, was the hope of these western metal miners and of the men they had rallied to the American Labor Union, and of the progressive forces around Trautmann in the Brewery Workmen, that the obvious inadequacy and misdirection of the labor movement might now make it possible, by mergers and re-organization and the organization of the unorganized, to build an organization large enough to give the brewery workers the power to boycott any scab beer, and to provide each affiliate with the unstinted backing of all.

The Western Federation of Miners was frontier unionism, the organization of workers who had become "wage slaves" of mining corporations rather recently acquired by back-east absentee ownership. They built their union when they were not yet "broken in" to the discipline of business management. It had the militancy of the undisciplined recruits who fought for the ten-hour day here in the 1830s, or for Chartism in England in the same era, or those who staged the sit-down strikes of France in 1936 and here in 1937. From the founding of the Western Federation in 1893, its story for twelve years is that of a continuous search for solidarity. Metal miners had been organized locally before that time, and formed their federation the better to back each other up in the increasingly hard battles forced upon them by well-heeled big business management. The idea of federating the various local unions was said to have been born "in the Ada County jail" and bull pens where hundreds of them were herded after the Couer d'Alene strike of 1892. It affiliated with the AFL, but its delegates to the AFL Cincinnati convention of 1896 came away not only disappointed with the refusal to aid their big fight in Leadville, but with a feeling that they had not been associating with union men, or with men possessing the moral or intellectual fiber ever to become good union men.[8]

They left the AFL and launched the Western Labor Union. The miners had reasons for building unions for non-miners. The mining territory was, apart from the miners, unorganized; the AFL outside of Denver and a few cities had done little western organizing except on the coast. Workers outside the miners wanted a union, and the Western Federation either had to take them in or build them one, for it needed to have them organized and on their side. How their strikes went depended largely on how the rest of the community that didn't work in the mines stood. Their strike experience had shown it made a substantial difference whether state politics was under labor-Populist influence or not. In the Cripple Creek strike of 1891-94 the Populist Governor had used the National Guard to restrain the private armies recruited by mine management. In the Leadville strike two years later the Governor swore the scabs into the National Guard and deputized the business element to give the miners a hard time. Gene Debs was on hand to help them organize the Western Labor Union and teach them socialism and solidarity. In the second battle of the Coeur d'Alene 1899-1901, Federal troops demonstrated the power of the back east owners, compelling some miners to work at gun point, others to build their own bull pens, inventing the rustling card system so no man could hunt a job without the sheriff's approval, and using Governor Steunenberg, whom the miners had helped elect as a Populist, to oust the elected local authorities who might have some sympathy with the strikers.

The miners wanted a nationwide labor movement that would not only help provide beans and bacon when long strikes had drained their own treasuries, but would exert some pressure to expose the daily press that lied about them and that thereby laid the carpet for atrocities by federal troops. Class-wide solidarity was not only an ideal with them; it was a bread-and-butter necessity, the only conceivable means to protect their wives against the atrocities of federal troops, and their children from the hunger imposed by absentee owners.

The Western Labor Union worried the Washington, D.C., heads of the AFL. Frank Morrison, secretary of the AFL, came to Salt Lake City in 1902 to attend the conventions of the Western Federation and its projection, the Western Labor Union. He threatened that if they did not re-affiliate, he would build a rival union. The delegates knew what that would mean: their dismemberment by crafts in an industry that made industrial unionism a matter of necessity, not one of choice. They feared too it would crush the spirit of their union, and they sensed that the anti-capitalist spirit that they cultivated in themselves and the community was an essential part of the defense of their bread and butter. Mark Hanna had launched the National Civic Federation in 1900 to housebreak unionism, to confine its growth to those fields where management could use it, and to emasculate it by a united front of labor leaders and captains of industry against all socialistic and insurgent elements. Miners knew that this growth of what was called "responsible unionism," in which the members were responsible to the leaders whom Mark Hanna called "the labor lieutenants of the captains of industry," meant more "sell-outs" of the sort imposed on the steel workers in 1901. So they met Morrison's threat by changing the name of the Western Labor Union to American Labor Union, a challenge to the AFL in its back east empire. To spice the retort they endorsed Debs' new Socialist Party, partly because it was an antidote to Morrison's and Gompers' and Mark Hanna's poison, partly because they thought socialism might be a good idea, and partly because they liked Debs who had been around in their strikes making speeches to help their families keep a stiff upper lip.[9]

Between then and this November 1904 conference they had fought a two-year war in Colorado. The union had spent over $400,000 in this struggle against the companies, the militia and the Citizens' Alliance. Its members had been put in bull pens, its officers repeatedly indicted. White-capped vigilantes had invaded its members' homes to deport them; the right of habeas corpus had vanished; the miners wives were subjected to outrages and terrorism. As the secretary of the Western Federation, Bill Haywood, told the January conference: "The miners of Colorado fought alone the capitalist class of the United States; we don't want to fight that way again."

The American Labor Union had grown only to about 16,000 members, not counting the 27,000 in its chief affiliate the Western Federation. But these included the two thousand or more in the UBRE which was affiliated with ALU, and those in Amalgamated Society.[10] Its paper *The Voice of Labor,* edited by a left-wing socialist, Thomas J. Haggerty, often called Father Haggerty, was an effective challenge to craft unionism, organized scabbery, and the Gompers-Hanna unholy alliance. It seemed plain that unless the progressive forces in the labor movement could be rallied to build something new, the metal miners would have to fight that way again, the brewery workers would be dismembered, and that an unbridled and reactionary autocracy would stifle these progressive forces that could be found to some degree in all unions. This is the chief explanation why these six men met in November 1904, to consider whether there was any chance of building a labor movement in which unions would support each other and not, in the name of sacred contracts, scab on each other.

As these six men met it was plain their combined mass lacked the gravitational pull necessary to start a new movement which it would seem prudent for progressive forces to join. The labor history of the last few years made them reckon, however, that a sufficient mass could be rallied. There had been great recent changes in the environment of the labor movement: first "the Morganization of industry" or mushrooming of great trusts starting with U.S. Steel in 1900; growth in the size of factories and consequent interdependence of crafts; the open shop campaign of the Citizens' Alliances from 1902 on a nationwide scale with backing of National Association of Manufacturers. The new model for capital organization, U.S. Steel, had promptly broken the old Amalgamated steel union in the strike of 1901 and had locked unions out of the nation's basic metal industry by lulling Gompers into inaction in the belief that Morgan was a "friend of labor." On the Great Lakes the Lake Carriers was organizing to drive off unionism. In the then very important molding trade, a much-prized national agreement had given way to a current attempt of the employers' association to rout the Molders throughout the nation. The Machinists similarly after the Murray Hill Truce now found themselves for several years in ceaseless conflict with the National Metal Trades Association. In the building trades, the racketeer unionism of Skinny Madden and Parks had played out; AFL unions had been compelled to merge with dual company unions; their sympathetic strike machinery was disrupted, and a most unpalatable arbitration scheme imposed in major cities. On the railroads the unions existed only for such crafts as the owners let organize; clerks were not allowed a union. On the Louisville & Nashville and other roads the shop crafts were engaged in long and unsupported strikes for survival. On New York's Interborough Transit, as these six men met, August Belmont, bell-wether of the National Civic Federation, was using the ace strikebreaker James Farley to build up an army of scabs should the men dare strike. The Butcher

Workmen had just collapsed before the onslaughts of the Beef Trust
in the strike (made famous by Sinclair's *The Jungle*) that ended with
unconditional surrender in September 1904.

Could a labor union of the sort needed for this new industrial situation be built by the reorganization of the crafts and the enrollment
of millions of unorganized? The six men decided there might be a
chance, and invited 36 of those they figured best able to help to attend
a secret conference to be held January 2, 1905.

The six men were all in the general sense of the term, socialist
as, in that age, were most staunch unionists, either espousing some
specific socialist program or expressing a general faith in some vague
"cooperative commonwealth" as the solution to the "labor question."
Even most old-line union preambles expressed such ideas, and rather
unavoidably, since the reason for their formation was to win quarrels
with employers, and these quarrels would arise no matter what they
won so long as the employer-employee relation continued. Consequently, to contemplate final or complete victory for labor had for
decades been recognized as the contemplation of some social order
successor to capitalism in which workers owned their jobs and the
equipment with which they worked either individually or collectively.
While the practical reason for their meeting was the need for greater
labor union solidarity, it was plain to them that the solution of this
practical problem would assure the solution of the larger "labor question," and this was emphasized in their invitation:

"Asserting our confidence in the ability of the working class, if cor-
rectly organized on both political and industrial lines, to take possession of and operate successfully ... the industries of the country;

"Believing that working-class political expression, through the Socialist ballot, in order to be sound, must have its economic counter-
part in a labor organization builded as the structure of socialist society, embracing within itself the working class in approximately the
same groups and departments and industries that the workers would
assume in the working-class administration of the cooperative commonwealth;

"We invite you to meet us at Chicago, Monday, Jan. 2, 1905, in
secret conference to discuss ways and means of uniting the working
people of America on correct revolutionary principles, regardless of
any general labor organization of past or present, and only restricted
by such basic principles as will insure its integrity as a real protector

of the interests of the workers."

Size was important for solving the practical problems that had brought these six men together. In retrospect, it appears that they erected a barrier to size by this prenatal injection of revolutionary theory. While the January conference in Wostas Hall was attended by 23 persons, representing nine organizations, it represented very little more union force than the November conference. Of them 18 came from these same unions, though now Moyer, Haywood and O'Neil represented the Western Federation directly; Sherman and Kirkpatrick came from the United Metal Workers; Trautmann had brought along Frank Kraft of the Brewery Workmen. New participants were "Mother" Jones of the United Mine Workers, Shurtleff of the International Musical Union, Schmitt and Guild from the Bakers, the former the editor of its *Journal*, and W. J. Pinkerton of the Switchmen. Debs was prevented from attending by illness. Though representing no union, A. M. Simons, editor of the *International Socialist Review*, was present, and though not originally invited, Frank Bohn, national organizer for the Socialist Trade & Labor Alliance, who happened to be passing through Chicago, was asked to participate, and did. This brought the gathering to 25. They decided to go through with the attempt, and issued a Manifesto calling for an Industrial Union Congress in Chicago on June 27. When this met, it became the Industrial Workers of the World.[11]

This Manifesto called for "the economic organization of the working class without affiliation with any political party"; industrial organization, with "industrial autonomy internationally"; transfers between local or national or international unions to be universal; a central defense or strike fund to which all members were to contribute equally; its general administration to be conducted "in harmony with the recognition of the irrepressible conflict between the capitalist class and the working class." It argued for the need for such an organization from the technological changes in industry, the organization of capital, and recent bitter experience in strikes.

The proposals of this Manifesto came, however, to be considered less on their obvious union merits than on the suspicion of what political motives might lie behind them. The Manifesto was much more a union document than the letter of Nov. 29. It went into the socialist issue only by including in its criticism of the craft union movement the comment that "it is blind to the possibility of establishing an industrial democracy, wherein there shall be no wage slavery, but where the workers will own the tools which they operate, and the product which they alone will enjoy." The committee circulated 180,000 copies of the Manifesto, and the reaction was largely the question, what were the bifurcated socialists planning to do to the unions now? One good indirect result: the industrial jurisdiction of the Brewery Workmen was temporarily restored.

To make at all clear the reception of this Manifesto it is necessary to consider at least briefly the past relations of the unions and the American socialist movement. Immigrants, especially Germans, had brought over the controversies of Marx, Lassalle and Bernstein; such books as Bellamy's *Looking Backward* had made a strong impression on American labor; the old Greenback and Populist movements had become impregnated with some of this more systematic socialist theory; the fact that the major labor movements of most other countries gave at least lip service to socialist ideals, had its influence; both the immigrant and native socialist movements had carried on propaganda and sought converts and positions in the unions.

A major argument within socialist ranks was over the role of unions in relation to their program. Complete Marxists said that not only was the will to build a new social order an outgrowth of the daily union struggle, but that the unions themselves were the "cells of the future society." They felt union activity was part of the work of a socialist. Complete Lassalleans said workers could gain nothing by unions, that the unions diverted the efforts of labor into futile channels from the building of a party by which to triumph. But all were sympathetic toward unionism and strikers. Some of both these divisions said that the future was one of increasing misery for labor until it reached the intolerable point where labor woke up and somehow made itself supreme; others of both these divisions held that either by union or legislative gains labor would steadily improve its lot as it increased its competence to run the world. Some said victory would be by ballots; some that it would come only by violent revolution. Some felt the way to win was to start colonies to practice socialism; some that it required the growth of select groups studying and agreeing upon fine points of doctrine; others that it was by building reform parties with a mass appeal, even if this involved slogans in which the leaders themselves could not believe. Socialism was far from a uniform body of thought, but most socialists felt that it was good to "bore from within" the unions, to seek converts votes, and positions.

Marx's First International, the IWMA, mortally wounded by the affright of British labor after the Paris Commune of 1871, and by schisms between himself and Bakunin, moved to New York in 1872 and was dissolved at a convention in Philadelphia, July 15, 1876. Four days later the delegates merged with a few American labor political groups to found the Workingmen's Party of the United States which bore the brunt of agitation in the spontaneous strike movement of 1877, and at the close of the next year changed its name to Socialistic Labor Party of North America. It sought friendly relations with the unions, particularly with those of the Gompers persuasion until 1890 when it began its quarrel with the AFL, and, with the final "ic" off the first term in its name, began its reshaping under Daniel De Leon. For five years it gave its attention to the Knights of Labor, then, losing out in that venture, De Leon grabbed what he could to form the Social-ist Trade & Labor Alliance, a union completely dominated by SLP. This body started out with 20,000 but dwindled rapidly though 228 charters were issued prior to its Buffalo convention in 1898; after that convention the Central Federated Union in New York with its locals quit, leaving the ST&LA little more than a "paper" union in which the members of the SLP doubled as union members. It reported 1,450 members in 1905 and entered about 1,200 into the IWW.

One circumstance that shaped its character was the "violence" ma-nia of the mid-eighties. Largely under the influence of Johann Most, a large section of the then-appreciable anarchist movement and of those socialists who placed little hope in the election process, adopted the Pittsburgh program of physical force in 1883 and pushed the dynamite philosophy that made the conviction of the Haymarket anarchists easy despite their obvious innocence. The aftermath was a strong employer offensive (the more effective as neither AFL nor K of L had defended the Haymarket victims) and the first clear triumph of conservative bureaucracy in the unions, denouncing all radicalism as tainted with this violence. This was easier as the dynamite enthusiasts had scorned the union movement and its 8-hour campaign. De Leon, appealing to leftists who tended to assume that the plutocrats would yield to nothing short of a triumph of arms, preached the doctrine as "unques-tionable" laws of society, that in election the workers must establish their right to rule, but that "right without might is illusory; in other words, the field of physical force is the unavoidable court of second and last resort," and thirdly "He who cannot vote right, ever will shoot wrong."[12] This he termed putting the class struggle "on the civilized plane," and jumped to the conclusion that for any group to advocate a major social change without endorsing a political party and program to legislate it implied "physical forcism."

From the 1890 breach with the AFL and the 1898 breach with the Knights, the De Leon group reached the further conclusion that the labor union movement was a corrupt mobilization of labor for the defense and perpetuation of capitalism, and that workers alike for everyday struggles and ultimate emancipation must build socialist industrial unionism. The possibilities of such unionism as visualized in the ST&LA and more clearly yet with the launching of the IWW, so long as the De Leonites could exert a substantial influence in it, tended to replace the prospect of "physical force" as the field of last encounter with the prospect of a lockout of employers by an organized working class, to supply might to the revolutionary SLP ballot.

Though the ST&LA had dwindled instead of growing, the De Leon movement was an irritant to the AFL leadership. The presence of Bohn, national organizer of the ST&LA, at the January conference, and his signature to the Manifesto, was taken by most union organs as evidence that De Leon was attempting to use this need of metal miners, brewery and other workers for a class-wide industrial union movement, to build a bigger ST&LA which he could dominate. The discussion on the Manifesto running for months in the columns of De Leon's *Daily People* clearly showed that this was the hope and plan of those SLP members who favored participation.[13] This hurt the chances for the new movement the more because of recent splits in the socialist movement.

Since most socialists felt it necessary somehow to get along with the unions, even when they were hostile to socialist ideals, and since the interest in the labor movement that led a worker to become a socialist often led him to be active enough in his union to become an officer of it, the switch of the only socialist party in the country to a policy of devoting most of its effort to an attack on the existing unions, created a demand for a socialist movement less doctrinaire than De Leon's and able to get along with the unions as they were. Debs' conversion to socialism after the Pullman strike provided this movement with its most popular and effective exponent. He turned the remnants of his American Railway Union into the Social Democracy of America, which, by merger with defections from the SLP, in 1901 became the Socialist Party of America. Between the two parties raged such a war as can be found only between competing radicals. The more Marxian and "class struggle" tendencies in the young Socialist Party were focused around the *International Socialist Review*, a monthly magazine issued in Chicago and edited by Simons, who also attended the January conference and signed the Manifesto. All this put the proposal for a new union movement to end organized scabbery and Civic Federation hobnobbing in the middle of vociferous arguments between different schools of socialists. Most socialist papers condemned the new effort then and throughout its formative years, chiefly, as Debs repeatedly insisted, not because of any principle or sound argument, but out of personal hostility toward De Leon.[14]

These circumstances not only prevented the proposals of the Manifesto from being considered on their merits, but beset the new union with internal quarrels that almost killed it in its infancy. From the advantaged view of hindsight it seems plain that had neither Simons nor Bohn attended that January conference, and had these extraneous political quarrels been sidetracked, it would have been much better for the IWW and the labor movement.

An indirect good was the preservation of the industrial jurisdiction of the Brewery Workmen. Trautmann, editor of their paper, was deposed for his participation in this new venture; the issue went to referendum of the brewery workers, so that according to Trautmann, with 10,481 votes cast for him and only 9,157 against, the AFL Executive counsel bought his ouster by restoring the charter revoked in 1904 in turn for counting out enough of these votes. The threat of the IWW was again to preserve industrial union jurisdiction for the brewery workers in 1908 and 1912.[15]

To the Industrial Union Congress June 27, 1905, came 70 delegates empowered to install the Western Federation, the American Labor Union, the United Brotherhood of Railway Employees, and the Socialist Trade and Labor Alliance, a total membership of 50,827 according to the memberships claimed by each. Also came 72 delegates without power to install, and 61 individual delegates able to install only themselves. With great oratory and repeated assurances by Debs and De Leon that here was common grounds for all socialists to meet, they launched the Industrial Workers of the World with little more actual backing than at that November conference of six men, minus the hopes then held of including the Brewery Workmen. There could be no blindness to the difficulties ahead; it was started because there was obvious need for a union of, by, and for the working class, and hopes that it might so conduct its affairs that locals and internationals would join, and great masses of unorganized workers become organized through its efforts.

Notes:

1. In article August 1906 in *The Worker,* a socialist publication, reprinted in *Daily People,* Aug. 12, 1906.
2. Quoted from Pinkerton, one of its delegates to 2nd Convention, in *Daily People,* Nov. 4, 1906.
3. Re Estes, *Daily People,* Feb. 23, 1905.
4. Re Sherman and United Metal Workers, *Daily People,* June 3, 1905.
5. Barou, *British Trade Unions,* p. 15.
6. Trautmann in *OBU Monthly,* October 1937.
7. Sources: *Daily People,* March 9 and April 30, 1905, and Perlman & Taft, Vol. IV, pp. 363-365.
8. See Jensen, *Heritage of Conflict,* p. 60.
9. All was not friendly between ALU and WFM, according to Trautmann in *IUB,* Feb. 22, 1908.
10. Membership of the American section of the ASE seems about 4,000; Trautmann reported to second convention that for one year its tax to ALU had been $2,688.13.
11. The Manifesto has been frequently republished, as in Brissenden's *Launching,* in *Bill Haywood's Book,* as a separate leaflet on several occasions, and is available as the first item in Kornbluh's *Rebel Voices.*
12. Editorial, *Daily People,* Feb. 3, 1905. For the general history of American radicalism in 19th century see both Vols. II and IV of the *History of Labor in the United States,* and David's *The Haymarket Affair.*
13. Examples: *Daily People,* Jan. 26: "With the conception of a Socialist Union comes the cessation of the struggle for higher wages and shorter hours, and the struggle for working class supremacy begins." On Feb. 3, W. Cox argued, "The new economic organization must be affiliated with SLP or party must fight it." The March 19 issue showed how completely SLP dominated ST&LA. On March 31, Olive M. Johnson writes: "It is impossible that the ST&LA can desire a separation of the political and economic organization of labor, ... or even passively submit to it." In the April 1 issue, H.J. Schade proposed that the initiation fee of the new union be used for subscription to *Weekly People,* and E.J. Rounier argues: "The Constitution of the SLP designates any union not under the control of the party as pure and simple. The SLP insists that the

economic organization be controlled by the political one."

14. Debs wrote in the *Worker,* August 1906 (reprinted *People,* Aug. 12, 1906): "It may be that DeLeon has designs upon the Socialist Party and expects to use the IWW as a means of disrupting it; ... if he succeeds, it will be because his enemies in the Socialist Party, in their bitter personal hostility to him, denounce the revolutionary IWW and support the reactionary AFL and thereby play directly into his hands."

15. Same sources as Footnote 7.

General Sources:

Brissenden's *IWW* is the best work available as yet (his 1913 monograph, *The Launching of the IWW,* offers a more extensive discussion of that topic), but covers the story with fullness only up to 1913, and sketchily to 1918. Gambs' *Decline of the IWW,* purportedly taking up where Brissenden left off, indicates no such familiarity with the subject as Brissenden had. The story of the IWW in short is given rather well in several chapters of Vol. IV of the *History of Labor in the United States,* that volume written by Perlman and Taft. The first 87 pages of Melvyn Dubofsky's *We Shall Be All* and his essay, "Origins of Western Working-Class Radicalism" (*Labor History,* Spring 1966) also treat the IWW's founding.

For the Western Federation of Miners, see Jensen's *Heritage of Conflict,* which is a detailed history of that union, but takes a rather hostile attitude toward the IWW. *Bill Haywood's Book* also contains much information. The most complete account of Father Haggerty is by Robert Doherty in *Labor History,* Winter 1962. The *Proceedings of the First Convention of the IWW* were reprinted in the 1960s, and are also available online through the IWW's web site, www.iww.org, and the Marxists Internet Archive, www.marxists.org.

A series in the *Industrial Worker* in 1950, entitled "Hard Rock Miner," considers the relations of the IWW and the WFM and SLP in great detail. Another series, "The IWW Tells Its Own Story," starting in *Industrial Solidarity* Dec. 23, 1930, and continuing in *Industrial Worker* to August 2, 1932, gives the story in much more detail than it is given in this book up to 1919. In 1945, to mark the 40th anniversary, the *Industrial Worker* ran a series, "The First Forty Years," and much other commemorative material, largely written by those who had participated in the making of the IWW's history, in issues from June to September. The *One Big Union Monthly* of 1919-1920 is now available in many libraries in Greenwood reprints and includes Harold Lord Varney's series on the history of the IWW. Because of space limitations, this book has avoided detail on those aspects where detail is readily available.

2. Getting Started (1905-1908)

Though the founding convention of the IWW ended with declarations of affiliation by bodies that gave it a claimed membership of about 52,000 to start with, it did not start with this membership. Apart from the individuals who had joined, it started out with the 1,100 members the American Labor Union entered on August 1, and the $817.59 that John Riordan of the ALU had left after winding up the affairs of the ALU. This was a substantial let-down from the 16,750 that ALU had reported to the first convention. Sherman's United Metal Workers entered 700 members, not the 3,000 it had claimed. When the Socialist Trade & Labor Alliance entered 1,200 members, this with the UBRE and individuals and miscellaneous groups brought the membership for September to 4,247. By that time individual recruiting was under way and raised the membership to 5,078 in early October and by Nov. 1, to 7,800. It stayed at about that level until the membership of the Metal Department doubled in February and again in March to 3,000 bringing the total on April 1 to 13,266.

This growth in the Metal Department was almost entirely in Schenectady among General Electric workers. Punch Press Operators Union No. 224 of that city was one of the bodies represented at the first convention. Now with the aid of a SLP group and others in a Workmen's Sick & Death Benefit Society, it promoted the IWW idea in this plant employing 17,000, some two-thirds of whom were under various AFL contracts. The IWW in the summer of 1906 built up a membership of about 2,500 among these workers, taking over some craft locals intact, and keeping them as 17 craft affiliates of its Industrial Council of Metal and Machinery Workers. The favorite method used in this first auspicious organizing campaign of the new union was to sit down until grievances in a department got adjusted. This tactic was devised to end the run-around that management and business agents had been giving the men on their grievances, and it was practiced also by the AFL union members in the plant. On hourly rates they drew their pay while staging sitdowns lasting from a few minutes in some cases to most of a shift in others.[1]

Strikes, almost entirely in the east, steadily drained the organization's resources, with no promising development outside of this in Schenectady, which led to the first stay-in of the century in December,

Moyer, Haywood and Pettibone's show trial preoccupied the Western Federation of Miners in the IWW's first two years.

noted later. In some of these the AFL sent in scabs. In Youngstown the tinners and slaters, previously divided in four crafts, joined the IWW and struck; the employer wired the AFL for scabs, and these were sent despite the protest of the local Painters. The AFL replaced IWW strikers in Yonkers and San Pedro. In contrast the IWW bricklayers in Cleveland walked out in sympathy with the building laborers of the AFL and refused to desert them even when offered a pay boost and a closed shop contract. In St. Louis and Butte an AFL boycott was put on IWW products. The Machinists, the Hat & Cap Makers, the Leather Workers, and the Carpenters all decreed no IWW could belong to their organization or work on jobs that they controlled.

On February 7,1906, Moyer and Haywood, president and secretary of the Western Federation, were kidnapped, along with a friendly nonmember, Pettibone, by government officers and taken to Idaho, charged with the murder of former governor Steunenberg. From that date to their trials in the summer of 1907 the IWW was preoccupied with agitation on their behalf and with raising funds for their defense. It raised $10,982.51 and secured the services of Clarence Darrow. Meanwhile the Western Federation was for the first time in its history free from strikes, and the new IWW beset with them, yet concentrating on this defense case which, while it got much newspaper space, called no attention to the new union, but only to the Western Federation and its past struggles. The WFM was not actually a part of the IWW until after its convention in June of 1906, when it entered 22,000 members. Haywood's imprisonment gave the right wing in the Federation control of its offices and a deal was worked out between these right wing forces, commonly called the "Denver Triumvirate," and Charles Sherman, president of the IWW, aiming to make the forthcoming second convention, in Sherman's phrase, "the Waterloo of the revolutionists." Sherman, the first and only president of the IWW, nominated by Moyer, had been elected at the first convention, chiefly because he stood nowhere, while all those who had taken definite positions felt it would be in the interests of harmony to decline the nomination.

The founding convention, amid its radical oratory, had elected an administration predominantly on the more conservative side, and provided for a system of departmental autonomy that entrenched the position of these conservatives. Simons warned at the first convention: "The men in one of those departments where we have a union today may go in there and adopt the name of that department and seize its machinery. ... A little handful of men can control the machinery of that department and keep up such a hubbub as to keep all opposition out." Sherman's United Metal Workers, which proved to have only one executive beside himself, did that with the Metal Department and kept out the Amalgamated Society of Engineers. Dictatorship developed in the Transportation Department, whittling it down to almost nothing by the second convention, through refusal to furnish dues stamps to those opposing the departmental heads; these ousted men sought a hearing and Sherman refused to do anything on the grounds

Vincent St. John   *William Trautmann*

of departmental autonomy. The only friends of the rebel railroaders were the two radicals in the administration, Trautmann, the secretary, who weakened his position by traveling, and "Honest John" Riordan, the one rebel on the Executive Board, who stayed in the office but had to content himself with writing "graft" across the checks drawn for the junketing trips of those who acted the customary role of labor leader.[2]

The second convention was supposed to have been held in May; then it was postponed so that the Western Federation could convene first and be duly installed. Had it been held then it might perhaps have ironed out these growing headaches but on the urging of Debs and his Terre Haute local, it was further postponed in the hopes of early trials for Moyer, Haywood and Pettibone, both to conserve funds for their defense and to make it a victory celebration for their acquittal.[3] When it was seen that their trial could not come until after Supreme Court had ruled on the kidnapping and related issues, it was called for Sept. 17, 1906. The delegates assembled, expecting it to be a short affair, and after ten days spent in wrangles over the seating of delegates from these dictator-ridden departments, many of them were out of funds. Sherman later explained in the *Chicago Record Herald* of October 7 how he had planned to handle the "revolutionists":

"We believed we could starve them out by obstructive tactics, but at the end of the tenth day, De Leon had a resolution passed that they be allowed $1.50 per day as salary and expenses while attending the convention. That was more money than any of them had earned in their lives and they were ready to stay with him until Christmas."

These remarks came rather poorly from one who in addition to his salary of $150 per month, turned in expense accounts that even his cronies on the Denver Triumvirate could not swallow, and who, it later developed, was planning to make a fortune from control of the Fraternal Supply Company, furnishing badges, buttons, etc. to WFM and IWW. Providing expenses for the delegates cost the IWW $450, and won by a vote of 380 1/2 to 251. The Sherman group argued this clearly violated the provisional constitution's provision that delegates should bear their own expenses, and the socialist and general labor press denounced it as the "coup of the proletarian rabble," and pictured it as a De Leon victory over the socialists. Actually SLP followers had only 60 votes at the convention while followers of the Socialist Party had 158, and the division was not between these two parties but between those who wanted to make a union in the accepted patterns and those who wanted to build an instrument for the emancipation of the working class. Of the five delegates from Western Federation, two, Vincent St. John and Albert Ryan, were consistently with the rebels.

With "'starve-out" tactics foiled, the convention soon attended to its business and ended Sherman's position by abolishing the office of president. When the new executive board went to the offices at 146 W. Madison they found that Sherman and his allies had hired the Mooney-Bohlen Detective Agency to hold it against all comers. As Trautmann reported to the 1907 convention:

"With no records or documents left, without addresses of unions or individuals, scarcely in possession of enough cash to communicate the outrageous proceedings to those who were expected to rush to the organization in its hour of need, with the whole press controlled by socialist party individuals, with one notable exception, as well as the capitalist mouthpieces, hurling their invectives against the 'tramps and beggars' and the 'proletarian rabble,' it certainly was a hard task to carry on the work and duties mapped out by the convention, which had adjourned a few hours earlier under the most favorable auspices."

St. John got an injunction against Sherman, but the funds were tied up. After long delays Sherman allowed the portion that had been raised for the defense of the Idaho cases to go to the Western Federation, and when the settlement was reached on Sept. 27, 1907, most of the rest of the funds went to the two lawyers. The "St. John-Traut-mann-De Leon faction" opened offices at 212 Bush Temple and won in the courts. Soon nothing was left of the Sherman faction which held the old address until June 1908 and then sold its assets to the Socialist Party for $250, while Sherman and Kilpatrick went on pay as speakers for the Hearst Independent League. Later Sherman was given a job with the Western Federation and still later a clerical job for the Socialist Party.[4]

Though the rebels won in the convention and in the courts and among the scattered locals, they lost the promising start in Schenectady and also the Western Federation.

In November 1906 some draftsmen at General Electric asked to join the IWW and were provided with a circular to solicit members in their department. They organized three dozen and then the three most active were fired. The IWW decided reinstatement or no production. On December 10 their 3,000 fellow workers folded arms and stayed in without working. The next morning the draftsmen walked out, followed by five thousand including many who belonged to AFL or to no union. Soon antagonisms between pro-Sherman and anti-Sherman forces, between radicals and conservatives, between supporters and opponents of De Leon, between the AFL and the new union broke up the early solidarity. The new draftsmen's local withdrew on the 14th, the electrical workers on the 18th. GE was much concerned over invasion of its white collar force and threat of IWW to organize other GE plants. By December 20th, when 200 new employees had been hired, the IWW called the strike off.

The craft structure of the industrial council and the dissension over the rift at the second convention wrecked the local organization. For a while there were two IWW bodies competing at the plant, the pro-Sherman Industrial Council, and its ousted locals 1, 34, 50, 55, 58, 76 and 77, which James P. Thompson, organizer for the rebel majority, reorganized in General Electric Workers Industrial Union No. 1. While some IWW support has existed among workers at this plant to this day, the IWW has not since then made any notable local history, despite the IWW sympathies frankly expressed for many years by General Electric's colorful "wizard" Charles P. Steinmetz.

The Executive Board of the Western Federation promptly issued a referendum after the 1906 convention asking: "Shall the acts of the

2nd annual convention of the IWW be held as unconstitutional and illegal?" This carried and the WFM refused to pay per capita to "either faction," even though the Sherman faction existed only on paper and could be given life – and pay its debts – only with WFM per capita. The 1907 convention of the Western Federation by majority supported this position, but manifested the enduring need for a class-wide union that had led it to bring on the scene in succession the Western Labor Union, the American Labor Union and then the IWW, by adopting a new preamble (by 283 to 66 votes) restating the same principles as were in the IWW preamble, and concluding, "Therefore, we the wage slaves employed in and around the mines, mills and smelters of the world, have associated in the Western Federation of Miners, Mining Department of the Industrial Workers of the World."[5] It issued at the same time a call for a conference of "the contending factions of the IWW, the United Brewery Workers, and all other labor unions ready to accept the principles of industrial unionism as formulated in the Manifesto issued at Chicago, June 2, 1905, to convene Oct. 1, 1907."

The instructions to the delegates for the proposed conference included that the joint body assume no debts of either faction, for Sherman's debts were extensive; that no officer of either side could become an officer of the new body; that departmental autonomy was to be preserved, for the provisional constitution adopted in 1905 gave the GEB the power to pull out all members in support of any group on strike, and the miners needed to protect themselves against this, though the experience with the Metal and Transportation departments had shown the need of some right of appeal to the general organization. It was felt that this proposal was an idle gesture, and it was almost impossible to get anyone to accept as delegates to the conference. It was repeatedly postponed. Haywood was acquitted a few weeks after this convention, and on Dec. 17, along with the other members of the Executive Board of the Western Federation sent an invitation addressed "To the Officers of Both Factions of the IWW" reading in part:

"As executive officers of the Western Federation of Miners we are determined to demonstrate to our membership, the membership of both factions of the IWW, and the working class generally, that we are not responsible for the continued dismemberment of the Industrial Workers of the World."

This call for a conference to be held April 6, 1908, was printed in full in the IWW paper, the *Industrial Union Bulletin* for Jan. 25, 1908, and flatly rejected. In rejecting it, the IWW, though its coming break with De Leon was already quite clear, evidently agreed with the arguments he was making in speeches and in his paper that ever since the founding of the IWW there had been a conspiracy to put it in the hands of those who would tame it and turn it from its declared purpose, and that this was the latest effort in this scheme.[6]

This decision ended the long struggle of the Western Federation to build a class-wide union. Thereafter it rapidly grew tame, futilely trying the approach of not antagonizing the employer in an industrial situation where that approach could not work, and steadily became more innocuous until the reawakening of American labor in the mid-thirties. Having gone back into the AFL in 1911, after invitations as early as 1907, it changed its name to International Mine, Mill & Smelter Workers. Already in 1908, two days after the April conference that never conferred, the Denver Triumvirate fired Bill Haywood. He had had no connection with the IWW other than as chairman of its first convention, and now went speaking for the Socialist Party, and in 1910 represented it at the International Socialist Congress in Copenhagen, toured Europe lecturing, and joined the IWW upon his return to America in the fall of that year.

Goldfield, 30 miles from Tonapah, in the silver region of Nevada had its 1,500 gold miners solidly organized in Local 220 WFM – a progressive local built largely of active unionists deported from the Federation's battles in Colorado and Idaho. In February 1906, an IWW local of newsboys was formed. Local 70 gradually organized the miscellaneous workers in the town, winning a strike of the Western Union messenger boys in May. In August, the *Tonapah Sun* declared war on the IWW, and the miners boycotted the paper so that it sold out to the *Goldfield Tribune*. Following the battle with Sherman at the September convention, these locals steadfastly supported the St. John faction.

In mid-December Local 220 tried to get $5.00 established as the minimum for all work in and around mines. The small leasers, largely former members of the Western Federation, were already paying this scale. They wanted to get all the ore out they could before their leases expired on Jan. 7; but the Florence and Mohawk Combination, owned back east, did not want this scale established and threatened to attack the small operators on the stock markets if they did not play ball. Thus work was stopped until two days after Jan. 7, when the scale was set at $5 minimum below ground and $4.50 minimum on surface.[7]

Once the big operators won out over the smaller, there was a more controlled production and many miners were laid off. They wanted to get some work out of the building boom, but the AFL carpenters objected to miners working even on the Miners Union Hospital. The Miners then demanded that carpenters working at mines carry WFM cards. The Mine Owners, recently reorganized on a straight anti-labor basis, sided with the AFL and locked the miners out March 10 to April 21. AFL organizers with sawed-off shotguns vainly tried to get miners to sign up for working the mines under AFL charters.

On the second day of the lockout, Silva, a restaurant proprietor, refused to pay a waitress her wages, and the IWW local struck his place. As M. R. Preston was picketing it in the evening, turning away prospective customers, Silva grew enraged and came out brandishing a gun. According to the parole board seven years later, Silva advanced on Preston for twenty-five feet, threatening to shoot, before Preston drew and shot in self-defense. (It was the custom to go armed.) Many were arrested, including St. John. Preston and Smith, the IWW delegate, were convicted on a conspiracy charge, though the parole board belatedly said there was no evidence of conspiracy. The Socialist Labor Party made Preston its vice-presidential candidate that year, over his objections, and though he was not a member of their party.[8] About a week before St. John's arrest, the *Chicago Journal of Finance* forecast that soon he and other radicals in Goldfield would be arrested. The intent seems to have been to prevent this camp from sending radical delegates to the WFM convention; this miscarried, as did a plot to lynch the victims, to prevent which miners stood guard around the jail house.

After the lockout had been on 10 days it was decided to have the miners and the IWW local of town workers meet separately. They had been merged early that year in what seems to have been an effort to submerge a radical minority. Though now separated, they stuck together. Mahoney, acting president of the Western Federation, came to settle the dispute. He found three-fourths of the businessmen in town had locked out the IWW, and that the AFL had sent in scabs. His concern was the miners, where the mine owners took the stand that they would not deal with a miners union connected in any way with the IWW, or that got involved in the troubles of the town workers. Mahoney evidently convinced them that the Western Federation would win out against the IWW. The lockout was settled, recognizing Local 220, affiliated with both WFM and IWW, at the mines and with wages and other terms the same as before the lockout.

Throughout the summer the IWW step by step got rid of most of the AFL scabs around the town, and the amicable Third IWW Convention increased respect for the IWW. In October, both Tonapah and Goldfield locals of the WFM – along with various others – passed resolutions in favor of continuing support for the St. John-Trautmann IWW.[9] How the WFM had been working meanwhile to undermine the IWW was explained in the following statement made by the Federation's counsel, Judge O. N. Hilton (later retained by IWW on the Joe Hill appeal and in Mesabi Range cases), to the *Goldfield Chronicle* during the Federation's last unsuccessful bid for the good graces of the Mine Owners Association there:

"Already we have accomplished much along the line of weeding out the undesirable trouble breeders, and we propose to continue the work until such time as there remains only a hard working force of good miners who will not be interfered with or led by undesirables. Last summer when I was in Goldfield, I spent $1,200 on transportation for a number of members of the organization whom I thought it was best to send away from camp. These men are now away from here and there remain but a small number who, we believe, should have no hand in affairs here. If our proposition is received and accepted, I dare say that there will be no more trouble and that Goldfield will remain a union camp and a camp only of good well-intending miners."[10]

In October the big nationwide financial crisis had hit. The Mine Owners asked Local 220 to permit part of the wages to be paid in checks drawn against ore in transit. The union was willing if the owners would guarantee eventual payment. While this was being negotiated with the mines in operation, an effort was made to kill St. John on Nov. 5, but the bullets hit another. When mine owners refused to guarantee payment to miners digging gold, the miners struck Nov. 27. The mine owners got the governor to ask Theodore Roosevelt for federal troops. There was no National Guard as the top layers feared that if one were formed it would consist largely of union men. The legislature was not called as required for a request for federal aid, as it was felt the legislature would not make such a request. Roosevelt sent in troops, and on the day they arrived, the mine owners cut wages and announced a policy of yellow dog contract. A commission investigated and reported there was no need for federal troops, but Roosevelt kept them there until Jan. 29, when the legislature enacted a state police bill. On the same day the mine owners announced the mines would run open shop.[11] WFM job control was over. Soon the rich ore played out; Goldfield eventually became a ghost town, but with Metal Mine Workers Industrial Union 353 of the IWW holding out and keeping some spark of unionism alive until the First World War.

A sawmill strike in Portland, Ore., starting March 1, 1907, and involving 3,000 men for 40 days, marked the first west coast progress of the IWW. There was a general public sympathy and a favorable press treatment of the demand for shorter hours and a minimum of $2.50 a day. A feature article on the strike, "The Story of a New Labor Union," by John Kenneth Turner in the *Sunday Oregon Journal,* was reprinted as a leaflet.[12] A quickie strike pulled at a busy time swamped the IWW hall at 298 Burnside with a demand for union cards. In two weeks 1,300 had enrolled. Soon the mill owners made a closed shop contract with the AFL, but the AFL managed to get no men past the picket line. Turner wrote of it: "Absolutely no violence, no lawbreaking, and no crying of 'scab.' Just one man was arrested for trespassing, and he imagined that he was standing in a public street. Other strange features were the red ribbons, the daily speechmaking, and the night and day shifts of organizers who received not a red cent for their services." The AFL issued public statements denouncing the strike and the IWW, and quoting extensively from the WFM *Miners' Magazine* in their attacks; yet WFM locals sent in over a thousand dollars. The strike committee had to send wires to send no more funds as their conduct of the strike kept expenses down: those not needed for picket duty were urged to go out and spread union doctrine on the various lumbering and construction jobs then in full swing. This was the seed from which sprang the IWW of the northwest.

A local of workers building a sewer and another local of harborcraft workers grew as sideshoots. In Tacoma the IWW smeltermen struck, and despite dissension over the WFM split, they won the 8 hour day and a 15 percent wage boost, but left the IWW. IWW lumberjacks struck in Humboldt County, Calif., and IWW bakers in San Francisco about the same time. In Montana the IWW had started organizing lumber workers and struck; the AFL gave them opposition, and as most of the logging was on Indian reservations, the bureau agents kept IWW organizers out.

In the east the IWW made progress prior to the panic in the fall of 1907 at American Tube in Bridgeport and in the textile industry, laying the foundations for its phenomenal victories five years later. In Bridgeport organizer French had started a local in June 1907, and when on July 15 the American Tube refused to alternate shifts, the local was ready to organize this indignation into an effective strike, with speakers in the various languages used, and a committee that rode bicycles up and down the parades of strikers around the two plants of the company. There the Machinists cooperated, happy to do so as these unorganized workers had helped them win a short time before. Victory in August came to a local that had enrolled 700 skilled and 1,000 unskilled among these workers.[13]

The IWW got its start in textiles in Skowhegan, Maine. The local there of Marston Mills workers demanded a 10 percent boost to be effective New Year's 1906, but settled for 5 percent then and 5 percent in July if conditions warranted. The manager tried to get rid of the active unionists. The entire force had met and decided upon policy; when fifty were put on notice by the manager, all walked out, including the boiler room crew who blew off steam and pulled their fires. This was Jan. 21. President Golden of the United Textile Workers offered "union scabs" and inserted his endorsement in ads through the New England press for other scabs. The IWW won on April 23 with reinstatement of all, abolition of the fining system, day's pay instead of piece rates for poor work, and a shop committee to meet with management twice a month on all grievances.[14]

In Paterson, N. J., scene of a more noted strike in 1913, the IWW struck a number of silk dye-houses in March 1907 over the discharge of members. Private detectives and uniformed police threatened and arrested the strikers, but after a short time the local press announced a "pleasant surprise" for the 6,000 dye-house workers of a dollar a week pay boost, without mention of the strike or union.[15] The union grew during the strike to a thousand members and in the fall tried to organize the American Locomotive plant there, resulting in a short strike of 300 workers. In November the IWW struck the international Stehli concern at Lancaster, Penn., and despite police interference came through the strike intact.

As a result of these activities in textiles, the General Executive Board called a convention in Paterson, May 1, 1908, to found the National Industrial Union of Textile Workers, the first industrial union, not a local, that the IWW had built. Progress was also made in the garment industry, with a local of cloakmakers in Chicago, a strike of 200 pressers in St. Louis, and a 12-week strike against Ratner Brothers in New York, white goods, which cost $2,012 but was defrayed locally by picnics, vaudevilles and other benefit affairs.

This eastern organizing – including a charter to the already striking flint glass workers of Marion, Ind., and a strike of 200 car foundry workers in Detroit – was in territory where De Leon held strategic advantages, and it was plain shortly after the peaceful third convention that a fight must be made to keep the IWW from becoming a tail to De Leon's kite. The decision to launch the National Industrial Union of Textile Workers, with James P. Thompson, an able exponent of nonpolitical industrial unionism, as organizer, was shaped by a desire to keep this development out of De Leon's hands. From even before its first convention the IWW had faced an opposition based largely on hostility to De Leon and his record of disruption in the labor movement. Its *Industrial Union Bulletin* had printed each week in large type across the front page that it was independent of any political party; but its readers could find in the *Daily People* discussion of its internal affairs and advice how to vote on its referenda.

The conflict grew hotter in the fall of 1907 over a question in economic theory: Does a rise in wages cause a rise in price such that workers achieve no real gain? De Leon said it did. In common with many radical politicians he was inclined toward such a conclusion as it focused attention on the abolition of the wage system rather than on union demands, and support for the conclusion can be obtained by misinterpreting the experience that in periods of rising prices workers are most moved to demand wage boosts and find it easiest to obtain them. The argument to the contrary by James P. Thompson and James Connolly, who was here from Ireland and helping the IWW, appeared in the *Industrial Union Bulletin*. It followed the Ricardo-Marx analysis that price is a monetary expression of value; that value is not altered by how it is distributed among wage earners and others, but it is determined by the real or labor cost of production; that it can be changed only by changes in the amount of labor required for production. They supported their position by the practical consideration that employers oppose wage boosts, while they would profit by them if De Leon's position were correct. It may have been theory, but it probed deeply into the question whether workers should consider unions worthwhile or concentrate on political activity.

The General Executive Board met in New York Dec. 22, 1907. Ever since the 1906 convention the rule had been that no GEB action was to be kept secret from the membership. Connolly appeared before it with a plan that, if acted upon promptly, might have brought 12,000 New York longshoremen, then independent, into the IWW. Action was hampered when De Leon induced the Board to go into secret session to try Connolly on his charge that his articles on economics constituted heresy. Even the SLP members of the Board felt all this was ridiculous, but indignantly rallied to their leader when the Board, in accordance with the rules, published its proceedings in *Industrial Union Bulletin* No. 49.

This brought the quarrel with De Leon to a head all over the country – and for that matter in the industrial union clubs that had been formed in Britain and Australia. Among the western membership there was a hearty disrespect for politicians, and the hard times starting in October 1907 had not abated IWW agitation in the west. An exceptionally enterprising organizer in that field was J. H. Walsh. In July 1907 he got enough support in Alaska to start the *Nome Industrial Worker.*[16] Coming down coast he found that the employment sharks provided a major grievance about which something might be done. They had tie-ins with bosses on out-of-town work to fire the men they furnished after they had worked a week so that they were back to buy another job. To reach these workers and build a concerted refusal to patronize the "shark" and thus force the employers to hire directly, street meetings in the skidroads were necessary. The Salvation Army ran interference with these meetings, and IWW speakers could not speak louder than the big bass drum. Walsh and his fellow workers hit upon the device of making parodies to be sung to the music furnished free by the Army. Thus the tradition of the "singing IWW" grew out of this conflict with the employment sharks. One satiric refrain, "Hallelujah, I'm a Bum," was particularly popular as its music was the customary "theme song" for the Army meetings.[17] Walsh headed a group of delegates to the fourth convention, who traveled by boxcar, stopping at division points to soapbox and sing and sell the song cards preceding the IWW song book. Their most popular ditty led the unappreciative De Leonites to call them "'the Bummery."

The convention met Oct. 1. De Leon's credentials were challenged on the ground that he represented a Store and Office Workers Union instead of belonging to the Printing and Publishing Local that as an editor he should have joined. De Leon argued for his seat on the contention that workers should be organized according to the tool each worked with, and he worked with a pen as did office workers. This was not accepted as sound industrial unionism. The convention then proceeded to recommend a change in the Preamble to the membership. Its second paragraph then read, as De Leon had insisted as a condition for cooperating in the first convention:

"Between these two classes a struggle must go on until all the toilers come together on the political, as well as on the industrial field, and take and hold that which they produce by their labor, through an economic organization of the working class, without affiliation with any political party."

When the present form of Preamble was accepted by the convention, the De Leon followers bolted, held a convention of a few eastern locals at Paterson, and founded what was known as "the Detroit IWW." De Leon followed up with attacks on the IWW as "slum proletarians" for which the GEB formally expelled him. The "Detroit IWW," like the ST&LA of earlier days, carried on chiefly as a union duplication of SLP membership, changed its name in 1915 to Workers International Industrial Union, and gave up the ghost in 1925.

In one sense this is the launching of the IWW. It is from here on that it exists as an organization with its own distinctive character. The Brewery workers were not in it or likely to be; the Sherman tendency was out; the Western Federation was gone, and now the De Leon forces that had alienated so many unionists. The five thousand members it had after this 1908 convention were no longer divergent groups trying to live together but a compact organization of men attached to the IWW rather than to something else, largely rebels who had been organized by the new union, but who had long experience in the struggle with the employer, and many of whom were very familiar with all the fine points that radicals argue about. This was the IWW that was to add something new to the American labor movement.

Notes:
1. On Schenectady see Trautmann's report to 1907 convention; *Industrial Worker,* Vol. 1, No. 7, Chicago, 1906 series; *Solidarity,* Feb. 17, 1931, and *Industrial Worker* summary, Aug. 18, 1945.
2. *Industrial Union Bulletin* reports of second convention; see also Hardrock Miner series, *Industrial Worker,* July 1950.

3. *Daily People,* May 26, 1906.

4. *I.U. Bulletin* editorial, June 27, 1908.

5. Jensen, *Heritage of Conflict,* chapter 11;WFM Preamble, quoted p. 189.

6. For details of conspiracy charge see Hardrock series, July 21, 1950, and for their substance, July 28.

7. To Goldfield, Brissenden and Jensen each devote a chapter; see also *Harper's Weekly* of June 22, 1907; St. John's account in *I.U.B.* No. 6.

8. Parole account, *Solidarity,* June 6,1914.

9. *I.U.B.* No. 35 and 37

10. Quoted *I.U.B.* No. 45, Jan. 4, 1908.

11. Details in Jensen's *Heritage of Conflict.*

12. Reprinted *I.U.B.,* April 13, 1907, in full.

13. Detailed accounts in *I.U.B.* Nos. 22, 23 and 27, quoted in *Solidarity,* March 3, 1931.

14. *I.U.B.* No. 1, March 2, 1907, quoted extensively in *Solidarity,* March 10, 1931.

15. *I.U.B.* No. 2, quoted *Solidarity,* ibid.

16. *I.U.B.* No. 32.

17. There are conflicting claims to authorship of "Hallelujah." Walsh in *I.U.B.,* April 4, 1908, says it was made up in Spokane hall, and is quoted in *OBU Monthly,* March 1938; various other claims to prior authorship in sundry versions exist; one in the pocket edition *Treasury of American Folklore,* p. 386.

General Sources:

On the Boise trial see Joseph Conlin's *Big Bill Haywood and the Radical Labor Movement* (Syracuse University Press, 1968) or same author in *Pacific Northwest Quarterly* 1969, pp. 22-32. Stephen Scheinberg in *Idaho Yesterdays* (Fall 1960) shows Pres. Roosevelt had a spy on the Haywood defense committee. J. Anthony Lukas' *Big Trouble* (Simon & Schuster, 1997) is a more recent, comprehensive popular history of the trial, fairly good until the last chapter where the author succumbs to a temptation to try to solve the mystery of who killed Steunenberg through speculation.

On Schenectady, a paper by David Goodall included in the IWW Archives at Wayne State University discusses the IWW as an outgrowth of earlier local militance. Russell Elliot discusses Goldfield in *Pacific Historical Review* (1950), pp. 369-384. It is also discussed in Brissenden, *IWW,* pp. 191-212, and in two more recent histories: Sally Zanjani and Guy Rocha's *The Ignoble Conspiracy: Radicalism on Trial in Nevada* (Univ. of Nevada Press, 1986) and Maryjoy Martin, *The Corpse on Boomerang Road: Telluride's War on Labor* (Western Reflections, 2004).

Foner's *History of the American Labor Movement: The IWW* (pp. 84-86) adds details on Bridgeport from the local press; the Hungarian radical press of the time is said to have the fullest account. Don McKee (*Labor History,* Winter 1962) and Glen Seretan (*Labor History,* Spring 1973) have written on De Leon, and Frank Girard and Ben Perry's *Socialist Labor Party, 1876-1991: A Short History* (Livra Books, 1991) is the best general history. General Executive Board Minutes for 1906-1910 at Wayne State show the situation following the 1906 convention and give much space to the Connolly-De Leon dispute. Priscilla Metscher's biography, *James Connolly and the Reconquest of Ireland* (Marxist Educational Press, 2002) discusses his years with the IWW.

Spokane and the IWW song cards are discussed in Richard Brazier's memoir published in *Labor History* (Winter 1968). Charles H. Kerr is preparing publication of a *Big Red Songbook,* which compiles all songs to have appeared in the IWW songbooks and discusses their role.

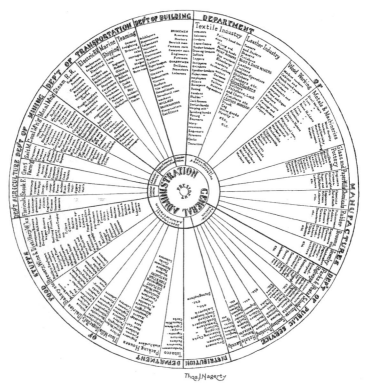

"Father Haggerty's Wheel of Fortune" was a widely circulated graphic depiction of the IWW's industrial union conception, illustrating how workers in each industry would organize into industrial unions welded together into one big union much as spokes come together to form a wheel.

3. Big Fights of a Small Union (1909-1911)

The hard times following the financial crisis of October 1907, the conversion of the previous SLP support into open enmity, added to the definite loss of the Western Federation and the collapse of the promising campaign in Schenectady, all put the IWW in a tough spot. Yet it grew and its secretary, Vincent St. John, figured a total membership of 9,100 in 1910 and 12,834 in 1911. Of these, 4,397 were in the textile industry, 2,000 were metal workers, 1,800 were engaged in railroad construction and 800 in lumbering.[1] It is possible that to avoid embarrassment he may have about doubled these figures. In any case the IWW of these years was a small union, yet it put up some memorable fights, winning free speech in Spokane and elsewhere, defeating the big steel companies in McKees Rocks and in the Chicago area, prodding the AFL into action in many places, and yet with enough surplus energy to take on a civil war in Mexico. During these two years, the distinguishing characteristics of the IWW were definitely developed, perhaps most clearly in the argument with William Z. Foster over his proposal to "bore from within."

The IWW was small, but widely spread. A list of locals in January 1910 shows 11 locals[2] scattered through California; three in Oregon, all in Portland; in Washington besides locals in Aberdeen, Bellingham and Anacortes, four each in Spokane and Seattle; in British Columbia, four. In Montana there were locals at Anaconda, Butte, Great Fails, Kalispell, Billings and Missoula; in Wyoming at Cheyenne; one in Denver, one each at Globe and Phoenix, Arizona – these locals all showing that some hold had been maintained in Western Federation territory. There were three in Minnesota, and one each at Omaha, Kansas City, St. Louis and New Orleans. East of the Mississippi there were locals in Chicago, Muncie, three in Ohio, 12 scattered through Pennsylvania; three in New Jersey; five in New York City and one each in Buffalo, Yonkers and Brooklyn; two in Rhode Island and three in Vermont.

Thus, over the map it had local organizations agitating, looking for opportunities and spreading its literature. Its official organ, the *Industrial Union Bulletin,* ceased in March 1909, but the membership in Spokane began at the same time to issue the *Industrial Worker.* With only one major break, 1913-1916, it continued there, or in Seattle, or in Chicago to the present time. On Dec. 18, 1909, *Solidarity,* also a weekly, appeared at first as the official organ of the Pittsburgh District Council, but issued at Newcastle, Penn. Later it moved to Cleveland, and in 1916 was brought to Chicago as official organ of the IWW, appearing with minor breaks and changes of name, until it was merged with the *Industrial Worker* when it too was moved to Chicago in 1931.

The strike at McKees Rocks (Pittsburgh suburb) got the IWW started in steel. It started June 28, 1909, as an unorganized protest against a pool system of payment at the Pressed Steel Car Company, U.S. Steel subsidiary, by which the foreman got the pay for his gang and distributed as he saw fit, which meant with considerable favoritism. That day 50 riveters walked out; half returned and the other half got fired. A third of the passenger car department staged a protest, and most of them were fired. On July 1, some of the porch department walked out and united with the discharged workers to picket the works. All came out except the tool and crane departments, which were under Machinist contract. AFL policy in the industry was against organizing the "unskilled foreigners"; Secretary Morrison of the AFL passed through town and turned them down. Among these foreigners, however, were men who had been in the Russian Duma in 1905, some who had been members of the Metall-arbeiter-Verband, and Italians who had been in the great resistance strikes.[3] Some of these asked Trautmann for help.

In their own preliminary organization two committees developed. One, called the "Big Six," was elected to take charge of the strike. The other developed of itself from among those previously active in the radical movement of Europe, and was referred to as the "Unknown Committee." This committee is credited with taming the Cossacks and with sending 60 strikers inside to bring out the 350 scabs who were living in the plant, and thus winning the strike.

Two troops of State Constabulary, commonly called Steel Cossacks, had treated the strikers with customary brutality, seriously wounding 76 by the end of July. On Aug. 12 when they killed Steven Horvath, one of the strikers, this "Unknown Committee" is reported to have written them: "For every striker's life you take, a trooper's life will be taken." One can neither verify nor refute this much-told story. Ten days later as strikers returning home from their meeting were crossing the O'Donovan Bridge, the constabulary attacked them. Four strikers and three troopers were killed. Secretary Trautmann reported in the first issue of *Solidarity:* "Then the chief of the cossacks called off his

Striking Pittsburgh stogie workers, July 1913.

bloodhounds. After that no striker or deputy was killed. Organized and disciplined 'physical force' checked the violence and wanton destruction of life." Following victory in the strike, six men, charged with participating in this riot, received sentences of 60 days in the workhouse. These light sentences may indicate that many in the community shared the view expressed by Trautmann. The socialist press of the area, heartily supporting the strike, contributed to this favorable attitude. Now that the IWW was definitely nonpolitical, relations with the socialists were sporadically more friendly.

The McKees Rocks strike ended the "pool system," improved the shop rules, and secured a 5 percent wage increase with another 10 percent to be paid 60 days later. Its indirect results were much greater. Steel depended on a supply of labor from Europe, much of it obtained by glowing misrepresentation. The IWW gave the facts of life as encountered by steel labor to the European labor press, and this diffusion of information became a major factor to raise wages. Trautmann reported to the Fifth Convention: "From data collected in several mills, the statement of a general increase of 15 percent and a reduction of five hours of working time per week for 350,000 workers

Solidarity staff in Newcastle jail, 1910. L-R, 1st row, G. Fix and V. Jacobs; 2nd row: Ben Williams, E. Moore, A.M. Stirton, C. H. McCarty.

would in sum total about express the results of the upheaval of workers in McKees Rocks." At the same time the AFL, appealing only to the skilled and preferably the Americanized workers in the industry, was losing strike after strike.

The IWW continued to win in steel, with victories against Inland Steel and Republic Steel, both at East Chicago, Ind., and another against Standard Steel Car in East Hammond.[4] At Standard the IWW had been organizing quietly, but when the committee representing the riveters got thrown out of the place for presenting a grievance, a strike was called. Special deputies, recruited from the red-light district in West Hammond, began an orgy of brutalities on Jan. 24, 1910, when the strike had been on a week. Resenting abusiveness, the strikers' wives formed a league for self-defense, and effectively stopped scabbing despite the arrest of 12 of the women. On the 24th, all officers were jailed early in the morning, but the picketing became even more effective, and at ten the company sent word to the committee in jail that it would accept all demands except immediate increases. Next day the strikers marched back to work in a body to make sure of no discrimination.[5]

The Pittsburgh District Council grew. It held its second convention in McKees Rocks Jan. 8, 1910, with 26 delegates from five locals, electing Joe Schmidt to assist Joe Ettor as organizer. Its organ, *Solidarity*, was edited for 90 days from jail, since it had neglected to specify its ownership, but it missed no issues while edited by men enjoying free board and room. It weathered efforts through that spring and summer to take away conditions won at Pressed Steel Car, including an attempted strike by company pets.

Organizers were kept there, and organization developed in other local industries, yet they were unable to keep the union among these victorious strikers more than a year. There are at least two explanations for this. One is that the growth of unionism is a widening of the occupational area in which unionism comes to be taken for granted; unionism first appears as organizing for immediate grievances, usually to strike, and only gradually among the workers lacking a skill that they might monopolize has the feeling developed that organization should continue between strikes. The IWW has always had to do its organizing on the periphery of the occupational area in which unionism has become an accepted practice, and its "failure to achieve stability" there has also been experienced by all other unions in the same field at the same time. It was not until the mid-thirties that permanent organization of all occupations came to be taken for granted widely throughout industry.

Another factor was pointed out by Secretary Trautmann to the Fifth Convention. Referring to a 10 percent increase just obtained at Republic Steel, he said: "While we cannot oppose too much the time-contract system of the craft union movement, in this instance and in others that cannot all be recounted, all of the enemies of the IWW used the fact of our not having anything black on white as an entering wedge to pull the workers away from the organization through which they had been able to win the strike."

Originally the IWW had put no restrictions, except requiring General Executive Board approval on contracts, and much of the discussion at the founding convention as to what constituted an industry proceeded on the assumption that industry-wide action would depend on the structure of the industrial union making contracts. The tradition of no contracts with specified duration had come from the Western Federation, and persisted until changed in 1938 to permit each Industrial Union to make its own regulations on this matter. Some Industrial Unions have persistently forbidden such agreements. Provisions adopted in 1946 ended the requirement of GEB approval, but stipulated that no agreement should provide for a check-off or obligate members covered by it to do any work that would aid in breaking any union's strike.

A strike of inside fabricators at Hansel & Elcock Construction, Chicago, on May 8, 1910, won an 8 percent increase and Saturday half holidays, after the crowd, first fed with speeches in Polish, Lithuanian and other languages, while AFL organizers looked on in bewilderment, turned down the AFL proposition to divide the 46 craftsmen away from the 246 lesser skilled that it was willing for the IWW to have. Trautmann's report of the victory stated: "The strikebreakers that came back with the strikers dismissed themselves within 24 hours when direct action methods were applied by the victorious strikers."[6]

This is the earliest instance noted in IWW publications of the term "direct action." Its meaning here may have been either ostracism or fisticuffs, as no further details are given. About this time the terms "sabotage" and "passive resistance" appear in the IWW press for the first time, in reporting an IWW strike of 580 men and girls against Lamm & Co., Chicago clothiers. There the IWW had been asked to aid an unorganized strike, and when scabs were brought in "workers in other firms where the material for the strikebound firm was made, 'sabotaged' their work to such perfection," to quote *Solidarity* of June 4, 1910, that the company yielded to all demands except that for the reinstatement of the man whose discharge had led to the walkout in the first place. Trautmann advised them to go back to work and use "passive resistance" methods to get the man back too. Here this meant putting so little heart in the work, out of regret for the absence of this fellow worker, that the employer decided to cheer them up by reinstating him. (For subsequent twists given to these words, see Chapter VI below.)

In Pittsburgh the district council set out to organize the meat packing plants. First it won gains from the big outside packers who wished to avoid a strike there. Later a general walkout was forced on the union and it struck all plants in the area, winning a reduction to 10 hours with an 8 percent pay boost, and shop control for a while in six plants. A less successful strike of the period was the IWW's first venture into the auto industry with a walkout against Parish, auto frame makers, in Reading, Penn. The men went to work in other shops and the strike petered out.[7]

Out west the IWW grew chiefly among out-of-town construction workers and lumberjacks, men on whom the employment sharks preyed. They worked on jobs with "one gang coming, one gang work-

IS IT ABOUT TO STRIKE?

ing and one gang going," and the more rapid the turnover, speeded up by firings, the more fees there were for the shark to split with the bossman who did the hiring and firing. The IWW urged that the men should collectively refuse to patronize the shark and thus force direct hiring by the employers or through agencies that charged no fee. There were 31 employment sharks operating in Spokane in 1909, and occasionally, against IWW advice, the fleeced men set out to wreck the employment shark's office for he sometimes took a man's last dollar for jobs that did not exist. The *Spokesman Review* of Jan. 18, 1909, give this picture:

"Hurling rocks and chunks of ice through the windows of the Red Cross Employment Agency, 224 Stevens St., several members of a noisy mob of between 2,000 and 3,000 idle men were about to attempt to wreck the place about 6 o'clock last evening, when James H. Walsh, organizer of the IWW, mounted a chair in the street, stemmed the rising tide of riot and pacified the multitude. In the opinion of the police had it not been for the intervention of Walsh, a riot would surely have followed, as the rabble was worked up to such a pitch that its members would have readily attempted violence. Walsh discouraged violence and summoned all members of the IWW to their hall at the rear of 312 Front Ave. The police dispersed the rest. ... At the hall Walsh warned the crowd against an outbreak. 'There were a lot of hired Pinkertons in that crowd,' he said. 'All they wanted you fellows to do was to start something and then they would have an excuse for shooting you down or smashing your heads in. ... You can gain nothing by resorting to mob rule.'"[8]

Throughout that summer as employment picked up, IWW street meetings, with the songs that had been born for this special purpose, turned the fury of more and more fleeced men into the constructive channels of building One Big Union. The sharks got the City Council to forbid street meetings in the area they infested, despite the several occasions on which these meetings had prevented riots. The IWW approached the City Council and leading citizens, pointing out the unconstitutionality of this ordinance, and that it would mean worse operation by the sharks and possible riots. Still, meetings were forbidden, and the *Industrial Worker* of October 28 sent out the call: "Wanted – Men to Fill the Jails of Spokane." A communication to all IWW locals stated: "Nov. 2, Free Speech Day – IWW locals will be notified by wire how many men to send if any. Meetings will be orderly and no irregularities of any kind will be tolerated." The City Council arranged for a large rock pile on which to put the free speech fighters to work.[9]

The first day of the fight for free speech, man after man mounted the box to say, "Friends and Fellow Workers" and be yanked down, until 103 had been arrested, beaten and lodged in jail. A legend runs that one man, unaccustomed to public speaking, uttered the customary salutation, and still unarrested, and with no police by the box, paused, with nothing more to say, and in all the horrors of stage fright, hollered: "Where are the cops?" In a month over 500 were in jail on bread and water. The Franklin School was used for overflow, and the War Department helped subvert the Constitution by letting the city use Fort Wright to imprison those upholding the First Amendment.

In succession, eight editors of the local *Industrial Worker* got out an issue and went to jail. The police tried to destroy all copies of the Dec. 10th issue in which Elizabeth Gurley Flynn, who had delayed her arrest by chaining herself to a lamp post while she spoke, charged that the sheriff was using the women's section of the jail as a profitable brothel, with the police soliciting customers. The *Industrial Worker*

FREE SPEECH IS YET MUZZLED IN FRESNO, CALIFORNIA

was moved to the quieter city of Seattle until May 1910, and then back to Spokane.

The constant arrests; the police brutalities; the appearance of men in court matted with blood; the disrepute into which Spokane had fallen in the more enlightened portion of the nation's press; the widely known evil practices of the employment sharks; the mounting cost to taxpayers; the boycott on Spokane merchants by men in many camps – all these made it harder for the city fathers to continue. Feeling was for the prisoners. On the rare occasion when they were marched through the streets to where they could get a bath, citizens showered them with Bull Durham, apples and oranges. On March 4 came victory – the release of the prisoners and the right to speak. Soon the licenses of 19 of the more offensive sharks were revoked, and the practice of direct hiring of men grew rapidly. The IWW's reputation boomed.

On the heels of this free-speech fight came another in Fresno, Calif. There the IWW was organizing agricultural workers, with Frank Little in charge, and the police, to oppose the policy of holding out for higher bidders, forbade three or more workers to talk together on the streets. Street meetings had not been part of the organizing campaign, but now there was a free speech fight. An influx of IWWs camped on land furnished by a friendly socialist – until the camp was burned one night by the vigilantes – and held surprise meetings to get some of their case to the public before each speaker was arrested. The jail was a forerunner of Hitlerian horrors, but this fight, too, was won.

Since IWW advocates frequently used the soapbox to spread their ideas, even where no definite organization campaign was afoot, these successes tended for a while to sidetrack the IWW into fighting for free speech on its own account. The 1912 fight in San Diego, where there was almost nothing to organize, is a case in point.[10] Similar enthusiasm took many members into the army supporting Magon in the civil war in Mexico. On Jan. 29, 1912, what is described as "an IWW army" took Mexicali and later Tia Juana, opening the jails as first order of business. They lost the war, but in July a number of Mexican unions confederated and adopted the IWW preamble.[11]

Elsewhere the IWW was trying to build up the global jurisdiction that its name implied; Tom Mann organized branches in South Africa; it was growing in Australia and New Zealand. James Roe, a one-armed telegrapher, attempted to launch it in Hawaii, but died or was killed in jail. In England a number of clubs, termed the Advocates of Industrial Unionism, formed a movement around the paper, *The Industrialist*. In the American melting pot, the IWW issued papers in various languages that were mailed to kindred spirits in mother countries: *La Union Industriale* (Spanish) at Phoenix, Arizona; *Solidarnosc*, in Polish, at Buffalo; *Emancipation*, organ of the Franco-Belgian Federation which consisted chiefly of textile workers; and the friendly *Proletarian* in Japanese, in San Francisco. On the international field, the IWW had challenged the AFL as a body denying the basic union principle of class struggle, indirectly at the International Socialist and Labor Congress at Stuttgart in 1907, and again through Wm. Z. Foster, its credentialed delegate, with the backing of the French CGT, at Budapest in 1910.

On Foster's return he urged a switch in policy to "boring from within" the AFL. The proposal was debated in the press and definitely turned down.[12] Arguments ran that the IWW could busy itself with the nine-tenths of the working class that the AFL had not organized; that to bore was to get kicked out; that the rebels in the AFL stood a better chance if outside it, there was the IWW to point to, to get into if they got kicked out or left in disgust, and to maintain a press pro-

Police turned fire hoses on the San Diego free speech fighters, while vigilantes tortured them with the connivance of local authorities.

moting their ideas; that vested interests and basic structure of the AFL would make the IWW impotent inside it; and that many of the IWW had occupations for which the AFL had no unions in which to bore. The few who supported Foster withdrew with him to found the Syndicalist League of North America, a very small propagandist society.

IWW relations with other unions formed a varied pattern. In San Diego, AFL carpenters refused to build a stockade to imprison free speech fighters. In Detroit the IWW did much of the work in the AFL's 8 Hour League and the McNamara Defense. In Philadelphia, where the AFL divided the men at the locomotive works into 17 different crafts, they struck, and the small IWW local, No. 11, went out with them June 8, 1911. Through dual membership in other unions the IWW had a majority on the joint committee, had access to various unions to seek support, and wound up reporting: "Instead of driving the men to use different tactics, we were showing them how to finance their fight, and this will not win." In New York the IWW organized the Western Union messengers, then the local organizers turned them over to the AFL on the grounds they could provide better halls and more help, but that strike flopped. In Brooklyn the IWW organized a number of shoe factories, enhancing their prestige after winning several victories by refusing to go back until the cutters, organized in a Knights of Labor local, had won too. This was a revolt against the policy of Tobin's Boot and Shoe Workers, who peddled the union label to employers in return for a check-off even with wages lower than in non-union shops. In this fight many AFL bodies supported the IWW instead of the AFL affiliate. The IWW ended 1910 with a large number of shoe shops on strike, but settled these strikes one after another from Jan. 22 on, until at the end of February only four plants were struck, involving 800, with 2,200 organized back at work. One reason for this was to use available funds for the defense of Buccafori, a striker who had killed his employer after the latter had knocked him down on the floor and kicked him. Bill Haywood, also returning from Europe at this time, renewed his interest in the IWW at this time and spoke for the Buccafori defense. His talk, "The General Strike," was issued as a pamphlet.

These big fights of a little union from 1909 to 1911 laid the foundation for its substantial growth and bigger battles of 1912.

Notes:
1. From table furnished in Brissenden, p. 70.
2. List from *Industrial Worker,* Jan. 15, 1920.
3. Duchez in *International Socialist Review,* October, 1909. A more detailed account of McKees Rocks is given in Perlman & Taft, *History of Labor in U.S.,* Chapter XXIII.
4. *Solidarity,* issue No. 52, Vol. I.
5. *Solidarity,* Jan. 29, 1910 et seq.
6. *Solidarity,* issue No. 25.
7. *Solidarity,* issue No. 51 et seq., and more detailed summary in series, "IWW Tells Own Story," *Solidarity,* May 26, 1931.
8. Quoted *Industrial Union Bulletin,* Feb. 7,1909.
9. Story of Spokane free speech fight from IWW papers, Spokane papers and *International Socialist Review* of the period.
10. See detailed series in *Industrial Worker,* July 16 - Aug. 9, 1947.
11. Lorwin, *Labor and Internationalism,* chapter 12.
12. Discussion starts *Solidarity,* Nov. 4, 1911.

General Sources:
The most complete account of the McKees Rocks strike is by John Ingham in *Pennsylvania Magazine of History* (1966, pp. 353-377), who also cites a related investigation into charges of peonage. Foner (pp. 281-195) and Dubofsky (202-209) also discuss the strike. The only sustained scholarly

treatment of Trautmann is Jay Miller's unpublished dissertation, "Soldier of the Class War" (Wayne State University, 2000). Mark Derby has a chapter on Trautmann's role in *Revolution: The 1913 strike in New Zealand*, edited by Melanie Nolan (Canterbury University Press, 2006).

The Free Speech Fights have received extensive attention, including in Kornbluh (pp. 94-104), Foner (172-182) and Dubofsky (173-197). Brazier wrote his recollections of the Spokane fight in the *Industrial Worker* (January and February 1967), and E.G. Flynn gives her recollections in a memoir variously published as *I Speak My Piece* or *Rebel Girl*. On Fresno, Ted Lehman's paper filed at Wayne State explores the role of Frank Little and his elder brother; Charles P. LeWarne published a lengthy account by E.M. Clyde of the trip to Fresno in *Labor History* (Spring 1973); also Ronald Genini in *California Historical Quarterly* (1974, pp. 100-128). On Aberdeen: "The Aberdeen, Washington, Free Speech Fight of 1911-1912" by Charles P. LeWarne in *Pacific Northwest Quarterly* (January 1975). On San Diego, to observe the 60th anniversary, the IWW branch there in 1972 reprinted as a pamphlet the *New York Call*'s account of that fight; McKay's participant recollections ran in the *Industrial Worker* (July 26 to August 9, 1947). See also Theodore Schroeder, *Free Speech for Radicals* (Riverside, 1916) and Phillip Foner, *Fellow Workers and Friends: IWW Free Speech Fights As Told By Participants* (Greenwood, 1981).

On the IWW and Mexico, see Norman Caulfield's *Mexican Workers and the State* (Texas Christian University Press, 1998), Lowell L. Blaisdell, *The Desert Revolution* (Madison, 1962), and Rey Davis' series on Magon in the *Industrial Worker* (May through August 1974).

Foster's case for boring from within is presented in Foner (415-434), and in Earl Ford and Wm. Foster, *Syndicalism* (1912, reprinted by Charles H. Kerr 1990 with an introduction by James Barrett). Critiques of Foster's position can be found in J. Conlin, *Bread and Roses Too*, and Jon Bekken, "The Tragedy of Fosterism" (*Anarcho-Syndicalist Review* 31, 2001, pp. 13-22, 36-37), much of which is devoted to reprinting debate on Foster's position from the IWW press.

4. The Textile Workers

Between January 1912 and the tough times that set in again toward the end of 1913, the IWW, with a series of good fights and substantial victories, won widespread recognition as the most forward thrust of the American labor movement. These were the years of victories in Lawrence, Lowell, New Bedford, Little Falls and other textile centers, ending in the hopeless fight at Paterson; of lumber battles in Louisiana and Gray's Harbor, Washington; of railroad construction strikes with thousand mile picket lines; of expansion into auto and other metal working industries; of fighting for the Pittsburgh stogie makers and the rubber workers of Akron; of the accession of longshoremen and seamen to start its Marine Transport Workers; and of sensational trials arising from its fight in Lawrence, Louisiana and the hop fields of California – trials that added to its fame as much as did the strikes that generated them.

A persistent myth about the IWW is that it plunged into strikes without previous organization, bringing out contented workers with spellbinding oratory, won great victories, then deserted the workers to repeat the process elsewhere. The myth is groundless.

Prior to its fame at Lawrence the IWW had been organizing textile workers for seven years, and these constituted roughly half of its membership. It had followed up its initial victory in Skowhegan, Maine, with organization and a victorious three-month strike at Mapleville, R.I., in 1907. By next year it had eight textile locals and these were formed into its first national industrial union with James P. Thompson as organizer. These withstood the depression, and in 1910 were all in good standing, and during the years in which strikes had been opportune, had added three more locals.[1]

This stability and steady growth of the IWW textile workers is the more remarkable since few of these workers could bargain through their union, and nowhere did it have "union security" in any form. They were men and women who had been educated into unionism with lectures on the history of the labor movement, with study classes in economics, with union fundamentals handed them in leaflets, and strike talks. Social activities and dramatic clubs, for most of their halls had stages, helped cement them. The National Industrial Union of Textile Workers of the IWW was held together by an understanding of what industrial unionism could accomplish, and its members were willing to transmit this vision to their fellow workers as volunteer organizers and leaflet peddlers. They aided various strikes of the small independent unions in their field and steadily built the reputation of the IWW.

Lawrence Local 20 had been formed in 1906. It almost died in 1907 but was brought to life again with aid from the National Industrial Union formed in 1908 and from a more thriving local nine miles away in Lowell. By 1910 it owned its own hall, and there the third convention of the Industrial Union was held over Labor Day. In January 1911, on invitation, it joined a newly formed Alliance of Textile Workers Unions of Lawrence with the reservation that it would not be bound to any action contrary to IWW principles. That summer the companies started changing the production system from one in which weavers ran 7 looms at 79 cents a cut to one in which they ran 12 at 49 cents a cut, giving them an average boost in weekly wages from $11.06 to $11.76 for almost double production. The IWW called a strike of the weavers against Atlantic Mills. It won, and the independent Lawrence Weavers Protective Association brought its 500 members into Local 20 on October 1.[2] On November 2 organizer J. P. Thompson was brought back to Lawrence for a two-month campaign, and throughout November expounded union fundamentals to enthusiastic noonday meetings. Stickers and circulars were issued in support of various small strikes called by other organizations, all urging a shorter workday and the One Big Union idea. Plainly the IWW was no flash in the pan when the big strike broke upon Lawrence in January 1912.[3]

Lawrence had a population of 85,892, of whom at least 60,000 depended upon mill wages. Almost everyone over 14 worked in its textile mills. The average wage was 16 cents an hour. About 15,000 got only 12 cents. With lost time the prevailing work week of 56 hours yielded an average pay of only about $7. Their labor had yielded such profits that they had more than paid for the mills in which they worked: Pacific Mills inside ten years had paid dividends alone amounting to 148 percent of its investment.[4]

Jan. 1, 1912, a state law became effective reducing the work week to 54 hours. Without a pay boost this meant 32 cents less a week for those working 56 hours, and 32 cents then bought 10 loaves of bread. For some with still longer hours it meant a still bigger reduction.

Wages were so close to starvation that many expected the weekly pay would not be cut. When the first pay envelopes for the year were distributed on January 11, some workers in the Washington Mills went through the plant calling their fellow workers to walk out with them. The strike was on.

Local 20 had not planned for a strike until summer, but seeing how feeling ran it called the entire local textile industry on strike the following day, and sent for Haywood, Ettor, J. P. Thompson and others to come in. By the middle of January 16,000 were out, and by the 27th 25,000, headed by a strike committee of 60 elected from the ranks of the strikers to represent both each major occupational group and each of the 16 major languages spoken. From these 60 various detail committees were elected. The first few unorganized days of the strike were disorderly. On the 15th militia and pickets clashed at the Pacific Mills. Once the IWW organized the strike it amazed all observers by the orderliness with which it was conducted, the only violence that of the police and National Guard who were there at a cost of $4,000 a day, or almost four times what it would have cost the companies not to have cut the weekly pay.

. Golden of the United Textile Workers came at once to break the strike, but failed completely. The rather diminutive AFL Central Labor Council refused to recognize the 25,000 textile workers striking under the banner of the IWW, with the result that the Molders Union withdrew in disgust leaving that sedate body without a presiding officer.[5]

On Jan. 20 a plant of dynamite was discovered. Strikers were accused, but soon it was shown that it had been planted by John A. Breen, member of the Board of Education. On conviction he was fined $500. On Jan. 29 a peaceful parade of the strikers was charged by the militia, and officer Oscar Benoit fired into the crowd, hitting striker Annie Lo Pezza and killing her. At once three organizers, Ettor, Giovannitti and Caruso, were arrested as accessories to murder, and held without bail to keep them from strike activity. They were acquitted Nov. 26 after a three-week trial. Nothing was done to Benoit or those who had ordered the vicious and needless attack on the parading strikers.

The view of the militia is disclosed by the remarks of an officer to a writer for *Outlook:* "Our company of militia went down to Lawrence during the first days of the strike. Most of them had to leave Harvard to do it; but they rather enjoyed going down there to have their fling at those people."[6] Harry Emerson Fosdick quotes a Boston lawyer: "Any

Some of the strikers' children leaving Lawrence to winter the strike with supporters in other cities.

man who pays more for labor than the lowest sum he can get them for is robbing his stockholders. ... The strike should have been stopped in the first 24 hours. The militia should have been instructed to shoot. That is the way Napoleon did it."[7] During the nine-week conflict 335 strikers were arrested, of whom 320 were sentenced on minor charges, with most of their convictions being reversed on appeal.

Feeding these impoverished people for nine weeks would have been an impossible task if it had not been for the help of the Franco-Belgian Cooperative that had its own bakery, and donated its services and also much material. Appeals to labor at large brought in donations totaling $74,011.39, but this figures out to only 33 cents per week per striker. A cotton broker, James Prendergast, connived with a minister and judge to tie the strike relief up by alleging donations were made without a name or address to which to send a receipt, and the contention that the strike funds were not properly handled. At the time the funds amounted to about $8,000, but these were withdrawn all but 48 cents to save them from seizure. Later an accountant appointed by the court certified that the IWW had spent some $3,000 more on strike relief than it had received, including donations from its own locals. The charge then shifted that some of this money had gone to buy railroad tickets for strikers' children sent out of town. This was dropped when the Boston Local of the Socialist Party testified that its donation of $3,000 was intended for whatever strike purpose it could best serve. The IWW was cleared in the courts, but the SLP, which, interfered throughout this wave of textile strikes, masquerading under the name IWW, issued a pamphlet again accusing the IWW of these exploded charges.

These railroad tickets had been bought to send strikers' children to sympathetic families away from hunger-and-militia-ridden Lawrence. This was a new strike tactic in America. The children liked it and were effective reminders of the strikers' needs in the communities to which they went. They traveled in guided groups, each child with an identification card signed by its parents. This went well until Feb. 24. That morning parents and friends assembled to see a group of children off on the seven o'clock train. When it pulled in, the militia crossed bayonets across all doors. The children had their tickets clutched in their hands and some who tried to run to the train were clubbed down on the platform while police beat the strikers in the station. "There was a hideous struggle," reported *Solidarity*. "The women fought and kicked and scratched with the mad frenzy of mothers fighting for their young. The police choked them and clubbed them and knocked them down. Finally the officers pitched the women and children into a great arsenal wagon and drove them off, a screaming, fighting wagon load, to the police station where the little ones were booked as neglected children."[8] Since this was interference with interstate commerce, the U.S. Senate investigated and brought forth two fat volumes on the strike.[9]

On March 13 a rank-and-file committee that could talk shop better than the company lawyers met with American Woolen that raised its previous best offer of a 5 percent flat increase to a 21 percent boost or 2 cents an hour for those getting 9 1/2 cents, ranging down to 1 cent for those getting 20, along with other improvements in reckoning the pay and bonus. Next day a mass meeting on Lawrence Common accepted these terms. Eight companies that refused were still struck until they gave parallel gains. There were sympathetic increases in mills elsewhere.

The impact of this strike on thinking about American labor was expressed by Harry Fosdick in *Outlook* of that June: "Wages have been raised, work has been resumed, the militia has gone, and the whirring looms suggest industrial peace; but behind all this the most revolutionary organization in the history of American industry is building up an army of volunteers. The IWW leaves behind as hopelessly passé the methods of the American Federation of Labor."[10] Others felt the same way about it.

Strike methods and oratory both contributed to this impression. Speakers talked of a day when the endless haggling with employers would be replaced by an industrial democracy in which those who did the work made the industrial decisions. They explained that the solidarity in the strike and the solidarity of labor toward the strike were steps, not only to two cents more per hour, but to the organized competence of labor to run industry for use instead of profit. The exodus of children to sympathetic homes was part of the strategy of making the working class feel as one. The endless chain picketing, devised in this strike when regular picketing was stopped, so that strikers walked one after another around the entire mill section of town, made each worker in that line feel that however helpless he might be as an individual, as a link in that chain he tied up industry. The democracy that welded these workers of 16 tongues together, and that enabled them to determine strike policy, was a foretaste of what labor, rightly organized, could do.

The Lawrence strike was followed by other textile strikes.[11] In Lowell 18,000 textile workers struck immediately after it. In New Bedford in July 15,000 textile workers responded to the call of the IWW to support the independently organized weavers who had struck against the fining system. The various craft unions refused to act jointly with the IWW but the 15,000 stayed out until the weavers on their own account had returned. In Little Falls, N.Y., a major center for knit goods and underwear, the state law limiting female labor to 54 hours per week became effective Oct. 1, 1912, and produced an unorganized walkout at the Phoenix and Gilbert Mills on the 10th, much like that in Lawrence. The IWW organized the Polish, Austrian and Italian workers, but had less success with the $6.40 a week "Americans." To hamper the strike, meeting places were denied and outdoor speaking prohibited. The socialists from Schenectady, including Mayor Lunn, furnished most of the force for the free speech end of the fight and won not only their constitutional rights, but considerable support from the English-speaking workers. On Oct. 30, when a thug struck a girl picket, a fight broke out with the result that organizers Legere (an actor) and Bochino got convicted of stabbing a detective "in the seat of the pants" and sojourned at Auburn until July 1914. There were hundreds of individual arrests, and a mass arrest of strikers meeting

The Little Falls strikers outside the Slovak hall.

in the Slovak Sokol Hall. On that occasion the police broke heads, musical instruments and furniture alike. The next day other strikers paraded, playing the Marsellaise and International on their broken instruments, and requested troops to curb the police. The request was denied. When, shortly after this, children were sent out of town, and truant officers attempted to stop them at the station, they had papers in proper legal form to assure their departure. On January 3 the strike was ended on terms arranged by state mediators: reinstatement for all, increases to range from 5 to 18 percent, no one to get less for the 54-hour week than for 60 hours.

A week later when the National Industrial Union of Textile Workers held its fourth convention, it was proud of its achievements. Then came Paterson.

Paterson was an old silk center, with some big firms and about 290 smaller ones. Its technology lagged behind that used in the newer silk towns, like Allentown, Scranton and other places where miners' wives and daughters worked on high speed looms. (Their wages averaged $7.01 in 1912; male earnings were lower, only $6.06) The industry was beginning to trustify. Haywood said: "The strike would undoubtedly have ended much sooner had it not been for the desire of the richer manufacturers to see the smaller ones starved out and driven into bankruptcy.... The competing Pennsylvania mills are largely owned by the same interests."[12] Under these circumstances victory required industry-wide solidarity; it could not be attained by lone action in the technologically backward center from which the industry was moving.

When the 4-loom system was introduced into the Doherty Mills in Paterson late in January 1913, the weavers, unorganized, came out spontaneously. In Paterson the IWW had a substantial local, including such capable organizers as Ewald Koettgen and Adolph Lessig, silk workers themselves. The weavers asked their help, and they took the gamble of trying to make the strike industry-wide. On the last day of February the local struck the 1,930 mills and dye-houses in Paterson, and, with the aid of socialist locals at or near the more modern silk centers, sent strikers and organizers to bring them into the fight too; but there had not been the necessary preparation, and the fight was confined to Paterson. There, 25,000 struck until September 24; 1,473 were arrested; five were killed. Outside labor support brought in $59,957.79 for strike relief, and this time to prevent rumors, the funds and expenses were checked by a public accountant. A pageant staged by John Reed, using the strikers to portray their struggle, toured eastern cities; the poster design was later used on many editions of songbooks and other pamphlets. But all this could not win in the old silk center against modern technology in other towns, with the better looms owned by the same large interests. By the time the strike was given up, hard times were on the way again, hitting, as they often do, the textile industries first. The IWW spent the last cent it could raise on this fight, and it almost did for the IWW as the Pullman strike of 1894 had done to Debs' ARU.

In April and May 1913, while the Paterson strike was on, the union engaged in a struggle in Ipswich, a town where the previous fall the IWW had won prestige by action enabling workers to collect $60,000 in back wages held from those who had quit without giving two weeks' notice. Arrests, police clubbings, and the impossibility of getting any place to meet except a churchyard made the strike a dead issue when an ordinance was passed forbidding meetings in churchyards.

The National Industrial Union of Textile Workers persisted until March 11, 1916.[13] Then the General Executive Board put its remaining members in directly affiliated locals until it should have a membership of 5,000 or more. Since then there has been only a scattered membership in that industry and a few minor efforts at organization.

Elizabeth Gurley Flynn addressing Paterson strikers, June 1913

Already at its 1913 convention, full of success, the older members whose persistent plugging had built it up in the lean years of 1908-1911, refused to accept nominations. The GEB reported to the 10th convention that immediately following the Lawrence strike "a campaign of slander and insinuation was launched against the officers and most of the old active workers." That 1913 convention resolved that only those who had worked in the textile industry should serve it as organizers, though the organization had been built largely by organizers from other industries. But most important factor was the unemployment and hard times that set in late in 1913.

The policies of the 1913 convention, the friendship of the socialists and these hard times all combined to undermine the newly grown union. Despite the arguments over "sabotage" and the unseating of Haywood from the National Executive Committee of the Socialist Party in 1912,[14] actual relations were friendly, and the harm done by the socialists was evidently done unwittingly, even though its policy right along had been and still was to favor the AFL. With hard times the socialist activities appeared to offer a better outlet for whatever aspirations for a new social order these workers had retained from their strikes and past experience. Dropping the old guard of organizers as strangers to the industry pushed them in this direction for they could have mapped out a program to make the union serviceable to its members no matter how hard the times, just as it had survived the bad years 1908-1909. While many had been organized for brief periods during the strikes, and while every effort, short of contracts, was made to hold them after the strike, post-strike locals were small. In Lawrence it was claimed that 10,000 out of the 25,000 strikers joined the IWW, but by the fall of 1913 the Lawrence local had only 700 members.[15]

To some extent this decline of the National Industrial Union of Textile Workers came from the difficulty of hitting the right balance between an industrial union program so different from prevailing thought that it struck most workers as alien, and a program so confined to job unionism that it lacked the spirit and vision necessary to hold workers together, as they had been held in 1908, when jobs disappeared and strikes were out of the picture.

Throughout the years since, some of the old battlers and some younger textile workers who shared their vision have maintained Textile Workers Industrial Union 610 of the IWW, mindful of the need for industry-wide bargaining to cope with geographical shifts and persistently low wages even as in the days of Paterson. They may yet provide the union the textile workers need, for their need very plainly has not yet been met.

Notes:

1. For general story of the period, see series "IWW Tells Its Own Story" for greater details, and articles by Chas. Miller who actively participated in these strikes, in *Industrial Worker,* July 1945.
2. *Solidarity,* Nov. 18, 1911.
3. Report of Organizer J.P. Thompson to seventh convention of IWW.
4. Chas. Miller, series, July 1945, *Industrial Worker.*
5. *Solidarity,* No. 114.
6. Al Priddy in *Outlook,* Oct. 1912.
7. H. E. Fosdick in *Outlook,* June 15, 1912.
8. *Solidarity,* No. 114.
9. They are 62nd Congress, 2nd session, Senate document 870.
10. *Outlook,* June 15, 1912.
11. Details of these strikes are in papers of period and summarized in "IWW

Tells Its Own Story," *Solidarity,* Sept. and Oct. 1931.

12. *International Socialist Review,* May 1913.

13. Proceedings, 10th Convention IWW, p. 73.

14. See below, chapter VI, on ideological conflicts of period.

15. Levine, *Political Science Quarterly,* Sept. 1913. Winston Churchill's novel, *The Dwelling Place of Light,* depicts the Lawrence strike fairly well.

General Sources:

The background of the Lawrence strike can be found in Donald R. Cole, *Immigrant City* (Chapel Hill, 1963), and all general histories have extensive accounts. Foner (329-350) gives the most detail on the Breen dynamite affair. William Cahn's photographic history, *Lawrence 1912: The Bread and Roses Strike* (Pilgrim Press, 1977) is an edited reprint of Cahn's 1954 *Mill Town.* Michael Miller Topp addresses the role of Italian-Americans in the strike (and in the IWW more generally) in *Those Without A Country: The Political Culture of Italian American Syndicalists* (Univ. of Minnesota, 2001). Ardis Cameron's *Radicals of the Worst Sort* (Univ. of Illinois Press, 1993) included much material on the role of women in the strike. Gerald Sider offers a strange take on the strike in his "Cleansing History: Lawrence, Massachusetts, the Strike for Four Loaves of Bread and No Roses, and the Anthropology of Working-class Consciousness" (*Radical History* 65, 1996, pp. 48-83, followed by responses by Paul Buhle, Ardis Cameron, and David Montgomery, pp. 84-117), which relies heavily on his plagiarism of Kornbluh's incorrect citation for Oppenheimer's poem "Bread and Roses." The most recent work on Lawrence is Bruce Watson's *Bread & Roses: Mills, Migrants and the Struggle for the American Dream* (Viking, 2005), a sympathetic account which nonetheless is unable to understand why the strikers, and the IWW, rejected capitalism.

Far more has been written about the Paterson strike than about any of the IWW's successful campaigns, demonstrating the quantitative distortion of the IWW story by even its sympathetic historians. The best history is Steve Golin's *The Fragile Bridge* (Temple, 1988), which focuses on the strikers' self-activity and the way it captured the imagination of radical bohemians in Greenwich Village. Anne Huber Tripp's *The IWW and the Paterson Silk Strike of 1913* (Univ. of Illinois, 1987) focuses on the role of IWW leaders. Salvatore Salerno's "Paterson's Italian Anarchist Silk Workers and the Politics of Race" (*Working USA,* Sept. 2005) explores the role of these radicals, who joined the IWW in 1906 and played a key role in laying the foundation for the strike. Graham Adams' chapter on Paterson in his *Age of Industrial Violence* (Columbia University Press, 1966) has material on the Scott and Quinlan trials; *Art in America* (May-June 1974) has an illustrated article on the Paterson Pageant; Martin Green's *New York 1913* (Scribner's, 1988) discusses the intersection of the Paterson pageant and modern art movements; African-American IWW organizer Hubert Harrison was one of the IWW's featured speakers during the strike – his role is discussed in Jeffrey Perry's *A Hubert Harrison Reader* (Wesleyan, 2001); Mel Most (*Sunday Record,* Nov. 11, 1973, and Sept. 1, 1974) interviews participants in the strike on both sides and concludes that local industry was ruined as a boomerang effect of employer lies about violence. The Botto home in Haledon, site for free speech during the strike, is now a national landmark and home to the American Labor Museum.

Henry McGuckin's *Memoirs of a Wobbly* (Charles H. Kerr, 1987) discusses the effort to bring out competitive plants. Little has been written on IWW activity in other textile plants. A generally ignored IWW silk strike in Hazelton, Penn., from Feb. 5 to April 2, 1913, is detailed in Patrick Lynch's M.A. thesis, "Pennsylvania Anthracite" (Bloomsburg State, 1974). Robert Snyder writes about the 1912 Little Falls strike in Joseph Conlin's collection, *At the Point of Production* (Greenwood, 1981), which also includes an essay by James Osborne on the role of immigrant strikers in the Paterson strike.

The textile strikes point to the key role immigrant workers played in the IWW, an issue given far more attention in Salerno's *Red November, Black November* than in other historical surveys. Salerno's "No God, No Masters: Italian Anarchists and the IWW" (in *The Lost World of Italian-American Radicalism,* 2003) offers a sympathetic look, while Topp clearly prefers the Amalgamated and uncritically accepts its perspective in *Those Without a Country.*

IWW organizers Hubert Harrison, E.G. Flynn and 'Big Bill' Haywood, photographed during the Paterson strike.

5. The Pre-War Crest

(1912-13: IWW activities outside of textile industry)

While the IWW was building a name in the textile industry, it fought some great battles among Canadian construction workers, Louisiana loggers, Washington saw mill workers, on the docks of Philadelphia and Duluth, in auto and other metal industries, in the Pittsburgh cigar industry, and for hop pickers in California. Its rapid extension – much like that of the Knights in 1884-86 – was possible only because it developed the organizing abilities latent in its ranks. It had not yet developed the program of "every member an organizer" and the job delegate system that grew in 1915 out of its activities in agriculture, but had as organization staff all its General Executive Board members, four national organizers, and 16 organizers with "voluntary credentials," weekly listing them in its papers and warning that no others were accredited organizers for the IWW.

The prestige of Lawrence resulted in victories in other fields: a victorious one-week strike of molders and others at National Malleable Casting in Indianapolis in March 1912; the organization of a successful strike of piano and organ builders in New York in April and May. Again in May, a two-week strike against American Radiator in Buffalo won boosts and better hours there and brought other nearby plants to do likewise so that over 5,000 benefited. In June the IWW won increases at Warner Refining in Edgewater, N.Y., and at Corn Products Refining at Shadyside, N.J.[1] In Peoria in June occurred one of the few events that give some substance to the myth of the IWW blowing into town, fomenting a strike and pulling out again. Visiting organizer James P. Cannon there turned a socialist meeting into a local of workers at Avery Implement. A couple of the boys were fired, and the rest pulled the whistle without any preparation for strike or getting many organized. It took aggressive picketing to make the strike click, and pickets got arrested, including Cannon's fellow evangelist, Tom Moore, who sent out a call from jail for "jail material and lots of it." It threatened to turn into a free speech fight to rival San Diego, but, to prevent this, new organizers came to town and arranged a settlement including the release of all in jail, and the evangelists departed.

Along a five hundred mile stretch where the Canadian Northern was penetrating the mountains of British Columbia, six thousand "dynos and dirthands" struck on March 28, 1912.[2] They soon tied up everything from Hope to Kamloops, and before it was over the IWW had another strike of similar size on the construction of the Grand Trunk. Some organization had been built among these men in the summer of 1911 as they flocked into the area waiting for this work to open up. Those doing preliminary work for the subcontractors, and others camping along the right of way waiting for work, sent for organizer J. S. Biscay to unionize them so they could start the big job with union demands. Their competition had brought down wages on this preliminary work to $2.25 a day. By Sept. 6, 1911, over 900 had been organized into Local 327 and the men on a 160-mile section decided to hold out for higher pay. The contractors asked for the army to force the men to work, but didn't get it. Local business interests hoped for a wage boost and businessmen even donated funds for Local 327 to build its hall in Kamloops. Organization had reached over 2,000, or a third of the men, before the big strike began.

This was the first time the IWW had to establish its "thousand mile picket line," extending not only over 400 miles of construction, but much further to employment offices in Minneapolis and San Francisco. The IWW kept many from shipping, and sent its missionaries among those who shipped to induce them to quit en route; the railroads were left holding many old suitcases filled with bricks and newspapers by those taking the trip part way.

The contractors, after finding that neither violence nor the remote recruiting of scabs could break the strike, hit on "station work," a form of subcontracting by small groups of "self-employed" workers, with "piece work" rates that appealed to many of the strikers. The strikers were now divided first over whether or not to accept station work at any rates, and secondly, if so, how those rates should be set. Solidarity weakened and the strike ended with minor improvements, and earnings at station work were no doubt raised by the strike and the sense of unionism. (A similar use of the "gyppo" system of piece work had much to do later with the decline of the IWW in Washington forests; and in postmortems many on the scene later argued that the effective tactic would have been to accept this payment by results system, but at rates that gave the employer no advantage over day work. In both instances, to introduce it, much higher earnings were permitted than men made by it once it was established.)

This and the strike on the Grand Trunk lasted until late fall. Both were well supported by the labor movement of western Canada. The *British Columbia Federationist* served it as a regular weekly strike bulletin.

It was at this time that the term "Wobbly" as nickname for IWW came into use. Previously they had been called many things from International Wonder Workers to I Won't Works. The origin of the expression "Wobbly" is uncertain. Legend assigns it to the lingual difficulties of a Chinese restaurant keeper with whom arrangements had been made during this strike to feed members passing through his town. When he tried to ask "Are you IWW?" it is said to have come out: "All loo eye wobble wobble?" The same situation, but in Vancouver, is given as the 1911 origin of the term by Mortimer Downing in a letter quoted in *The Nation*, Sept. 5, 1923, with the additional information:

"Thereafter the laughing term among us was 'I Wobbly Wobbly,' and when Herman Suhr during the Wheatland strike[3] wired for all footloose 'Wobblies' to hurry there, of course the prosecution made a mountain of mystery out of it, and the term has stuck ever since." Mencken in his *American Language* doubts this explanation. Some credit the term to Otis of the *Los Angeles Times*, an avid opponent of the IWW. Some lingual difficulty seems most likely to have been behind it, for in its sense of vacillating it fits no accusation ever made against IWW, and about the only meaning of wobbly that could conceivably fit is that of "wobble saw," a circular saw mounted askew to cut a groove wider than its own thickness.

In February 1912 the second national industrial union of the IWW was formed, the Forest and Lumber Workers. That summer the young Brotherhood of Timber Workers, centered in Louisiana joined it as an autonomous division. In contrast to the northwest, the Louisiana lumber worker was a "homeguard," often a "sodbuster."[4] Previous efforts from the Knights on had failed to give them stable organization. In 1902 around Lutcher they had formed a union, won, and dissolved. Again they had organized in 1907 to resist a wage cut, holding out longest around Lake Charles, and the union had died again. In 1910 the Brotherhood was formed, "swarming" around some 90 IWWs and "red" socialists – that is those who preferred Debs to Berger and Lee – and from the beginning was attacked by the lumber barons as IWW and alien. Its fights were lockouts, not strikes, and it was a revolt

Louisiana timber worker.

of the local people, including farmers and preachers and merchants and doctors, against the outside capital that was walking off with the riches of the area. (During its fights the lumber interests said they would deal with a respectable AFL union, yet in 1919 when AFL Carpenters tried to organize around Bogalusa, a mob of deputized thugs killed three at the union hall and stopped it.) The Brotherhood organized black and white workers together. It sent fraternal delegates to the 1911 IWW convention; its convention in May 1912 was addressed by Haywood, and by referendum it joined the IWW that summer and was duly installed at the 1912 IWW convention.

The lumber companies opposed the Brotherhood with off-and-on lockouts, discrimination and "tin-panning," or the raising of such a din by beating circular saws that speakers could not be heard at union meetings. On July 7, 1912, at the crossroads in Grabow, A. L. Emerson, president of the Brotherhood, held his audience together through such a "tin-panning" until shots came from the office of the Galloway Lumber Company, killing three. In the ensuing fight several more were killed. No company thugs were arrested, but 58 union men were lodged in the "Black Hole of Calcasieu" until after a two-month trial they were acquitted in December. The jury was much influenced by the frank admission of state witnesses that their story had been framed in the offices of Congressman Pujo. Their victory in court was greeted with general jubilation by all southern labor.

After the strike the American Lumber Company discharged all who had testified for the defense, and, expecting further discharges of union militants, Emerson asked the 1,200 workers involved to line up on one side of the road, and those who wanted to risk a strike to cross the road. The 1,200 African-American, Mexican, French, Italian and native white workers crossed in a body, and a seven-month fight was on that the Brotherhood lost. It had one more skirmish at Sweet Home, in December 1913, also lost. The Brotherhood persisted until 1916, but had been virtually killed by the blacklisting of 5,000 members. They went west and later helped organize the oil fields of Oklahoma.

On March 4, 1912 the Forest & Lumber Workers Union of IWW struck all the sawmills in Hoquiam, Washington, and within a few days the strike had extended to Raymond, Cosmopolis and Aberdeen, tying up mill operations throughout the Gray's Harbor area. The demand was a wage boost from $2.00 to $2.50 per day. When the mayor of Aberdeen tried to turn city laborers into deputies to break the strike, most of them quit. The Aberdeen Manufacturing Company turned out a load of heavy clubs to crack strikers' heads; the strikers went into the plant and seized them.[5] A Citizens' Committee prevailed on the Aberdeen Trades Council not to endorse the strike. This Committee was headed by bourgeois direct actionists whose vigilantes raided the union hall, arrested strikers, clubbed many in town, and kidnapped hundreds more, whom they took into the surrounding swamps, clubbed and left there. At Hoquiam these vigilantes put 150 strikers into boxcars for deportation, but the Mayor and the railroad workers stopped them. There were mass deportations of Greek and Finnish workers in particular from Raymond. Hindus were brought in to scab, but refused. Finally the Citizens' Committee recommended a raise to $2.25, but preference for native-born American workers. The companies agreed, and the strike committee called a meeting and recommended that the men go back with this gain, and build organization for a further fight.

Next year, in May, the Forest and Lumber Workers, IWW, put out a ballot in all logging camps in that area on whether or not to strike for the following demands: a minimum of $3 for 8 hours; "clean, sanitary bunkhouses without top bunks and having springs, mattresses and bedding furnished free of charge, all camps to be supplied with baths and dry rooms"; and an end to employment fees. Though the vote ran 85 percent to strike, the strike was called off July 3 for lack of pickets.[6] A similar short-lived strike in the Missoula region also failed. The lumber worker was doomed to remain an unwashed timberbeast until 1917.

In August, 1912, Local 101 of IWW, tobacco workers, won short strikes in its old battlefields of Pittsburgh and McKees Rocks, making the Penn, Zasloff and Webster companies revoke a cut. It followed up with a strike against Standard Cigar in both towns, precipitated by a fire in one of its factories that killed four girls and injured 17 others. The union had overcome a prejudice stirred up by the company between the McKees Rocks girls who were mostly Jewish and the Pittsburgh girls who were mostly Irish, and thereby won an 8 hour day, wage boosts ranging from $3 to $4 per week, and a cleanup of the shops and greater protection against further fires.[7]

The following summer the employers in the "hill district" of Pittsburgh, where the three for a nickel variety of stogies were made, locked out the IWW when it struck a member of their association, Dry Slitz Stogie. Twelve hundred were locked out, and the IWW called the remaining 800 stogie workers out. It was an unfavorable time, the beginning of the summer slack season, but the IWW held these workers, mostly girls, together to victory. The lack of organization in this field points up the craft viewpoint. In the nineties the stogie makers had organized, but been turned down as outcasts by the Cigar Makers, and for a time were part of the Knights. When the machine-made "four for a nickel" variety came in, this union turned these down too. The IWW welcomed them all. In the Labor Day Parade the IWW local entered a float depicting child workers and tuberculosis in the Dry Slitz factory. On Sept. 4 the agreement binding employers into an association ended, and many made separate offers. The IWW demand had been 12 to 15 cents for stogies, per hundred, and soon all settled at 11 to 14 – all but Slitz. It had moved out of town.

In Akron on Feb. 10, 1913, 150 Firestone tire builders walked out when their piece rates were cut 35 percent. This led to a six-week strike in which the local socialists and IWW with the aid of Haywood and other outside speakers competed with John L. Lewis, then an AFL organizer, and William Green, then an Ohio state senator, the one side to organize the rubber workers industrially, the other to stampede them back to work rather than see the IWW grow.[8]

It was an unorganized industry. Unionism had been held back by

Akron rubber strike, 1913

craft claims of Boot & Shoe Workers. When the Amalgamated Rubber Workers, AFL, was launched in 1902, Akron rubber workers welcomed it, while the companies launched an Employers' Association and fought it by discriminatory discharge, espionage through Corporations Auxiliary Company, "voluntary" increases, and company unionism. The Amalgamated had lost its push by 1904 in a major defeat in Trenton.

When these 150 tire builders walked out, unorganized, they soon brought the rest of the Firestone tire building department after them. There was an IWW local of 50 or 60 members, closely associated with the Socialist local, and the hall they jointly used was offered as strike headquarters. In a short time they brought out the entire local rubber industry, about 20,000 workers. It was a revolt against industrial poisoning, lack of sanitary facilities, and especially the speedup and Taylor system of which Sieberling boasted. No one had expected this spontaneous revolt, yet it was orderly. The *Akron Beacon-Journal* of February 14 said: "It is safe to say that no strike was ever started so peacefully or with less excitement," and again on the 17th: "With the factories depleted," it commented, "throughout Akron there is only praise for the very orderly way in which the strikers have behaved up to date."

The mayor promptly asked for the National Guard. The governor instead sent in the State Board of Arbitration, and Senator William

Green, later president of the AFL, set up a committee to investigate, and the AFL sent in John L. Lewis and other organizers to take over. The AFL issued a statement explaining that it had intended to organize in Akron earlier, but had been delayed "on account of the enormous work devolving upon its organizers in textiles and iron and steel, as the result of interference... by the people who have assumed control of the strike in the rubber industry."

It took the strike committee of 100 close to two weeks to iron out a wage scale acceptable to all occupations. The AFL drew up its own wage scale, but withdrew it as workers protested against the obvious inequities in it. Later, as in regular Mohawk Valley formula style, the loyal citizens were equipped with badges and clubs to crush this "invasion of alien unionism," and with meetings and picketing stopped a back-to-work movement was promoted to the tune of clubbings. Then, says Roberts in his study of the Rubber Workers, "The AFL put itself in the unfortunate position of aiding the back-to-work movement, thereby helping defeat the strike."

The dirty work of the AFL went deeper than that. The issue was whether or not there was to be collective bargaining. Sieberling, who had done much with his stopwatch to promote the strike, hurried back from his Pacific cruise to say he would deal with no union, and to denounce the strikers as anarchists. Organizer Bessemer replied that in the common usage of anarchist as an extreme individualist, Sieberling's refusal to deal with a union made him the leading anarchist in town. The entire managerial side, in its dealing both with the State Board of Arbitration and with Senator Green's Committee, made it clear that there would be no collective bargaining. Yet the AFL forces, including Green's committee, made much of IWW aversion to contracts as though this could prolong the strike in an industry whose management refused contracts. On the contrary, the IWW proposals were workable ways to settle the strike and achieve some progress in industrial relations. Since the companies refused to deal with any union, the strike committee proposed instead: "The right of employees to present grievances collectively by committees of their own selection, composed of employees of each factory, to negotiate with each manufacturer, should be established for the adjustment of all grievances in the future. The right of workers to organize in labor organizations of their own choice should not be infringed upon."

This was a workable basis for unionism and collective bargaining without official union recognition. (In most instances the criticism of IWW for not making contracts in these years falls equally flat for almost identical reasons.) The language of the proposal, considering its adaptation to the specific circumstances, later acquired a familiar ring in the proposal by which Gompers broke up Wilson's Industrial Conference of 1919, and was later incorporated in section 7a of NIRA to go on down into the Wagner and Taft-Hartley Acts. It appears to have originated in this proposal made by the executive committee in an IWW strike on March 7, 1913. The committee also proposed that the 8 hour day it demanded could be introduced gradually. Probably the greatest damage the AFL did to the rubber workers was their denunciation of the IWW as an impossible organization that could not carry on collective bargaining. This and the similar line of Green's committee did much to ease the conscience of the Citizen's Police Association, and its recruitment in churches and YMCA. The employers refused to meet even with committees of their own employees, insisting that strikers were not employees, and issued statements that made the local AFL inclined to pull a general strike. At that point the sheriff put the city under martial law, the more loyal AFL local leaders joined in the back-to-work movement, police clubbing grew, and on March 31 the IWW called off the strike by a vote of 140 to 58 – a marked contrast from the thousands who had gathered in Perkins Park to hear Haywood say: "We are standing in the shadow of a monument of John Brown to discuss and fight a greater problem than he ever faced." The strike is usually called a defeat. It did not establish the collective bargaining it aimed at, but it did stop the 35 percent cut that precipitated it, and so properly cannot be called a defeat.

The following January a startling disclosure was made in an affidavit by James W. Reed, secretary-treasurer of the Akron local, that he had hired out as a spy in 1908 to look out for labor agitators at Diamond Rubber, and that during the years 1912-13 almost all officials of the local had also been in the pay of this Employers Auxiliary Corporation, an industrial espionage outfit.[9] While few knew of this, several of those involved attended the Jan. 14 meeting, and a picture of all was taken first, and then the story disclosed. The incident shows the futility of such espionage in an organization of the IWW type, where the strikes are handled by committees of strikers and not by the secretaries or other officers. Thus there seems to have been no great harm done by the spies, and instead a rather good technical performance of the clerical duties to which they were elected.

In the auto industry of Detroit the IWW had a small local, No. 16, which for several years had sought members by speaking in parks about social evils or distributing occasional leaflets without much success. In the spring of 1913 it too began to concentrate on industrial unionism at factory gates, and it began to grow. An able speaker was Matilda Rabinowitz, one of the four national organizers, who had come to Detroit originally to raise funds for the Paterson strike. She was a little woman and after one noonday meeting a police officer complained, "You take advantage of us because you are a woman." Within the one month of May Local 16 grew from a mere skeleton to a promising start of 200.

In June Studebaker changed from weekly to monthly pays. There was dissatisfaction over this and members of the local in the Delray or west end plant of the company sent in a committee to ask about it and to report to a meeting for all Studebaker workers that the Local had called for June 14.

All the committee got for an answer, was the discharge of one of its members. The Sunday meeting elected another committee to see management; it got told that the company would give its answer in a week. The men feared that week would be used to thin out union ranks, and struck on the morning of the 18th at Delray. They all held a meeting in an adjacent vacant lot and marched in a body the seven miles to Plant No. 1, arriving there at noon and bringing out its 2,000 workers. Next day the men from both plants brought out plant No. 5, bringing the total on strike to about 6,000 or a tenth of the local auto workers at that time. They accepted the police restriction of 30 pickets to a plant, but somehow the urge to soapbox turned the strike into a free speech fight, and it seems the entire strike evaporated into this evangelistic activity.[10]

Industrial unionists in the local then went to work on the three companies providing most of the wheels for the auto industry. First they won a short strike at Metal Wheel, gaining a 10 percent boost, a 9 hour day and better sanitation. This enabled them to get similar gains by strike threat next day at Toledo Metal Wheel, and on July 29 by a four hour strike at Foyer Brothers.[11]

The IWW in Detroit must be distinguished from the stillborn faction of De Leonites who left the IWW in 1908 and were known as the "Detroit faction." The factual Detroit IWW plugged along, but found it could not build a strong union in autos, though neither were AFL nor independent attempts successful either. This period should make plain that in all these fields – textiles, rubber, autos, out-of-town construction, and whatever the IWW hit – it was there simply because all those who disdainfully spoke of IWW instability, had proven even more unable to organize than were the Wobblies. The IWW did not leave Detroit, but has been there ever since, though many workers it has organized and won gains for have deserted it.

In 1911 the IWW had gone on record against "boring from within." The urge, and often the need, to belong to whatever union one's fellow workers were in, led, of course, to many IWW members belonging to other unions in those fields where they had organization. In three fields this resulted in efforts to alter union programs: in the Western Federation of Miners, among the Hotel and Restaurant Workers of New York, and in the maritime industry. On the New Years Eve that ushered in 1913 a strike accredited by press to IWW started among the members of the Hotel & Restaurant Workers, AFL, first at the Astor, and soon extended to other leading hotels. The *New York Times* of the period makes much of accounts that Elizabeth G. Flynn urged an end to tipping and an exposure of food adulteration or that Ettor urged strikers to poison food of patrons, which he plainly did not advise. A running fight between AFL and IWW in that local field ran through the year.[12]

In the spring of 1913 the Marine Transport Workers of the IWW was launched. In February the Marine Oilers, Firemen and Watertenders moved to affiliate with the IWW.[13] No such event occurred, but the desire for industrial organization led a number in this and other maritime crafts to build up an IWW organization that by 1916 was to have considerable say about conditions aboard ship on the Atlantic coast.

In Philadelphia on the docks the IWW found a chance to build its first clear example of stability, a longshore organization that lasted from 1913 to 1925 and exercised job control through most of those twelve years.[14] About May 10, the small Philadelphia local got wind that the unorganized longshoremen were in a mood to organize and favored the IWW. An organizer was assigned to the job, but he could not find those who had such ideas. George Speed of the IWW was addressing a meeting of sugar workers, and a group of longshoremen came in and asked if he would organize them. He said he would and got it settled that in this industry, where African-American and white workers had regularly been pitted against each other, a union would have to unite them, and got them to formulate the demands they felt the union should go after. Word of these demands spread along the 20 miles of dock like prairie fire, and resulted in a strike which the IWW had not called. But the response to its appeal for African-American and white workers to stick together so took the company by surprise and so shattered its customary means for keeping these African-Americans, Poles and Lithuanians apart – through threats to assign docks to men of another hue – that the strike was won in a short time. In the early stages of the strike, the strikers calmly deliberated on the proposals of both AFL and IWW and chose the Wobblies. After the strike the AFL, with booze parties and a press accusing the IWW of mismanaging the strike, tried to recover but the MTW-IWW held the fort and grew.

An effort was made to build this Marine Transport Workers on the Great Lakes, where the AFL had just given up a three-year strike, but the only Lakes success was on the docks at Duluth and Superior, where an IWW strike put in the safety devices still used on the ore docks. On the Superior docks two workers were killed through what their fellow workers felt to be company negligence. Organizers Leo Laukki and J. P. Cannon were there and built up strike sentiment, and were soon joined by Frank Little. Many of the workers were Finnish and at this time the Finnish socialists were leaning toward IWW views, and had founded the daily paper *Socialisti*, made into an IWW paper in 1916, and still published as an IWW Finnish daily, *Industrialisti*, in Duluth. [*Industrialisti* ceased publication October 21, 1975.] With this support they spread the strike to the ore docks of the upper end of the Lake. On August 8, GEB member Frank Little was kidnapped and taken to a farm 35 miles out in the country and held there until newspaper reporters caught the trail and rescued him. He got back in time to make a dramatic entry, haggard and unshaved, at a strike mass meeting in the Duluth Armory. The demand for safety equipment was won, the strike called off and other concessions obtained in the settlement were spread by the Finnish socialists to other docks.

In this period of active industrial organization there were many smaller strikes not mentioned here. One strike of workers employed by Utah Construction near Soldier's Summit, Utah, resulted in a mass deportation from the camp, an incident that later became part of the background of the Joe Hill case.[15]

Another sortie that achieved fame out of its aftermath was the strike at Durst's hop ranch at Wheatland, between Marysville and Sacramento, Calif.[16] Durst advertised for pickers to flood the market. Some 3,000 camped on his land, whole families, waiting for a chance to work, though the earnings averaged only $1.28 a day and tents were rented to them for 75 cents a day, and all groceries were to be bought at his "pluck 'em" store. The camp had no facilities for garbage, nine crude toilets, and five wells, garbage contaminated and usually dry. To the thirsty pickers he sold a mixture of citric acid and water for five cents a glass. Dysentery and other sickness was common. Among them a few, perhaps a hundred, had IWW cards, for the IWW had been making repeated efforts among west coast agricultural workers. These called a meeting to consider strike action Sunday noon, Aug. 2, 1913, using a dance pavilion to speak from. On it Dick Ford took a sick baby from its mother's arms and said, "it's for the life of the kids that we're doing this." At that moment two cars filled with drunken deputies, brandishing their guns, broke into the peaceful meeting and proceeded to arrest Ford. The crowd hollered, and some drunken deputy started shooting. Before it was calmed down, two strikers and two of the sheriff's group lay dead. Hop pickers believed that one of the wounded strikers, a Puerto Rican, had grabbed the gun of a deputy before he died and evened the score.

Hundreds of hop pickers were arrested, "investigated," and put under pressure to turn state's evidence, but among all these 3000 starvelings not one such could be found. At the trial in 1914, Ford and Suhr were convicted of the murder of Deputy Sheriff Riordan. In 1928 Ford was released on parole and promptly rearrested on orders of District Attorney Manwell for the murder of his father, the other officer killed in the scrimmage. The trial resulted in such an exposure of the previous miscarriage of justice that both Ford and Suhr were liberated – fifteen years too late.

Thus ends the story of the pre-war crest of the IWW. Focusing its attention on industrial activity, it had jumped from the approximate 4,000 members of its first six years to have an average membership, as reckoned by per capita of 18,387 for 1912, and 14,851 for 1913.[17] A figure for all who were members at any time during those two years would be at least double, and probably quadruple, these figures. In 1912 it had been almost consistently winner in its fights; it won some

Striking hop pickers at the Durst Ranch, Wheatland, California.

in 1913, but was progressively less successful. When hard times hit in the fall of 1913, they fell on an organization that had spent its resources on Paterson and Akron, on the trials arising from Paterson and Wheatland and Louisiana – a union in bad shape to face tough times and with many enemies, both in and out of the labor movement.

Notes:
1. *Solidarity* of period, especially issues 122, 128 and 148.
2. British Columbia accounts from IWW press and *International Socialist Review* of period.
3. See Wheatland strike, end of this chapter.
4. For account of Louisiana lumber, see Jensen, *Labor and Lumber* (Farrar & Rinehart, 1945), pp. 87-92; also Spero & Harris *The Black Worker* (Columbia Univ. Press, 1931), chapter 15. This account taken largely from writings of Covington Hall, including article in *International Socialist Review,* Sept. 1912, reports in IWW press, 1912-1914, series on Louisiana in 1945 *Industrial Worker,* July 14, 21 and 28, and [recently.published] manuscript, "Labor Studies in the Deep South."
5. *Solidarity,* No. 119. For general account of strike, Jensen, *Labor and Lumber,* p. 121, etc., and Bureau of Labor Statistics *Bulletin* 349 (1924), though Jensen repeats confusion of 1913 woods strike with 1912 mill strike. Woehlke in *Outlook,* July 6, 1912, has a story of strikers scaling fences around Lytel Mill to pull out scabs that is not corroborated by accounts or memories of participants. Account of end of strike, *Solidarity,* No. 124.

6. *Solidarity*, No. 178.

7. Pittsburgh cigar: *Solidarity* Sept. 7, 1912, and No. 198; extensive account by Cooper in *Survey* for Nov. 29, 1913.

8. For details of Akron read *The Rubber Workers* (Harper's, 1944) by Harold S. Roberts, senior economist National War Labor Board. Other data taken from *Solidarity* and *ISR*, April 1913.

9. Affidavit given in full, *Solidarity*, Jan. 17, 1914.

10. *Solidarity* No. 127.

11. Ibid., Nos. 184 and 192.

12. *Solidarity*, through Jan. 1913, and *N. Y. Times* 1913, see own index.

13. Grover Perry in *International Socialist Review*, May 1913.

14. Spero & Harris, *The Black Worker*, chapter 15, give the more commonly held account of IWW start on Philadelphia docks, based on reminiscences. This follows record in *Solidarity* by McKelvey, Oct. 4, 1913; also *N.Y. Times*, May 13, 1913, for May strike.

15. Soldier's Summit account, *N.Y. Times*, June 13, 1913, p. 13.

16. For details of Wheatland read Report of Executive Secretary of State Housing and Immigration Committee, by Carlton Parker, published as appendix to his book, *The Casual Laborer*. (The rather Freudian analysis of migratory workers in this book has struck some of them as much like the distorted descriptions of primitive peoples by well-meaning outsiders, including even anthropologists.) Both the story of Wheatland and a record of the failure of AFL attempts to organize agriculture in California is given in Williams' *Factories in the Fields*, Little Brown & Co., 1939.

17. Figures from table in Brissenden, p. 354.

General Sources:

The British Columbia strike is treated in Mark Leier's history of the IWW in British Columbia, *Where the Fraser River Flows* (New Star Books, 1990); in Foner (228-231); Agnes Laut has good pictures but a distorted account in *Illustrated Technical News* (Oct. 1912). There is good footage in the CBC film on Joe Hill (part of the Other Voices series); details of the strike and Hill's involvement are included in Louis Moreau's recollections at Wayne State. Henry McGuckin's *Memoirs of a Wobbly* adds much detail on Aberdeen, British Colombia, and Paterson.

Labor folklorist Archie Green reviews the evidence for competing theories on the origin of the term "Wobbly" in chapter 3 of his *Wobblies, Pile Butts, and Other Heroes* (Univ. of Illinois Press, 1993), but while establishing that it came into common use by 1913-14 does not ultimately reach a conclusion.

There are a number of sources on the IWW in Southern lumber including James R. Green, "The Brotherhood of Timber Workers, 1910-1913" (*Past and Present* 50, August 1973); James Fickle, "Race, Class and Radicalism," in Conlin, *At the Point of Production*; Merl Reed, "IWW and Individual Freedom in Western Louisiana" (*Louisiana History*, Winter 1969) and his "Lumberjacks and Longshoremen" (*Labor History*, Winter 1972); and Covington Hall, *Labor Struggles in the Deep South and Other Writings* (Charles H. Kerr, 2003). Grady McWhiney's article on area socialists (*Journal of Southern History*, August 1954) gives that part of the background. M.R. Brown's "The IWW and the Negro Worker" (Ball State Ph.D. dissertation, 1968) studies this and other efforts to organize black workers.

On Akron, Harold S. Roberts' *The Rubber Workers* is the major published source; Roy Wortman discusses the strike in his *The IWW in Ohio 1905-1950* (a 1972 Ohio State Ph.D. dissertation that was also issued in a limited printing), and in an essay in Conlin, *At The Point of Production* (his interview with striker Paul Sebastyan is part of the Labadie Collection at the University of Michigan); Foner, pp. 373-390; Journal, Ohio 80th General Assembly 1913, Reports of Committee Investigating Akron Rubber Industries.

The Studebaker strike is discussed in Henry Faigin's "The IWW in Detroit and Michigan, 1905-1919" (M.A. thesis, Wayne State, 1937). For the Pittsburgh stogie workers, see Patrick Lynch's "Pittsburgh, the IWW, and the Stogie Workers" in Conlin, *Point of Production*.

An unpublished memoir by Matilda Rabinowitz (Robbins) is among her papers at Wayne State University, which also include the manuscripts of many of her articles for IWW newspapers, including an autobiographical column in the *Industrial Worker* in the early 1950s. Joyce Peterson's "Matilda Robbins: A woman's life in the labor movement, 1900-1920" (*Labor History* 34:1, Winter 1993) focuses largely on her years organizing with the IWW.

Prosecution pressure and the California power structure in the Wheatland Hops strike is discussed in Richard Frost's *The Mooney Case* (Stanford, 1968); Foner, pp. 258-280; Kornbluh, pp. 236-239; and P.W. Eldridge, "The Wheatland Hop Riot and the Ford and Suhr Case," *Industrial and Labor Relations Forum* (May 1974, pp. 165-195). Eric Chester addresses the role the case and some IWWs' attempts to secure Ford and Suhr's release played on the union's reputation in an article in *Anarcho-Syndicalist Review* #42/43 (2005), excerpted from a forthcoming history of the IWW in the World War I era.

The definitive account of IWW organizing on the Philadelphia waterfront is Peter Cole's "Shaping Up and Shipping Out: The Philadelphia Waterfront during and after the IWW Years, 1913-1940" (Ph.D. Dissertation, 1997, Georgetown University), slated for publication in 2007 by the University of Illinois press. Cole's *Black Wobbly: The Life and Writings of Benjamin Harrison Fletcher* is forthcoming from Charles H. Kerr. Other sources include Howard Kimmeldorf's *Battling for American Labor* (Univ. of California Press, 1999), which also features extensive discussion of IWW organizing of New York City restaurant workers; Myland Brown's dissertation, Irwin Marcus in *Negro History Bulletin* (October 1972); Foner in *Journal of Negro History* (January 1970); and Spero and Harris, *The Black Worker*, Chapter 15.

6. "Those Bomb-Throwing I Won't Works"

The hard times that set in toward the fall of 1913 cut down chances for job organization and strike activities and turned the attention of the IWW toward agitation, particularly among the unemployed. The first effect of the war in 1914 was to cut jobs further. Joblessness, this war for trade and dynastic ambitions, the breakdown of international socialism, the evils of militarism and conscript armies, the obvious need for worldwide working-class solidarity – all these gave soapboxers much to talk about, and audiences to talk to.

When the IWW again became effective in industry, it was in new fields: lumber, metal mining, oil fields, agriculture and construction projects. Its area of influence, outside of the Philadelphia waterfront and east coast shipping, was chiefly west of the Mississippi. The prewar depression and early war years make a definite break in the story of the IWW, the more so because of a change in its reputation. Before this, it had been derided as being ahead of its time and had been called the "International Wonder Workers." After this break in its story, it was ridiculed instead as the "I Won't Works" and depicted as a bunch of bums with bombs in hip pockets, advocating violent sabotage.

This weird reputation has no relevance to the facts, but it became so widespread and such an influence on its subsequent history that the history of the myth must be told alongside the history of the actual organization. Perhaps the simplest answer to the myth is the finding of an extensive study issued by Johns Hopkins University in 1939: "Although there are contradictory opinions as to whether the IWW practices sabotage or not, it is interesting to note that no case of an IWW saboteur caught practicing sabotage or convicted of its practice is available."[1]

Brissenden, whose studies should have enabled him to know better, writes in the *Encyclopedia of Social Sciences* that the Socialist Party was so deeply incensed by the sabotage propaganda of the IWW that its national convention in 1912 put a provision into its constitution excluding those who advocated sabotage. This is a widely accepted opinion. The facts indicate instead that IWW discussion of the subject developed as a consequence, not as an antecedent, of this Socialist Party action, and that the roots of the entire hullaballoo lie not in any American situation at all, but were transoceanic migrations of earlier quarrels between socialists and other theorists in Europe.

Prior to the May 1912 convention of the Socialist Party, the only reference to sabotage or kindred ideas appearing in any IWW publication is to sabotage and direct action in Chicago strikes in 1910 mentioned in Chapter 3. The connotation of sabotage there is that of malingering or inefficient work. The currently accepted sense of malicious destruction is a later development, attaching itself to an absurd etymology. As Veblen, in his *Engineers and the Price System,* and other scholars have pointed out, the relation of sabots or wooden shoes to sabotage is this: the use of wooden shoes persisted among French peasants after industrial workers had shifted to leather shoes; the clumsiness of peasants, particularly when they entered industry as strikebreakers, led to their being called saboteurs, in much the sense that "hayseed" was once current here; and defeated strikers going back to work and expressing their discontent by work as bungling as the strikebreakers had done, referred to this imitation of the sabot-wearers as sabotage. The alternative derivation, to support the connotation of destruction, alleges a practice of kicking a wooden shoe into a loom, and thus involves the unlikely picture of the culprit with one shoe off, one on, standing by the damaged loom trying to deny his depredation.

The entire story of these disputes about violence physical force, sabotage and direct action is a tale of strange fantasies told in words that keep changing their meaning. Not only has "sabotage" shifted in meaning from malingering to malicious destruction, but "violence" in the earlier discussions was an accusation against unionists that they violated the social concord of democracy by refusing arbitration; "physical forcism," dead as a social program since the decline of Johann Most's influence after 1886, was a DeLeonite epithet used to imply that any radical movement lacking an electioneering program must therefore anticipate the overthrow of government by force of arms; and "direct action," used originally to contrast action by workers for themselves with action for them by legislative or other representatives, has been contorted to cover all the implications of mayhem and destruction implied in these other terms.

The background of the IWW myth lies in France. (The background of the actual IWW is American industry.)[2] A class-struggle unionism had grown in France whose leaders, as Lewis Lorwin says, were "annoyed and hampered by the overshadowing prestige of the political socialist groups and by the disruptive competitive bidding of these groups for the loyalties of the workers."[3] Their Confederation Generale du Travail developed as antidote a philosophy hinging on the doctrine of union self-sufficiency: that whatever workers needed done for them, they could do for themselves through their unions by union action. This CGT philosophy was one of world labor solidarity, and thus anti-patriot, anti-militarist and distrustful of all government. It projected an increasing competence of organized workers to determine what should be produced, with union quality control, and where it should go, and pictured the final showdown with the old order as a social general strike, with folded arms, that would so demoralize the old order that soon all or almost all sections of society would be happy to see the resumption of the work necessary for social survival by union workers producing for use under their own direction.

There was no scope in this program for the politician. All parties seeking the labor vote felt the urge to attack it, and the more so because then, even more than now, mid-19th century Utopianism had left as a hangover the notion that every program should be a complete procedure for performance in some social vacuum where nothing but the specified program itself went forward.

Liberals and reformist socialists, believing that the role of government is to settle all conflicts in the general interest, urged arbitration of industrial disputes and assured workers that they could get a better settlement that way than by striking, and without any trouble, if only they would elect friends of labor to office. French liberals argued that even the most peaceful strike, if it stopped work the community needed done, or stopped income that the shopkeepers needed, did violence to the social concord and was a crime of "lese democratie." In 1906, Sorel answered these arguments with a series of essays, "Reflections on Violence," emphasizing the demoralizing influence of compulsory arbitration or of statism in general, and urging that the will of the working class to create the good world could develop only from daily practice of a class struggle ethic. This was the content of the term "violence" in this dispute between French radicals, and it continued as the content in British discussions, such as Ramsay MacDonald's articles on syndicalism; but when this discussion moved to America where labor disputes had often become pitched battles, "violence" was taken to mean Most's "physical force."

The more Marxian wing of the socialists used a different attack. It

We Are Coming Home, John Farmer---We Are Coming Back to Stay

conceded that in times of business activity, strikes could be effective but argued the final battle might come instead when masses already unemployed could not effectively strike. To counteract this argument, the syndicalist movement elaborated various forms of possible sabotage: that of the "open mouth" by which workers let out trade secrets or disclosed the wrongdoing of employers, particularly in the foodstuff industries; that of "misdirection" of shipments; that of giving employers the services of "hands" only, if workers were to be treated and hired and paid only as "hands" – and sundry other forms of the "conscientious withdrawal of efficiency." There was disagreement among syndicalists as to the effect of these practices on proletarian morale and the development of labor's ability to create a good world, but the syndicalist consensus was that by the discriminating choice and adaptation of these means, the morale of capitalism could be shattered and organized labor emerge as a constructive force. This became official CGT doctrine in 1897.

In the socialist movement of pre-war years, particularly throughout Europe, there were internal power disputes presented as conflicts of theory as to the nature of the state, the relation of politics to unionism, the determinants of historic development, the choice of programs of reform or programs for the simple abolition of capitalism, acceptance of posts in capitalist governments, attitudes toward nationalism and war, and whether to oppose war by a general strike or by parliamentary action. While there was no neat polarization on these issues, in a general way all socialists denounced syndicalists as sinners, and the gradualist-reformist socialists denounced the doctrinaire "impossibilists" as sharing the sins of the syndicalists.[4]

In America, the fact that many of the "doctrinaires" were outside the Socialist Party and in the SLP delayed the breaking out of this dispute until 1912. Then the IWW replaced the CGT as the goat. Those who hoped to catch support by catering to the AFL pushed through the new Article II Section 6 by a vote of 191 to 90, which read: "Any member of the party who opposes political action or advocates crime, sabotage or other methods of violence as a weapon of the working class to aid in its emancipation shall be expelled." In consequence of this, Haywood was recalled from the National Executive Committee of the SPA in February 1913. On local levels, IWW and socialists remained as friendly as ever, often sharing halls. In 1917 the Socialist Party rescinded Section 6.[5]

The argument over violence led to a resolution adopted at the seventh Convention of the IWW, September 1913:

"At all times it is the rulers who, being in power, are in a position to determine in great measure just how and when the struggle will be fought... It is the employing class and their agencies who provoke violence and then cry out the loudest against it. ... The program of the IWW offers the only possible solution of the wage question whereby violence can be avoided, or, at the very worst, reduced to a minimum. If the ruling class of today may decide, as their prototypes in the past have decided, that violence will be the arbiter of the question, then we shall cheerfully accept their decision and meet them to the best of our ability – and we do not fear the result."

The weird reputation that the IWW acquired in this period is the outcome of this right-left quarrel inside the socialist movement, combined with a depression situation that led to sensational soapboxing. Although many writing in the IWW press were familiar with the European labor press, the only portion of CGT philosophy prior to the 1912 convention in IWW publications were statements by Vincent St. John supporting the doctrine of union self-sufficiency. In other literature, a reference exists to a pamphlet issued by Trautmann in Pittsburgh in 1912, entitled "Direct Action and Sabotage," but no mention of it occurs in the IWW press. In February of 1913, *Solidarity* ran a series of articles on the CGT by Leon Jouhaux, with editorial comment that it was necessary to get a clear picture because of misrepresentation in socialist and capitalist press, and pointing out that the IWW was not antiparliamentary but nonparliamentary, asking the politicians only to leave the labor movement alone. Later that year as Andre Tridon's *New Unionism* came out, the IWW press promoted its circulation, and took note of translations from the French being issued of Pouget's *Sabotage* and Pataud and Pouget's fictional description of the general strike, *Syndicalism and the Cooperative Commonwealth*. In Spokane, on his own account, an IWW speaker, Walker C. Smith, issued a booklet on sabotage and it was advertised in the IWW papers in 1913; this was followed by another booklet describing sabotage by Elizabeth G. Flynn issued in Cleveland in 1915. For neither of these could the IWW be properly held responsible. It was this irresponsibility of the Cleveland autonomous "IWW Publishing Bureau" that led to its dissolution next year and the consequent move of *Solidarity* to Chicago. For a while a few internal critics of the IWW in Los Angeles, who attacked IWW policy as "centralist," issued a paper, *The Wooden Shoe*.

Soapboxers found that talk of sabotage gave their audiences a thrill, and since the dispensers of the above publications were happy to send them for sale on commission to all who would handle them, there was nothing to stop spielers, whether they were IWW members or not, from procuring these booklets, mounting a box, talking about the IWW, taking up a collection and selling the literature. The actual effect on IWW practices was evidently nil, as shown by the Johns Hopkins study given at the start of this chapter; but its effect on the popular conception of the IWW was definitely damaging. There are curious consequences of this disparity of practice and reputation: in one IWW strike after another local papers commented on the amazing orderliness and peacefulness of the strike despite the "known fact" that the IWW was notoriously violent everywhere else; the imprisonment of hundreds of exceptionally nonviolent men for allegedly aiming at the violent overthrow of organized society; or the confusion of the North Dakota farmer who regularly hired IWW help and who made the distinction: "The IWWs I know are swell fellows, but them

IWW textile workers display union newspapers during the frame-up trial of IWW organizers Caruso, Ettor and Giovannitti. They were acquitted of accessory to murder charges stemming from the Massachusetts militia killing of a picketer during the Lawrence strike.

alleged IWWs I read about in the papers are holy terrors."[6]

IWW ideas on violence have been shaped by practicality. Organizers regularly pointed out to strikers that if they used violence or induced violence toward themselves, they handicapped their strike by putting the police openly on the side of the scab-herders; and that the violent strikes of labor history are almost regularly the lost ones; that violence was often found to be the work of employer agents. At all times their concept of the "social revolution" in an industrial society was that of industrial action, not violence. In February of 1913 when a mysterious explosion in a New York rooming house occupied by radicals (incidentally not Wobblies) led to much talk of dynamite in the local press, Joe Ettor wrote in *The Call:* "The IWW has neither advocated nor participated in violence against the social order. The general strike is the method we favor for overthrowing the capitalist system, and that is the only kind of force we are in favor of." E. G. Flynn took exception to this stand; Ettor and others replied with arguments that there was too much talk of violence and it would be best to stop it. But there was no puzzle why strikers felt like punching scabs in the nose; and when McNamara of the Structural Iron Workers, which had systematically blown up scab-erected bridges, always with certainty that no lives would be lost, was induced by the promise that his fellow workers would be let off, to "confess" to 'blowing up the Los Angeles Times Building (which evidently went up from a defective boiler), the IWW frankly called him a victim of the class war and, with all his friends deserting him, provided him to his death in San Quentin with tobacco money.

Before the IWW got back to substantial organizing, war came. The IWW stuck to the position that had been typical of the labor movement in peace. When Gompers wrote his "Labor in Europe" in 1910, he did not hesitate to concur with the CGT slogan "the workingman has no country" or to assert that "workers will forever refuse to kill one another merely because authority has put them in different uniforms."[7] Because the IWW did not change its tune with the new winds of war, it became the wartime bogy of the propaganda press, which picked up all the canards that had developed about the IWW and broadcast the cartoon conception of the Wobbly as a bomb-toting "I Won't Work."

Notes:

1. *History of Criminal Syndicalism Legislation in the United States,* by Eldridge Foster Dowell, John Hopkins University Studies in Historical and Political Science, 1939, Series LVII, No. 1, p. 36.

2. Both Levine, in 1913 article cited next note, and Brissenden in both his books on IWW and in article in *Encyclopedia of Social Sciences* point out the native American origins of IWW, and its industrialist program a response to the more developed American industry.

3. In article "Direct Action," *Encyclopedia of Social Sciences.*

4. Socialist background of this period given in WE. Walling, *The Socialists and the War,* Holt, 1915, or L.L. Lorwin, *Labor and Internationalism,* McMillan, 1929.

5. James O'Neal and C.A. Werner, *American Communism,* Dutton, pp. 29 and 37. Theoretical differences in SPA given in John Macy's *Socialism in America,* Doubleday, 1916 (very readable with considerable information bearing on IWW).

6. For a positive presentation of IWW philosophy, see Frank Tannenbaum, *The Labor Movement,* Putnam, 1921, or the section on Syndicalism in Bertrand Russell, *Roads to Freedom,* or pamphlet "IWW in Theory and Practice" by Justus Ebert.

7. Gompers: *Labor in Europe,* esp. p. 274 *et seq.*

The data and place of publication of the following material is significant of the migration of the content of the questions discussed in this chapter: Sorel, *Reflexions sur Violence*, Paris, 1906; Roller, *Die Direkte Aktion*, Berlin, 1910; R.A. MacDonald, *Syndicalism*, London: Constable, May 1912; Arthur D. Lewis, *Syndicalism and the General Strike*, London: Unwin, 1912; Levine, *Syndicalism in France*, Columbia University Press, 1912; A.W. Kirkaldy, *Economics and Syndicalism*, University Press, Cambridge, 1914. In America the following, in 1913: John G. Brooks, *American Syndicalism*; Spargo, *Syndicalism, Industrial Unionism and Socialism*; Hunter, *Violence and the Labor Movement*; Tridon, *The New Unionism*, and the following scholarly accounts: Levine, Sept. in *Political Science Quarterly*, and Brissenden, *The Launching of the IWW*, University of Berkeley Press, and in 1914, Hoxie, "Truth about IWW," in *Journal of Political Economy*.

Fictional treatment of IWW follows similar diversity later, ranging from Zane Grey's poisonous *Desert of Wheat*, Harper, 1919, which helped send many Wobblies to jail, to such sympathetic treatment as Upton Sinclair's *Oil*, Boni, 1927. Winston Churchill's novel, *The Dwelling Place of Light*, uses the Lawrence strike of 1912 as general situation with a rather neutral treatment. Eugene O'Neill's *Hairy Ape* has a scene in IWW maritime workers' hall that realistically dramatizes the conflict of myth and reality; Stavis' *The Man Who Never Died* is a somewhat Stalinoid drama of Joe Hill, with very informative preface. Probably favorite IWW fiction has been Jack London's *Iron Heel*, 1907, and *Dream of Debs*.

General Sources:

The best discussion of the relationship between the IWW and European syndicalist ideas is Salvatore Salerno's *Red November, Black November* (State Univ. of New York Press, 1989). Three IWW pamphlets on direct action were reprinted as E. G. Flynn, Walker C. Smith and Wm. E. Trautmann, *Direct Action & Sabotage* (Charles H. Kerr, 1997), introduced by Salerno. Kornbluh, pp. 35-64, includes a survey and samples of the sabotage argument from 1911 to 1917. The most extensive study is by Joseph Conlin in *Bread and Roses Too* and his essays "IWW and Question of Violence" (*Wisconsin Magazine of History*, Summer 1968) and "Case of the Very American Militants (*American West*, March 1970). Mark Karson, *American Labor and Politics* (Southern Illinois Univ. Press, 1958, pp. 150-211), gives a sketch of the IWW from 1905 to 1917 in terms of ideological disputes in it and Socialist Party, assuming the IWW anti-parliamentary rather than non-political. Extensive treatment in Foner chapters 5, 6 and 17, and in Dubofsky, chapter 7.

Pataud and Pouget's *How We Shall Bring About the Revolution* was reprinted in 1990 by Pluto Press, with an introduction by Geoff Brown reflecting on its significance in the syndicalist movement of its day.

7. Hard Times (1914-1915)

When the prewar depression hit in 1913, IWW members were as jobless as any. Inclined toward collective action, they felt their chances for food and a place to sleep were better if they went after these necessaries organized. First notes of their activity among the unemployed are in the various organizations that grew spontaneously in different cities. In some instances the IWW substantially directed these. In other instances it formed unemployed auxiliaries with dues usually at a nickel a month. Soon these began the collection of food and the provision of lodging for their members, not only to meet creature needs, but to escape the demoralizing influences of the soup lines and missions and to provide a sociability and sense of solidarity that was needed as much as soup. By September 1914, when the ninth convention met, it was agreed that it was folly to join parades to City Halls where there was nothing to eat anyway, but that the unemployed should be organized to give them union principles, to enable them to go after what they needed, and to prevent their being used to batter down wages.

There were various outcomes: free speech fights; fire hoses turned on "unemployed armies"; a busboy became a college professor; "Solidarity Forever," marching song later of millions of American strikers, came to its author, Ralph Chaplin, out of an unemployed demonstration in Chicago;[1] Henry Ford announced $5.00 a day minimum; the hall of Butte Mine Workers Union No. 1 got blown up; in Sioux City a group of jobless men descended upon a banquet at which the Chamber of Commerce was considering their plight, and relieved their plight by eating the banquet. Probably the chief consequence for the IWW was that their activities laid the foundation for building a substantial organization of agricultural workers, and thus later for substantial victories in western lumber and other industries.

Early in March 1914 a big snow storm hit New York City. The IWW agitated that the unemployed should not shovel the snow for less than 30 cents an hour. Shelter from the cold was important for the penniless. A busboy, Frank Tannenbaum, led a number of jobless men to the Church of St. Alphonsus on West Broadway, to sit there for the night; but a fight developed and Tannenbaum was sentenced to a year on Blackwell's Island. Agitation for his release merged with protests against the Rockefeller Ludlow Massacre and the brutal treatment of the striking Michigan copper miners as major issues at the unemployed demonstrations, including the Union Square riots of April 6. (Tannenbaum went ahead with his education, and his early book *The Labor Movement*, especially in its opening chapters, is an outstanding constructive statement of basic IWW attitudes.)

In Detroit on February 12, 1914, the IWW staged an unemployed demonstration in front of the Employers' Association to demand a municipal lodging house; about 3000 jobless gathered before the police started cracking skulls.[2] In December, IWW organizer John F. Leheney formed the Unemployed League as an IWW auxiliary which set up kitchen in a former church building donated by the Unitarians. There it combined public forums with mulligan stew and found that even with a shortage of Wobbly speakers, the IWW points could be made by systematic Socratic questioning of invited orators. This IWW effort managed also to maintain close cooperation with the AFL.[3] With street meetings and leaflets the Unemployed League steadily argued that to get rid of depression it was necessary to cut the hours and boost the pay; Ford's policy of $5.00 minimum has been attributed to this pressure.

On the West Coast the trend was to participate in other organizations of the unemployed. There were frequent arrests at the daily mass meetings held in 1914 at 5th and Howard, then a vacant lot, in San Francisco. Kelly's Army was starting its parade eastward and at Sacramento got chased off the sand-lots with firehoses.[4] When the millionaire hobo Eads Howe obtained the San Francisco Civic Auditorium for an Unemployed Convention (February 18th to 23rd, 1915) the IWW participants took substantial control from the big names, on the grounds that the term unemployed meant workers seeking work, and not the habitually idle, rich or poor.[5] Taking it over yielded nothing much but resolutions on behalf of various imprisoned workers, such as the McNamaras, Niles, Ford and Suhr, and Pancner.[6]

In Butte hard times brought the automatic blacklist system to a head. It had been started in December 1912 by connivance between the companies and the copper clique, as those in Butte Miners' Union who sought to propitiate the companies were called.[7] Under the new scheme all miners had first to go to the Butte Mutual Labor Bureau, maintained by the companies, and get a rustling card without which they could not apply for work at the mines. The militant and especially the pro-IWW element, which up to 1912 had exerted a healthy influence in the Butte WFM local, could readily be deprived of employment by this scheme – an objective common to some of the local labor union leaders and management. However, so many of the more competent miners were in the red-tagged group that it had not been practicable to try to get rid of them until slack times had set in. The separation of the WFM from the IWW in 1908 had set it out on the futile path of trying to imitate the union-company collaboration of various AFL unions in a field where management was not inclined to collaborate with even the most supine of unions. In 1913 the Moyer faction had brought it back into the AFL where it was to be the International Mine Mill & Smelter Workers.

The rustling card, the affiliation with the craft separationists, the futility of discarding militancy as shown at Hearst's Homestake and elsewhere, and distrust over handling funds for the Michigan copper strike, all produced dissension and a substantial decline in members in Butte Miners Union. When the latter insisted that all miners show their cards to go to work, dissidents launched a new organization, the Butte Mine Workers' Union, often called "Muckie McDonald's union." The IWW forces supported the new venture, and the Socialists, who administered Butte in 1914, were also friendly. The dispute between the two organizations was used by company provocateurs to rid Butte of miner unionism – and it stayed that way until the spontaneous rebirth of unionism after the speculator disaster of 1917. In the dispute, against the instructions of the new union, a mob was led against the old union hall; shooting broke out evidently from inside the hall; dynamite was obtained from the mines and the old hall was blown up with 26 separate blasts, Miners Day, June 13, 1914. Many accused the IWW of this, but even the editor of the Western Federation *Miners' Magazine* wrote that he had reliable information that the dynamiters were gunmen of the Waddell-Mahon agency.[8]

In Sioux City the IWW opened up a hall in October 1914 as it was a strategic point for new plans to organize the wheat hands. IWW activity on behalf of the unemployed led to a series of skirmishes and free speech fights, in which IWW had the backing of a substantial local Socialist movement. The Sioux City free speech fight was "good stage." Every night crowds of about a thousand witnessed a Wobbly mount his box and talk until arrested; 82 were in the stockade by mid-April. The police started a rock pile and led the prisoners there. They sat

IWW agricultural workers meeting

down in passive disobedience. A fight developed with police over this refusal to work and over the burning of lousy blankets issued to the prisoners; three cops got laid out with a pop bottle. Public sentiment grew for the Wobs, and as more free speech fighters arrived, the city sought terms, proposing that the men would be freed if they would promise to leave town. The men insisted that whether they went or stayed was up to the individual preference of each. They were released and, as a final gesture of contempt for the rock pile, they gathered the ingredients for a mammoth mulligan stew, built fires there, cooked the stew in Standard Oil cans, and ate their "victory banquet" on top the rock pile.[9]

More significant was the beginning of organization among the wheat hands. Kansas City Local 61 set out in earnest in the spring of 1914, aiming at $4.00 a day, but pushed the going wage only to $3.00 from a previous $2.50. Organization of agricultural workers had been attempted by AFL and other unions without success except for an independent local of sheepshearers.[10] The 1914 experience showed how the problem shaped up, and what structural changes would be needed in the IWW to handle it. Reduced to bare elements, building unionism in a factory or on a construction project amounts to getting men together, agreeing on terms of employment, and enforcing the terms by collective refusal to work on lower terms. Here the job was the vast wheat belt of America, running up into Canada. The job seekers gathered in box cars, rode empty gondolas, huddled in hobo jungles, idled around the one Main Street of a thousand towns and villages. But hardly any lived in the wheat belt; they came into it from outside. It was too big a job for Kansas City Local 61. It would require the coordinated effort of IWW members all around the wheat belt, organizing the jobseekers as they came in, and proceeding inward with the new recruits to maintain wages and enforce union terms.

The 1914 convention arranged for a spring convention of the locals directly concerned with such a campaign for Kansas City, April 16, 1915. This led to several new developments that soon became the general plan of operations throughout the IWW. Up to this point IWW members had been members of locals, with these locals occasionally, as among the Textile Workers, banded together into a National Industrial Union. Membership cards were issued by the secretaries of the locals, but no secretary of Local 61 could write cards all over Kansas and the Dakotas, nor was there reason for forming local unions scattered through this area. Thus one organization was set up – the Agricultural Workers Organization 400 (later changed to Agricultural Workers Industrial Union 110) with a national secretary issuing blank cards and dues stamps to job delegates, and an organization committee to be responsible for operations everywhere in that industry. This system of industrial union secretaries issuing organization supplies to local secretaries and even more to job delegates, soon became the regular IWW pattern in all industries.

The new organization was tempted into free speech fights, but soon learned to avoid these as distractions from its main job, organizing, raising the pay and cutting the hours. It did find it was necessary to clear the jungles and freight trains of hijacks and cardsharps. At first the policy was to get the jobseekers to withhold their labor waiting for farmers to meet the union demands. Soon they found this meant that the work got done by "wicks" below union scale. Policy then changed to going on the jobs at the going wage, then pulling a quickie strike at an opportune moment for their demands.[11] This often resulted in benefits to their successors rather than themselves, but, if acted upon generally, as later it was in the lumbering industry, it became of mutual benefit to all workers.

To achieve better conditions, it was necessary to deter those who would not cooperate with the union from reaching the harvest fields. Since they rode boxcars, this meant keeping them off unless they joined or talked like union material. Soon many train crews aided them by asking all free riders for their red cards, or else get off. This speeded up initiations, so that for quite a few years, up to 1925, the dues collected by the Agricultural Workers ran to about half of the total IWW dues collected while initiation fees were an even more disproportionate share of the total. A further consequence was that the process of sifting out the non-unionists or "wicks" was the more complete the further one penetrated the wheat belt. This difference gives some measure of the union's effectiveness. In the interior of the wheat belt a 10 hour day prevailed, and on the fringes the day was sunup to sundown, and wages in the center of the wheat belt were usually double those on the fringe. This sort of organization remained effective to about 1926, when the wide use of the combine, previously restricted to Kansas, cut down the labor market, and the cheap second hand car brought in the wicks on rubber tires in a manner difficult to organize. The net effect of the IWW on agriculture is perhaps most clearly shown in the statistics in Louis J. Ducoff's *Wages in Agriculture in the United States* issued by the Bureau of Agricultural Economics in 1944. These figures show that if farm wages in 1943 bore the same ratio to industrial wages that they had during World War I, they would need to have been 80 to 85 percent higher. That difference is attributable to the fact that the Wobs were there in World War I, but not in World War II and largely because union demands had made it pay to mechanize agriculture.

Looking backward in 1945 one of the IWW organizers active during the First World War period, Joe Ettor, wrote in a series of articles "The Light of the Past"[12] that this relatively easy way of obtaining about 15,000 initiation fees per year had sidetracked the IWW from other fields of industry that might have yielded more permanent results. Others point to the fact that many of those recruited in the harvest field became active for the IWW elsewhere, and that the large amount of literature circulated in these harvest drives resulted in an understanding of IWW unionism that both made for a readiness to respond to organizing efforts elsewhere and for some insistence that other unions come closer to IWW ideals.

The most popular piece of IWW literature was the little red song book. In box car, jungles and on the job, its songs were sung, until even the farmers and their boys were singing them too. Many of the more favorite songs were written by Joe Hill. When it became known that he faced death on flimsy and unconvincing evidence, public con-

Joe Hill's funeral procession, Chicago.

cern developed into international proportions comparable only to that shown in the Sacco-Vanzetti case. A grocer (an ex-policeman) had been shot along with his son by masked men who, according to the remaining son, had entered his store at closing time crying out "We've got you now." Since no theft was attempted, the obvious motive appeared to be revenge. However, Joe Hill was arrested and convicted on the grounds that he had been wounded about the same time. Conceiving that the grocer may have shot, the lower and finally the Supreme Court of Utah proceeded on the strange logic that to have a bullet wound for which no explanation was offered by the defendant was as damaging evidence in this murder trial as the possession of goods from his store had it been a charge of burglary. However it is very doubtful whether the grocer shot at his assailants. Had he hit Hill, since Hill's wound went through his body and clothing, the bullet would have been in the store; but it wasn't. Further the bullet hole was high in Hill's chest but low in his coat, showing that he had been shot with his hands up. Also, the bullets that killed the grocer and his son had not been fired from Hill's revolver.[13]

To the IWW, and to many outsiders who investigated the case, there was no doubt that Hill was prosecuted because he was considered a dangerous agitator, a writer of rebel songs that growing thousands sang, and out of vindictiveness for previous skirmishes in the mines of

Utah, free speech fights in Salt Lake City, and particularly for winning a victory at Tucker against the Utah Construction Co. On November 19, 1915, Hill was executed, despite the protests of the AFL and the labor bodies of other countries, the objections of the Swedish government and the intervention of President Wilson. His funeral in Chicago was attended by an unexpected 30,000 mourners who blocked traffic for their long parade to the cemetery in an amazing demonstration of concern for a framed-up working stiff.

Notes:

1. R. Chaplin, *Wobbly*, University of Chicago Press, 1948, p. 168.

2. *Detroit News*, Feb. 12, 1914, quoted in *Solidarity*, No. 215.

3. *Solidarity*, No. 272.

4. Account of Kelley's Army at Sacramento with good photos, in *International Socialist Review*, May 1914.

5. *Solidarity*, No. 269.

6. Niles was in San Quentin on trumped-up charge of horse-stealing and subjected to brutalities described in Jack London's novel, *The Star-Rover*. John Pancner: Public Service Workers Local 111 had won the 8 hour day in all miner boarding houses in Tonapah, Nevada, except two, which it boycotted. Drunken thugs raided its hall July 11, 1914, tore down the boycott signs, and seized a member, threatening to lynch him. Pancner shot one thug in the leg and they fled; he was convicted on charge of assault with intent to kill.

7. Brissenden: "Butte Miners and the Rustling Card," in *American Economic Review*, Dec. 1920, and Perlman and Taft, History of Labor in U.S., p. 257 (good summary).

8. *Miners' Magazine*, July 2, 1914, quoted in Jensen's *Heritage of Conflict*, Cornell University Press, 1950, p. 336. Jensen gives detailed account, marred however by a bias that leads him to imply on page 347 that the IWW had an impossible three-month advance knowledge of this occurrence, on the basis of a letter from Leheney to Dan Liston, sent in care of Bradley, subsequently secretary of the new union, containing the statement, "Fearing that the hall may have been lost, am addressing this letter in care of him." The reference in letter is plainly to IWW hall, for Wobblies at that time might as well have used the Anaconda as a mailing address as the Butte Miners' Union. The dispute ended with martial law, despite objections of the mayor, and the imprisonment of McDonald and Bradley on charges of deporting objectionables, i.e., requiring that they leave town. See also P. F. Brissenden's pamphlet "Labor Conditions in Butte," and *Solidarity*, Nos. 233, 254 and 255.

9. Sioux City affairs described quite fully by Wallace Short in *Survey*, Oct. 15, 1915; see also *Solidarity*, Nos. 263, 264, 273 and 277.

10. AFL lack of success in attempts to organize agricultural workers, detailed

in Williams, *Factories in the Fields,* Little Brown and Co., 1939, and in Jamieson, "Labor Unionism in American Agriculture," *Monthly Labor Review,* Jan. 1946.

11. The role of the IWW in devising and developing union techniques is roughly indicated in chapter 16 of Taft's *Economics and Problems of Labor,* Stackpole, 1942.

12. Series in summer of 1945, especially issue of July 21.

13. Most complete account of Joe Hill available is the nonfiction half of Barrie Stavis, *The Man Who Never Died,* Haven Press, New York 1954. (The other half of the book is a fictional drama about Hill.) A summary of the evidence is given in special Hill edition of *Industrial Worker,* Nov. 13, 1948, answering attack on Hill by Wallace Stegner. A boiled-down version of same article in *New Republic,* Nov. 15, 1948. In Swedish there is Ture Nerman's *Joe Hill,* Federatovs Forlag, Stockholm, 1951, giving his original name as Joel Haaglund, born Gavie, Sweden, July 12, 1887. Detailed account of Hill's funeral is given in Chaplin's *Wobbly.*

General Sources:

Several accounts of IWW organizing among agricultural workers have been published in recent years, including Greg Hall, *Harvest Wobblies* (Oregon State Univ. Press, 2001); Nigel Sellars' *Oil, Wheat & Wobblies: The Industrial Workers of the World in Oklahoma* (Univ. of Oklahoma, 1998), and Frank Tobias Higbie's *Indispensable Outcasts: Hobo Workers and Community in the American Midwest, 1880-1930* (Univ. of Illinois Press, 2003). Cecilia Danysk's *Hired Hands* (McClelland & Stewart, 1995) has two chapters that address IWW organizing on the Canadian prairies; see also Michael Sideman, "The Agricultural Labor Market and the Organizing Activities of the IWW 1910-1935" (MS Thesis, Univ. of Illinois, 1965); Philip Taft, "IWW in the Grain Belt," (*Labor History,* Winter 1960).

On Joe Hill, the definitive biography is now Gibbs Smith's *Joe Hill* (Univ. of Utah Press, 1970; reissued by Peregrine-Smith, 1984); Franklin Rosemont's *Joe Hill: The IWW & the Making of a Revolutionary Workingclass Counterculture* (Charles H. Kerr, 2003) is a hefty tome reviewing everything published on Joe Hill and his impact in the larger culture; Phillip Foner's *The Case of Joe Hill* (International, 1965) dissects the prosecution case. On film, there is a good CBC documentary on Joe Hill in its Other Voices series, in which Hill's songs are sung by Don Francks; a lengthier feature film directed by Bo Widerborg that IWWs found disappointing; and a documentary by Utah Public Television, "The Return of Joe Hill," that carries the story through the release of the last of Joe Hill's ashes from the National Archives in 1988 and their scattering. The *Washington Post* reported on the ashes Nov. 19, 1988, "Joe Hill Remembered" (pp. C1, C6); the *Chicago Reader* ran a piece by Roger Kerson, "What Ever Happened to Joe Hill?" (Nov. 25, pp. 8-9, 30-32).

8. Events of 1916

In 1916 the IWW became involved in an inter-union dispute in the Baltimore garment industry. It had started a local for clothing workers there on May 1, 1911, which remained small until the spring of 1913 when the independent Lithuanian Tailors' Union joined it, followed a little later by a body of Italian clothing workers. By September 1913 it had control of some of the largest shops in the city, among them Schless Brothers' four big shops. A 14-week strike against Schless ended dismally when the United Garment Workers furnished scabs. For nearly two years the IWW remained ineffective in the Baltimore garment industry but began to grow rapidly again in 1915. The United Garment Workers (AFL) relied less upon the organization of workers and putting up a battle against employers than it did on the demand for union label clothing by other workers who did not question under what conditions or for what wages the clothing had been made. Consequent dissatisfaction led to a split and the formation of the Amalgamated Clothing Workers after the 1914 convention of the UGW.[1] During the early part of this split the IWW was the largest union in the industry in Baltimore. IWW policy forbade time agreements with employers and it sought no closed shop. The pattern of unionism throughout the local industry was less like the current "sole collective bargaining agency" device and more like the pattern that until recently prevailed in Europe, with workers in the same unit acting through whichever union tendency they individually preferred. The IWW was the majority in some shops, the minority in others; in either case, although it competed with both ACW and UGW for members, it took action to defend members of either union. For this "it got about the same thing as the neutral Belgians" observed organizer E. F. Doree.[2]

Grief & Company had five plants, one of which in the Coca Cola Building was three-quarters IWW, the rest UGW with a few members of the Amalgamated. In 1916 the UGW and ACW began demanding closed shop and wanted the IWW to pull this plant in support of their respective demands. The IWW issued a circular stating: "The IWW always has and always will work in conjunction and strike with any group of workers anywhere, whether organized or unorganized, when they have a grievance against any boss, but will not permit itself to be used as a club by any organization to fight another union."

The Amalgamated sent pickets with clubs and knives to bring out the Coca Cola Building; other members rallied to the free for all to even up the odds with the result that ACW left them alone there.

Soon after this the pocket makers at Strouse – 20 of them IWW and ACW – decided to strike for the abolition of the subcontract system and a straight price of 15 cents a pocket. The ACW tried to settle for less, proposing to replace any who struck against its settlement. The cutters in the plant were UGW and decided to strike in support of the original pocket makers whether IWW or not. A long strike of 700 AFL and IWW followed with 300 ACW recruits inside working. The clothing industry in Baltimore went to the unions that bid against each other for collective bargaining agreements and the IWW faded out of the picture.

Organizer Doree pointed out to the 10th Convention that the IWW was handicapped by its provision that no time agreements could be made and argued that as a result the IWW organizes, fights and lets other unions derive the benefits. However, the reluctance to let agreements prevent sympathetic action continued this constitutional ban to 1938 when the constitution was amended to permit industrial unions to adopt their own regulations for agreements provided that nothing in the agreement obligated the workers covered by it to undertake any work that would aid in breaking any strike.

In contrast, on the Philadelphia waterfront similar IWW policies achieved substantial union stability. The Marine Transport Workers there had a branch of 3,000 members in the spring of 1916 and on May 20 with a parade of all 3,000 members – and a band – to the three nonunion docks, won union recognition (without any written agreement) and the same conditions as prevailed on the docks previously organized. In June, with all docks now acting jointly, it struck and raised the scale to 40 cents for day work, 60 cents for night work and 80 cents for Sundays, holidays, Saturday afternoons and meal hours. The union branched out to other industries. Shoe Workers Local 162 won a strike in 23 shops. A local of coopers was organized, and a Spanish-language local with a paper *Cultura Obrera*. An AFL local of lumber handlers left the ILA even though it meant leaving their treasury behind to join the IWW. In 1917 it began the organization of the sugar refineries.[3]

In Detroit, workers at the Solvay Process plant struck without organization for a nickel pay boost, showers and lockers. A couple came to organizer Weber who arranged a meeting attended by 700 strikers. There was some difficulty over forming a committee, so it was decided to get the manager, Mr. Greene, to come to the meeting and negotiate with all. Mr. Greene said that only the back east directors could grant their demands and urged the men to return to work while he saw what he could do for them. Weber pointed out that the long distance lines were open to New York and said the men would continue their meeting while Mr. Greene talked to the directors. Soon he reported that they had been considering a one cent raise but agreed to the demands. Weber insisted this meant that penny plus the five cents just granted, showers and lockers. On these terms the men returned, but no permanent organization resulted. The local IWW auto workers did better with a strike of 3,000 against Kelsey Wheel, adding a tenth of them to its local.[4]

The most novel of IWW organizing campaigns was that of Jane Street among the housemaids of Denver. By persistent contact with them she compiled a card index by employer giving the "salaries paid in each of these positions, the number of people in each of the homes, the kind of work, the hours, and the characteristics of the mistresses," later adding a turnover record. The list soon grew to cover 2,500 homes hiring servants with the pay going up largely because each time a girl managed an increase her successor would know of it and insist upon starting in at that figure. Both the *Post* and *News* in Denver ran cartoon-illustrated articles about the new union, implying it sabotaged the soup with too much pepper and won raises by putting too much starch in shirts. The union provided job information, employment service and social gatherings for the girls on their days off. It planned on having its own clubhouse in the residential area where girls could also stay between jobs, but it fell flat when its index list was stolen from its office. Unsuccessful efforts to imitate it were made in Seattle, Chicago and Duluth.[5]

In May 1916 the IWW began organization efforts on the Mesabi Iron Range on the urging of the Finnish socialists who were strongly entrenched in that area. In Duluth they had a daily paper, the *Socialisti*, a residential labor college and a fine hall. Throughout the Iron Range they were responsible for the election of scattered socialist administrations. They favored the IWW; some had participated in the IWW strike at Gray's Harbor in 1912 and others in the Duluth and Superior dock strike of 1913; they had earlier been staunch supporters of the Western Federation, but had been alienated by its futile efforts at company collaboration and in particular its rustling card deal in Butte which first victimized several hundred Finnish socialists over a socialist proposal to tax mine tonnage for the benefit of the city.[6] Though enthusiastic socialists, their ties with the Socialist Party also had been loosened ever since Article 6 was born over disappointment with the effect of the McNamara confession on the Los Angeles mayoralty campaign, and now they saw a chance to help build a union that would give them socialism on the job.

In April the staff of *Socialisti* advised Walter Neff, secretary of the IWW Agricultural Workers Organization in Minneapolis, that there was unrest on the range, and that if the IWW could provide organizers speaking English, Italian and the various Slavic tongues, it could assure the support of the Finns and Swedes. There were already Finnish-speaking delegates, including Geo. Humon, on the Range.

Before organization had proceeded far, a strike broke out at Aurora on June 2. It spread rapidly, for the strikers paraded to nearby mining towns and when miners there struck, they did likewise. By June 14 the entire Mesabi range was out, 16,000 strong, and 4,000 IWW cards had been issued. Demands had been formulated into one program: "$3.50 per day for wet places; $3.00 per day for dry places; $1.75 for surface work; 8 hours to constitute a day in and around the mines; miners to enter and come out on company time; pay twice a month; Saturday night shift to be abolished and miners receive full pay; abolition of all contract work; all miners to be paid as soon as they quit work for a company." They had been working 10 to 12 hours per day and getting from $1.38 to $2.50.

The IWW tried to run a peaceful strike, but the companies recruited over a thousand thugs from various cities, often with the aid of police chiefs who had "something on them," to break up meetings and to prevent even small groups of miners meeting on the streets. On June 9, as the miners were parading from Aurora to Biwabik, eight organizers were nabbed from their ranks by the company police. An Oliver Mining Company gunman shot a miner, John Allar, as he and some other miners stood talking to each other on a street in Virginia. There a Citizens Committee ordered all IWWs out of town. The *Duluth Herald* held that resistance to this illegal vigilante group, which represented about two percent of the citizens of Virginia, was a defiance of law and order. Company lawlessness overruled local administrations

Carlo Tresca (L) with other IWW organizers during the Mesabi Iron Range strike.

that allowed civil liberties. On July 6 a posse of deputies, led by one who had recently been a bouncer in a roadhouse, entered the home of Phillip Masonovich to arrest him and a miner who boarded with him, Joe Hercigonovich. Mrs. Masonovich objected, and was knocked down on the floor. Somehow two of the deputies got shot. According to a boy in the house, they were shot by the previously mentioned roadhouse bouncer. The two Montenegrin miners already mentioned, and another, Joe Nicich, and others were arrested as directly participating and also a group of organizers who were not in the vicinity, Carlo Tresca, Sam Scarlett, Joseph Ahlgren, Joe Schmidt, Frank Little and James Gilday, on the theory that their speeches had led to the deaths of the deputies. No trial was held; though the coroner's verdict had been "death at the hands of persons unknown," Judge O. N. Hilton, who had been called in as defense attorney, arranged for the three Montenegrin miners mentioned to plead guilty to manslaughter and for the others to go free. It soon developed that this arrangement had been proposed by Elizabeth Gurley Flynn who was handling publicity, and that she had sacrificed these miners to secure the release of her friends among the organizers. Her connections with the IWW were promptly terminated.

In mid-August a meeting at Crosby brought out the Cayuna Range. Organizers were busy in the Michigan iron mining country. At Ironwood the vigilantes drove eight organizers out of town. On August 16, Frank Little was arrested at Iron River, Michigan, taken out of jail, beaten, and threatened with lynching – with a rope around his neck – in a futile effort to make him lead his persecutors to the organizers speaking Italian and other languages. They knocked him in the head and he woke up dazed in a ditch near Watersmeet.

The labor movement felt obliged to support the strike. The *Duluth Labor Herald*, AFL, commented: "In 1907 there was a similar strike on the Iron Range. At that time there was a responsible labor organization supporting the strike. ... Were not the same arguments being used in 1907 as are being used in 1916? Did not the press condemn the WFM as it condemns the IWW today?" On July 17 the Minnesota Federation of Labor convened in the strike town of Hibbing and promised support to the strike. The official organ of the Western Federation attacked the strike but its locals sent donations. Following the strike the State Federation attempted to organize the miners, but they wanted the IWW.

With mine production crippled, stock piles were shipped and then lower grade material. In Two Harbors the dock workers struck and stopped shipment; in Duluth a dock strike was broken by police; on the Allouez dock a 15 percent increase was promised if the men would stay at work. In Superior the coal dock workers struck for a 60 percent boost. Mayor Conklin told them he would help if they would join the AFL; instead they joined IWW.

There were tips that the companies were less reluctant to grant improvements to the miners than to grant them formally to the IWW; so in September with the Mesabi, Cayuna and Vermilion ranges out, the central strike committee discussed the proposal of going back to work with a strong organization, a market hungry for ore, and winning their points by action on the job. The proposal was referred to all locals; all voted in favor, and on September 19 the central committee called the strike off. A week later it reported: "The men are returning to work and thus far there has been no evidence of any discrimination against them and none is expected as the mining companies confess themselves exceedingly hard up for help." On April 1 next year Metal Mine Workers held its first conference in the Socialist Opera House in

Virginia. Reports submitted showed that the gains anticipated when the strike was called off were being won; there was a 10 percent increase and a promise of the eight hour day May 1. To make sure of it the miners decided on a 24-hour strike that day – but meanwhile America was taken into the war.[7]

At the same time the IWW was recruiting miners on a smaller scale in the copper country of Arizona and in the Joplin lead district. In the coal fields of Pennsylvania it had a dozen locals who held a conference at Old Forge, Feb. 6, 1916. They established a district organization committee, uniform dues and initiation fees and formulated uniform demands: abolition of the contract system; an 8 hour day with Saturday a half day; $4.00 for miners, carpenters, engineers and motor runners; $3.50 for laborers; $2.50 for mule leaders and $2.00 for breaker boys. A strike in the Lackawanna region to enforce these demands was broken by the State Constabulary, and of course hampered by the fact that the miners were under a four-year UMWA contract against which they were chafing.[8] On June 14 a meeting of 268 members at Old Forge was raided by mounted troopers in a combination cowboy and Indian and Keystone cop manner. All were lugged off to jail and released by October for lack of any evidence against them, but the *Scranton Republican* on October 4 complained "The sheriff's opera bouffe at Old Forge has cost this county several thousand dollars."[9] This terrorism prevented further IWW organization in the field, but IWW influence still had one effect: while bituminous miners were kept tied during the war years to their contracts, the anthracite field permitted upward adjustments.

The Agricultural Workers had a successful year. Their policy had taken the form of announcing in the IWW press what wages it demanded for different operations and areas, and where these terms were met the farmers had no labor trouble. The more intelligent farmers realized that no gain came to them from beating down labor, so long as they were not put at a differential disadvantage with other farmers, and the experience of 1916 led the farm organization, the Non-Partisan League, to propose all-over collective bargaining for the next year, an outcome prevented only by the anti-IWW war hysteria. This fact is far afield from the bogey tales of sabotage. Harvest over, the AWO sent its members into organization efforts in the woods of Minnesota and the West Coast and the western fruit area. In Yakima, Washington, the IWW was organizing among the apple pickers and opened up a hall. A

THE NEW EVERETT HALL
WATCH US GROW!

few hours later the police closed it. The members started an open air meeting to discuss their grievance, and 60 of them were thrown into the city jail. This was lousy; they held a meeting, condemned it and proceeded to demolish it from the inside out. Police and fire department turned the fire hose on them, then marched them soaked to iced refrigerator cars and told a train crew to take them out of town. The train crew refused and told the vigilantes to get going. The men were released from the refrigerator cars and taken to the county jail, for the city jail was a relic. Protests from union officials resulted in permission to open an IWW hall and the release of the men.

A similar effort to drive the IWW out of Everett, Washington, became a tragedy. The lumber barons ran the town through the Commercial Club and their lackey Sheriff McRae. They wanted no union, IWW or AFL. On August 19 the striking Shingle Weavers were beaten by company thugs who waylaid them as they went over a trestle 30 feet above the water. When an IWW hall was opened, McRae closed it. On September 11th his thugs, sworn in at the Commercial Club, took IWW organizer James Rowan to the woods and beat him severely. During October various groups of IWW members, totaling altogether about 400, were driven out of town by these organized hoodlums.

On October 30, forty-one members arriving from the wheat fields were taken to Beverly Park, beaten, and forced to run a gauntlet over a cattle guard at a railroad crossing while the Commercial Club thugs beat them. A church committee investigated and found men's hair and skin still sticking to the cattle guard and the ground soaked with blood. On the advice of these ministers, the IWW issued a circular to the people of Everett announcing an open meeting for Sunday, November 5, at 2:30 and urging them to "come and help defend your and our constitutional rights." Wobs took passage on the steamer Verona, and the overflow came on the Calista. As the Verona drew in to the dock, the free speech fighters were on the side facing it. One lad, Hugo Gerlot, had climbed the mast and all were singing. At a signal from McRae his thugs on the dock and others hidden in a warehouse opened fire. Gerlot fell dead to the deck. At least five more whose bodies were recovered were shot. The pilot house was riddled with bullets, and without a pilot the engineer backed the vessel away through the bloody water, the Commercial Club thugs shooting at it until it was out of range of their high-power rifles.

As the vessels returned to Seattle, the men were arrested, and 74 held on the charge of having killed two deputies who were among those hidden in the warehouse where the men could not have even seen them. All demanded separate trials. During the trial of the first, Thomas Tracy, the lawlessness of the sheriff's thugs became a matter of record, along with their plans to murder the free speech fighters; also that the two deputies had been killed by ricochet of bullets inside the warehouse; and that the bullet holes in the boards of the warehouse all showed that the firing had been from inside it toward the Verona. Tracy was acquitted May 5, 1917. The others were released. But the bloodthirsty Commercial Club and its murderous hirelings were not even indicted.[10]

Organization in the woods went ahead despite this terrorism.

The Duluth District is a winter logging area. On December 24th a meeting of 1,500 sawmill workers in Virginia voted to demand a pay boost and the 8 hour day, and struck on Dec. 28th. They were soon followed by the lumberjacks who demanded a minimum of $40 per month, free hospital treatment, and the right to go to and from work in daylight. In Idaho, spring drive country, the men went to work at the going rate of $3.50 for 12 hours, struck at the opportune moment, and won $5.00 for 8 hours. The Seattle district was busy laying foundation for the history-making strike of 1917.[11]

Although the country had re-elected Wilson on the slogan "He kept us out of war," pressures were growing to bring America into the war.

Australian Wobblies mounted a vigorous campaign against conscription and participation in World War I.

Through the British Empire, where the IWW had some degree of organization in England, South Africa and Australia, the IWW was already being victimized. The general viewpoint of its members was that the primary purpose of unionism is to prevent workers from being used against each other, and that a sense of their common interests should prevent them from shooting each other just as it should prevent them from scabbing on each other. The frank expression of this attitude in Australia led to the trial of its more active spokesmen for treason. They had been arrested in a raid on their headquarters by the militia on September 30, 1916. On December 3, seven were sentenced to 15 years, and others to 10 and 5 years. A press account states that one of them, Beatty, aged 30 when sentenced to 15 years, "startled the assembly by saying that he had been sentenced thirty years ago to penal servitude for life, and that any sentence the court could pass would not trouble him." In contrast to America, these men were released promptly when the war was over.[12]

The 10th Convention – the last before 1919 – met on November 1916 with an organization well recovered from the slump of 1914, and, as shown in the reaction to the Mesabi strike and the Everett tragedy, winning recognition from most labor unionists as a significant part of the labor movement. The two chief outcomes of the convention were the reorganization of its forces and its stand on war. Out of the former grew substantial industrial unions: Agricultural Workers 400, Lumber Workers 500, Construction Workers 573, Metal Mine Workers 480, Metal and Machinery Workers 300 and a General Recruiting Union to administer both mixed and industrial locals that lacked an industrial union on a national scale, and to encourage the formation of industrial locals until enough of them existed to warrant the formation of an industrial union structure for them. (These were renumbered in a decimal system in 1919.) This was a swing from the decentralist tendencies manifest in 1913 and not to crop up again until 1923, and reflected the need to coordinate recent gains. To make its publicity more responsible, the IWW Publishing Bureau was moved to Chicago and the GEB held responsible for publications, with *Solidarity* as the official organ. On the West Coast the *Industrial Worker* had been resumed; the Finnish *Socialisti* of Duluth, a daily paper, had changed its name and become an IWW daily which continued until 1975; for non-English readers there were the following: *Il Proletario, A Bermunkas, Pruslovy Delnik, Solidarnosc, Conscience Industrial, L'Emancipation* and *El Obrero Industrial.*

The IWW stand on war took form in the following resolution:

"We, the Industrial Workers of the World, in convention assembled, hereby reaffirm our adherence to the principles of industrial unionism, and rededicate ourselves to the unflinching, unfaltering prosecution of the struggle for the abolition of wage slavery and the realization of our ideals in Industrial Democracy.

"With the European war for conquest and exploitation raging and destroying our lives, class consciousness and unity of the workers, and the ever-growing agitation for military preparedness clouding the main issues and delaying the realization of our ultimate aim with patriotic and therefore capitalistic aspirations, we openly declared ourselves the determined opponents of all nationalistic sectionalism, or patriotism, and the militarism preached and supported by our one enemy, the capitalist class.

"We condemn all wars, and for the prevention of such, we proclaim the antimilitaristic propaganda in time of peace, thus promoting class solidarity among the workers of the entire world, and, in time of war, the general strike, in all industries.

"We extend assurances of both moral and material support to all workers who suffer at the hands of the capitalist class for their adherence to these principles, and call on all workers to unite themselves with us, that the reign of the exploiters may cease, and this earth be made fair through the establishment of Industrial Democracy."[13]

Notes:

1. Perlman & Taft: *History of Labor in the United States,* McMillan Co., 1935, being the 4th volume of the *History of Labor* by Commons and Associates, p. 312 et seq.
2. Doree's report on Baltimore in Proceedings of 10th Convention. Budish and Soule in their *New Unionist* give a very garbled account.
3. Philadelphia account taken from *Solidarity,* Nos. 330, 333, 340 and 348. The 10th Convention proceedings indicate friction between the MTW and the centralizing tendencies of 1916.
4. Solvay account, *Solidarity,* No. 329; Kelsey Wheel, No. 331.
5. Denver housemaids account, *Solidarity* No. 328; cartoons reproduced in *Solidarity,* No. 342.
6. A clear account of the victimization of Finnish Socialists by the copper trust unopposed by WFM is given in Perlman and Taft *History* cited above, page 258.
7. The account of the Mesabi strike is taken from *Solidarity,* and *Survey* of the period, Proceedings of 10th Convention, Industrial Commission and conversations with participants.
8. The two four-year contracts accounted Perlman & Taft, pp. 342 and 470.
9. The Old Forge arrest vividly described in *Scranton Times* of June 15, 1916, as quoted in *Solidarity,* No. 350.
10. Everett most fully described in book *The Everett Massacre*; also *Survey,* Jan. and May 1917, in two articles by Anna Louise Strong, and 30th memorial issue of *Industrial Worker,* Nov. 2, 1946, with detailed memoirs of Jack Leonard, one of the participants. For general background see Jensen *Lumber and Labor,* Farrar & Rinehart, 1945.
11. Lumber strikes: *Solidarity* No. 364, and article by C.E. Payne in *International Socialist Review,* June 1917.
12. Full account of Australian arrests in pamphlet "Guilty or Not Guilty," by H.E. Boote, published by the Committee Appointed by the Labor Council of New South Wales to Secure a Royal Commission to Investigate the IWW Cases.
13. Minutes 10th Convention, 1916, page 138.

General Sources:

For the Mesabi Range strike, Donald G. Sofchalk, "Organized Labor and the Iron Ore Minders of Minnesota, 1907-1936" (*Labor History,* Spring 1971) proves AFL abstention from organizing these miners in hopes of freedom to organize other trades and details the 1916 strike; also Neil Betten, "Iron Range Strike of 1916," *Minnesota History* (1968, pp. 89-94). Foner (486-517) and Dubofsky (319-333) include opposing views of E.G. Flynn's defense strategy. Gerald Ronning's "Jackpine Savages: Discourses of Conquest in the 1916 Mesabi Iron Range Strike" (*Labor History* 44, 2003, pp. 359-382) and Robert M. Eleff's "The 1916 Minnesota Miners' Strike Against U.S. Steel" (*Minnesota History* 51, 1988, pp. 63-74) offer more recent accounts.

On Finnish involvement, see Douglas Ollila, "A Time of Glory: Finnish-American Radical Industrial Unionism, 1914-1917," *Institute of History, General History Studies* (1977, pp 31-53), "From Socialism to Industrial Unionsm," in Michael Karni et al., *The Finnish Experience in the Western Great Lakes Region* (Univ. of Turku, 1975); "The Emergence of Radical Industrial Unionism in the Finnish Socialist Movement," *Institute of History, General History Studies* (1975, pp. 25-54), "The Work People's College" in Ollila and Michael Karni, eds., *For The Common Good* (Tyomies Society, 1977); "The Finns of Minnesota," by Walfrid Jokinen (M.A. Thesis, Louisiana State, 1953).

The only detailed study of the IWW in anthracite is Patrick Lynch's MA thesis, "Pennsylvania Anthracite: A Forgotten IWW Venture" (Bloomsburg State, 1974).

For the Agricultural Workers Organization and the NPL, see agricultural references in Chapter 7, and Robt. Moran, *Political Prairie Fire* (Univ. of Minnesota Press, 1955). Joel Watne ties the changed outlook to dollar wheat in "Public Opinion Toward Non-Conformists," in *North Dakota History* (Winter 1967); Charles Haug, "IWW in North Dakota, 1913-1917," *North Dakota Quarterly* (Winter 1971-72).

On Everett, Norman Clark's *Milltown* (Univ. of Washington Press, 1970) probes the social history background and his "Everett, 1916 and After" (*Pacific Northwest Quarterly,* 1966, pp. 57-64); Walker C. Smith, *The Everett Massacre* (IWW, 1918); Robert Tyler, *Rebels of the Woods* (1967) and "The Everett Free Speech Fight," *Pacific Historical Quarterly* (1954, pp. 19-30); Kornbluh, pp. 105-126, includes contemporary and participant accounts.

On Minnesota lumber, John Haynes' "Revolt of the Timberbeasts" (*Minnesota History,* Spring 1971) summarizes a 1,500-page report by the governor's investigating committee.

On the Australian IWW, the leading sources are Verity Burgmann, *Revolutionary Industrial Unionism* (Cambridge, 1995), Frank Cain, *The Wobblies at War* (Spectrum, 1994), and Ian Turner, *Sydney's Burning* (Alpha Books, 1969). Burgmann offers the most comprehensive overview, and understands the IWW the best, but Cain and Turner each are useful as well.

9. The Fight with the War Profiteers

From the summer of 1916 through the summer of 1920, IWW efforts to improve job conditions met with an unparalleled campaign of terrorism. During this period the IWW won some of its most enduring victories and built up its strength to what is probably its peak membership of about 40,000 in 1923.[1]

The campaign of terrorism was directed by employers anxious to resist unionism of any sort. At first these employers relied on their own plug-uglies and local vigilante movements; throughout this period this was the chief force the IWW had to fight. They were soon abetted by the local politicians and judiciary, all covered by the smokescreen of a subservient press. In March 1917 the Idaho and Minnesota legislatures passed the first Criminal Syndicalism laws, and the first victim of these was James Dunning, a Minnesota lumberjack convicted Sept. 29, 1917. From the spring of 1917 federal troops began herding off pickets, and in June several hundred sailors from the Bremerton Yards were given special leave and wrecked the IWW hall in Seattle; it was quite unofficial, yet before the event the Roseburg, Ore., *News* announced that these men had been given a few hours leave to drive the IWW out of the city. The Washington end of the government acted with at least outward propriety until September 5, 1917, and in August had assured the editors of *Survey* that Washington had received no information on which to take action against the IWW despite horrendous stories in the press depicting the IWW as a gang of arsonists in the pay of the Kaiser.

That this campaign, masked with the patriotism that Johnson called the last refuge of scoundrels, was the work of corporations fevered with high profits, is plain from the geography of the struggle and the acts and assertions of the corporations themselves. Where the IWW had already made employers take unionism for granted, as in Philadelphia, no campaign against it developed; the impetus to destroy the IWW came from the nonunion fields it was invading: lumber, copper, iron mining and oil. Federal prosecutions were based on opposition to the war and interference with conscription; where the IWW had small propaganda locals there was evident sentiment against registration, but where it was engaged in substantial union activities it avoided being sidetracked from the struggle with the employer by such issues; yet the men arrested were those engaged in practical union effort, and of them all but one of draft age had registered. The copper corporations fought the IWW with thugs, deportations and lynching, all on the pretext that the IWW interfered with war production; yet these companies were selling the government copper at 30 to 34 cents a pound which it cost 7 to 10 cents to produce, and to maintain the scarcity had to store away over three billion pounds of the essential metal;[2] moreover, to fight the unions Phelps Dodge kept the ablest miners out of the mines, thus restricting production.[3] In the oil industry when the Tulsa tar and feather outrage, the federal raiding, the closing of halls by force and the Wichita indictment had not stopped organization and a strike started in January 1918, the oil companies told the federal investigators that they would close down their wells rather than permit government interference with their labor relations.[4] Or, as a large lumber operator told Robert Bruere: "We have fought the IWW as we would have fought any attempt of the AFL unions to control the workers in our camps, and of course we have taken advantage of the general prejudice against them as an unpatriotic organization to beat their strike."[5]

In these war years, profits soared to where they equaled capitalization, but the average real wage, which had climbed from its 1914 base of 100 to 125 in 1916, fell to 116 in 1917 and did not get up to its prewar level until after the war. Yet in those industries where the embattled Wobblies fought, substantial gains were won.

The foundations laid in 1916 enabled the IWW through 1917 to organize rapidly on several fronts. Efforts that had been made in the southwest oil fields now blossomed into an Oil Workers Industrial Union chartered January 1. When the Metal Mine Workers were chartered on January 29th they already predominated over the AFL Mine Mill in the Globe and Miami districts of Arizona, and the Miami scale became the standard for bargaining in other areas. On the east coast the IWW was rapidly organizing seamen and a major chore for its MTW secretary in Boston was to make up menus for all vessels on the Atlantic run; these were stamped with the IWW seal, posted in every mess hall, and the stewards were instructed to abide by them.[6] The U.S. Shipping Adjustment Board recognized the IWW as the bargaining agency for the Philadelphia longshoremen and on February 7, 1918, asked that it provide a member for its three-man adjustment commission empowered to settle wage disputes. The General Executive Board wired that this was autocratic and the Shipping Board made an exception for IWW democracy and accepted the MTW representative on the understanding that he was at all times under the instruction of the union.[7] As a result no strikes were necessary on the Philadelphia waterfront until 1920. At the same time on the Great Lakes, where AFL unionism had been wiped out in the long strike of 1909-13, a fair start at organization was made, but with entrapment into war, arrests and hysteria stopped it.

A new national Industrial Union for General Construction Workers was launched at a conference in Omaha April 29, 1917. It conducted a strike on an irrigation project at Exeter, Calif., in April. On May 14 a short strike won complete job control on all grading jobs around Seattle, including the arrangement that all workers be hired through the IWW hall. At Rockford, Illinois, an active construction local won a strike about the same time; here there was also a budding Furniture Workers' local, but both got strangled in the anti-draft activities that made Rockford briefly famous. Throughout the Inland Empire, as construction work opened up in the spring job delegates got busy recruiting. It was the age of the mule team and fresno for most of this work and the Wobbly mule-skinning clan was known to hold tightly enough together so that without formal agreements, their announcement of wage rates enabled the contractors to reckon their labor costs with certainty. Through most of 1917 the organization efforts of this Industrial Union 573 went ahead relatively unmolested, until Guthrie, Grant and similar large operators turned loose the same campaign of terrorism as had been loosed on their fellow workers in lumber, copper mining and the oil fields; yet their organization survived to be a major part of the IWW in postwar years as Industrial Union 310.

During the early months of 1917 there was wide apprehension that America would be taken into the war and that conscription would follow. A division of opinion grew as to how to apply the 1916 resolution on war. A minority that included many of the Finnish and Irish members in Butte and on the Iron Range, and GEB member Frank Little, and Clyde Hough, secretary of the Rockford Furniture Workers, and a number of propaganda locals, felt the IWW should concentrate on open opposition to the war and defiance of the draft. The majority felt this would sidetrack the class struggle into futile channels and be playing the very game that the war profiteers would want the IWW to play. They contended that the monstrous stupidity by which the governments of different lands could put their workers into uniforms and make them go forth and shoot each other was something that could be stopped only if the workers of the world were organized together; then they could put a stop to this being used against themselves; and that consequently the thing to be done under the actual circumstances was to proceed with organizing workers to fight their steady enemy, the employing class, for better wages, shorter hours, safer and more sanitary working conditions, keeping in mind the ultimate ideal of world labor solidarity. There was no opportunity for referendum, but the more active locals took this attitude, instructing speakers to confine their remarks to industrial union issues, circulating only those pamphlets that made a constructive case for the IWW, and avoiding alliance with the Peoples Council and similar antiwar movements.[8]

Lumber Workers Industrial Union set out at its initial convention in Spokane, March 5, 1917, with the set of demands they aimed to achieve in lumber camp and sawmill. The lumber worker of that day was still the victim of the employment shark. He was a "timber beast" set off from the rest of his fellow workers; he had to furnish his own blankets, and these with his working gear were enough to carry without ordinary dress clothes; as a result when he came to town he was permitted entry only to the dives that lived off him and so tolerated the caulk shoes his work required and that would soon tear up a floor. Camps lacked shower baths or facilities for washing clothes, and the timber beast was often a smelly, scratching specimen of humanity in town; at camp he spent his little leisure after a 10 hour day in a bunkhouse of double deck bunks, redolent with the acrid odor of sweaty work clothes drying. The Wobbly demands ran:

1. 8 hours with no work on Sundays or holidays;
2. Minimum wage of $60 per month and board;
3. Wholesome food in porcelain dishes, no overcrowding; sufficient help to keep kitchen clean and sanitary;
4. Sanitary sleeping quarters, not more than 12 men in each bunkhouse; single spring beds and mattresses with good clean bedding to be furnished free by company; bunkhouse to be well lit and furnished with reading tables; dry room, laundry room and shower baths;
5. Free hospital service;
6. $5.00 per day minimum for river drivers;
7. Two pay days per month by bank check without discount;
8. All men to be hired on job or from union hall; free transportation

from place of hiring to job;
    9. No discrimination.
    Quick victories were won on the river drives in the short log coun-
try during the last part of April. The 12 hour day was cut to 8 and the
pay raised to $5.00 from $3.50. Militia raided the hall at Whitefish,
Mont.; men were arrested for refusing to work, but the river drive
strikes were complete victories. IWW plans for the woods had been
for a July strike in the short log country, then later a strike on the
coast, but events moved faster. Scattered victories along the hump
between the two areas were won in May and "in camp after camp the
union was moving from the hall to the bunkhouse." Spontaneous action started the wave of short log strikes on June 20th, general by July
16, on which date, in response to strike calls by both AFL and IWW,
the long log country came out solid too.
    The use of federal troops in the lumber and other strikes lacked
legal sanction. The National Guard had been called into federal service as soon as America was taken into the war, and so only federal
troops were available. No record seems available that any governor
or state legislature certified that insurrection or disorder beyond the
capacity of the state to suppress required such intervention, though
such certification is required by law. To the contrary, "prosecuting attorneys in Montana and Washington and special agents of the Bureau
of Investigation testified to the peacefulness of the lumber strike and
the lack of violence and intimidation by the IWW." Though the law
of 1878 provided that federal troops may not be used as a posse comi-
tatus to federal law officers, War Department authorizations to local
army officers passed down the line of authority to platoon level, in
effect provided for such service to sheriffs and district attorneys. Arrests could be made to protect public utilities essential to the war or
for "acts in pursuance of prearranged plans contemplating violence."
These pretexts were used to arrest strikers committing no offence.
Those arrested were not subject to habeas corpus, as the local Councils of Defense agreed that the sheriffs should answer any such petition that "the prisoners are held by military power."[9]
    Concurrent with this general northwest lumber strike was the cop-
per strike in Montana and Arizona. The repressive measures urged by
the copper barons and behind the scenes moves in Washington shaped
the novel and successful process of carrying the lumber workers' strike
back to the job. A correct depiction requires a switch of attention here

Bisbee deportation.

to these copper miners, then a return to the lumber strike.

By June 1917, the IWW in Arizona had edged ahead of the old Western Federation, then known as AFL Mine Mill & Smelter Workers, but neither organization was in position to engage in effective bargaining. The Mine Mill members often carried two cards and favored joint action by the two unions; most local officials didn't, yet were opposed enough to Moyer policy to want statewide autonomy. At Globe and Miami the two forces working together had pushed wages up to the highest in the industry. Early in June the IWW won a 12 1/2 pecent pay boost at the Humboldt smelter at Prescott and in the mines at Mayer with a short strike. Mine Mill had given notice to the Clarke interests that it wanted a wage boost at Jerome and a contract with check-off. The IWW called a mass meeting there, explained that it would support any strike for improved conditions, but opposed the check-off and contract, proposing instead that where two unions were involved a policy of no discrimination and a grievance committee elected by all workers would protect all miners. The men were solid for this policy, and the company promptly met these demands, including the Miami scale. At Swansea the same company granted the same demands after the IWW had staged a strike for one half shift.[10]

At this point things began to move in Butte where there had been no miner unionism since the turmoil of 1914. On June 5 many Irish and a number of Finns were arrested for demonstrating against the draft. On the 8th came the Speculator Mine disaster. With flames blocking the shafts, men rushed to the bulkheads that separate the level of one mine from adjoining levels of the next mine. To save a few dollars for iron manholes in them required by safety law, they had been concreted solid, and 190 miners were burned to death. Indignation resulted in a strike on June 11 and a new union, the Metal Mine Workers, formed to ensure mine safety, end the rustling card and espionage system, and bring wages up with the high cost of living. The new union was unaffiliated; the miners would have none of Moyer's Mine Mill, nor of the handful still liquidating the assets of old Butte Miners' Union No. 1, and the IWW avoided any action that would jeopardize their solidarity. The AFL, however, would not let them use the Carpenters' Hall, so they met in the hall of the Finnish Socialists. On the 18th the AFL electrical workers, as the result of a long-standing dispute, walked out and soon were followed by other AFL crafts. The miners and electrical workers cooperated and until July 20th issued a joint strike bulletin.

Arizona miners quickly saw that with Butte struck, a strike throughout Arizona was the best help they could give to restore unionism to the Butte mines and to settle their own grievances, particularly their safety demand of two men on all piston and Leyner machines, two men in all raises and stopes, and no blasting in raises, stopes or drifts during shifts. By June 26th IWW organizer Grover Perry could wire: "Bisbee, Jerome, Miami and Swansea strike in support of Butte; other camps await call." On the 27th the Silver Bow Trades and Labor Council resolved 44-28 that the new mine union was "in the best interests of organized labor" though the AFL crafts still disowned it. There was some talk of getting an AFL charter, but Mine Mill's jurisdiction prevented that and the miners were told they would have to join Moyer's union as individuals – which they didn't.

With Arizona mines tied up tight, the federal government sought a settlement by its Conciliation Service, to which it appointed former Governor Hunt, who had been re-elected but had been temporarily counted out by the copper companies for his friendliness to unions. The IWW insisted that settlement should be nationwide so as not to leave the Butte miners holding the bag, and proposed that the government could save a lot of money by granting union demands and taking over the mines. Since the government was paying Phelps Dodge three times the production cost of copper, it was horrified and denounced the IWW as working for the German government. Then, working on a plan laid out by a German army captain for him, Walter Douglas, head

IWW organizer Frank Little.   *The IWW issued the Daily Bulletin during the Chicago trial.*

of the Phelps Dodge Copper Queen Division, set out to rid Arizona of Wobblies. On July 10 at Jerome, the company officials with a posse of business men and a handful of Mine Mill members, rounded up those they considered IWW agitators and jailed them. A Mine Mill organizer secured the release of 37 of the 104 on his assurance that they weren't IWWs and the rest were shipped to Needles, sent back and released. At Bisbee before dawn on July 12, a similar posse rounded up the strikers as they prepared for break-of-day picketing, and searched homes until they had a total of 1,164, not counting the three they killed, marched them to Warren, and held them in a ball park until they could be put into cattle cars and shipped to the desert. They were packed tight, standing up, parched with thirst, and many had been clubbed in the round-up. After 36 hours of this torture they were put into a detention camp at Columbus, N.M. All was carried out under the direction of Mr. Douglas of Phelps Dodge.

Scattered strikes continued in Arizona, but with many of the more experienced Wobs at Columbus or in jail at Prescott and Tombstone (for protesting these outrages) settlements were made for wage increases and other improvements, leaving the Copper Queen run with imported scabs, and the Butte miners fighting the copper trust alone. There on August 1, again in the dark early hours, a gang came to the boardinghouse next to the Finn Hall where Frank Little lay in bed, his leg recently broken, and dragged him to the Milwaukee railroad trestle where he or his already dead body was hanged. Instead of intimidating the miners, it put them the more solidly behind the IWW whose spokesman Frank Little was. His funeral was the largest Butte had ever seen, even the AFL unions joining the procession with their banners. On August 11, Federal troops began to patrol the streets. Phelps Dodge stirred up additional wrath when, upon taking over a coal mine at Gallup, N.M., it declared open shop, and subsequently deported the UMWA coal miners. William Green of UMWA threatened a national strike of coal miners unless these men were protected in their right to return. The fight between labor and the war profiteers everywhere (the AFL had of course far more strikes than the IWW) was threatening to demolish the fabric of lies against the IWW woven by the press and to lead to recognition of the IWW as spearheading this fight with the profiteers in the areas where it was most competent to do so. On August 25 the new union in Butte, by this time usually thought of as pro-IWW, closed the Anaconda smelter by a picket line and the Anaconda shut down what mines it had been able to operate and its smelter at Great Falls. On September 5th federal authorities abruptly changed face and raided IWW offices and halls across the country all at 2 p.m. central standard time and seized all records – over five tons of them.

This was the situation that led the lumber workers to switch tactics. By September 1 the short log country had been out from eight to ten weeks in different sections and the west coast six weeks. On the coast the IWW had been hesitant about calling the strike because most of the workers had gone back nearly broke after the July 4 holiday. In the short log country, in particular, repression had been rough. At Troy, Mont., Frank Thornton had been put in a wooden jail and the jail burned down. All halls had been closed, Spokane being the last to remain open; as it was being closed and the authorities at one end were taking possession, at the other jacks were still lining up to have their cards written out. In Klamath Falls strikers had been kangarood; local lawyers refused to defend them while lawyers from out of town were told to travel. In Portland when strikers were arrested, the MTW answered by tying up river transportation. Arrests for vagrancy and other charges grew on the coast, and in its issue of August 15, the *Industrial Worker* pointed out that if this continued the strikers would be compelled to shift to a new kind of strike – one on the job where the police would not be so handy to club them. On August 31 the District Organization Committee for the Seattle District carried the following motion: "That we ask all branches and picket camps to call a meeting for September 7th to determine the sentiment in regard to transferring the strike to the job for the purpose of enforcing the eight hour day. We wish to impress on the minds of the membership the importance of understanding this motion clearly. The meaning of the motion is that if we did transfer the strike to the job we would only work eight hours and quit. Kindly inform the District Office of the results of your meeting of Sept. 7."

The nationwide raids of Sept. 5 ended any doubts about the proposed tactic. To the employers it seemed that the men were accepting defeat; the lumber workers who had discussed their tactics, and agreed upon them almost unanimously, went to the camps as they opened up. Some took their own whistles with them, blew them at the end of eight hours and went in to camp. If they were fired, the next crew did the same. In some they soldiered on the job; in others they played "dumb" – but whatever their form of the new tactic, they were eating and sleeping on company territory, away from the police, and the employers did not know what to do. Senator Borah explained: "The IWW is about as elusive a proposition as you ever ran up against. ... It is intangible. ... You cannot reach it ... it is simply an understanding between men" – and it could not be jailed.[11]

The case of the lumber workers was clear. The president sent Carlton Parker as a peace envoy and he said they should have their demands. Secretary of War Baker and the Governor of Washington urged the 8 hour day. But the west coast operators said no. As the strike on the job tactic was enforcing the 8 hour day in camp after camp, the operators of the Inland Empire passed a resolution calling on the government to establish the 8 hour day for industrial peace. The Spruce Division headed by Colonel Disque of 4L fame announced it officially May 1, 1918 – but the lumberjacks knew that they themselves had got it. They had celebrated May 1, 1917, with a big parade to strew Joe Hill's ashes. They observed May 1, 1918, with a bigger celebration in camp after camp, burning the old bedding rolls so that the companies had to furnish bedding or have no workers. Where double deck

The New York City IWW hall after it was raided by federal agents.

bunks persisted, the top sections got thrown out. By a continuous battle, intermittent but never lost sight of, the process of "conditioning the job" went on to transform the shunned timber beast of 1916 into the respected lumber worker of 1919, eating the best and dressed the best of any worker in the country, and also sobered up. The IWW had changed not only the conditions of the timber beast, but also his wants and habits. A wage boost can at times be taken away – but not the habits and standards of an entire occupational area; the gains of 1918 have withstood depressions, wars and complete disorganization to this day.

In the copper strike no such permanent victory was achieved. Following the raids of Sept. 5, 1917, it seems that the higher brackets of labor leadership effectively clamped down on sentiment in their ranks favorable or even tolerant toward the IWW, though to that date its prestige in the labor movement had been gaining. In the Butte, Anaconda situation, on Sept. 11 the AFL staged a meeting to urge the return to work; the Butte miners were left out, and their strike and their new union faded out by December 28th. Once the new union had given up, the IWW job delegate system felt free without imperiling solidarity to build for itself, and achieved sufficient strength by September 1918 to pull short strikes protesting the convictions in the IWW and Socialist cases, and by March 1919 there were over 5,000 in the Butte IWW local. In Arizona the Mediation Commission set up machinery for union representation, but with the proviso that those belonging to organizations refusing to make contracts or disloyal to the government be excluded. Thus, by excluding the IWW the commission slapped the war profiteers on the wrist for their lawless interference with production and gave them exactly what they wanted.

The espionage charges, to support which the nationwide raids were made, had nothing to do with espionage, and were an improvisation hit upon after other plots to wreck the good work of the IWW had proved ineffective. The first scheme was to rely upon the new deportation provisions enacted in 1917, which allowed deportation for beliefs acquired by the foreigner during his stay here. Deportation procedure was felt to have the stealthy advantage of permitting no "snail-paced court trial," little or no publicity, and putting the burden of argument on the deportee. It was felt that extensive deportation arrests would intimidate enough to prevent the IWW from using the war to establish decent working conditions. This snagged on three facts: the Wobs didn't get scared; most of them were native born; and the employers didn't want them removed from the labor market, but only wanted to stop them from having any voice in that market. Use of federal troops got snagged on the same facts. Western governors proposed that all IWW agitators, without any bother about court procedures, be apprehended and secretly interned somewhere so as to "mystify and frighten" the remaining members. This plan was considered and then given up for the program said to have been formulated by former governor John Lind of Minnesota for the state Commission of Public Safety – arrest all officers, editors, etc., under the wartime provisions of the Espionage Act.[12] IWW membership lists secured from the raids were given to Samuel Gompers to arrange for general blacklisting.

On the basis of the five tons of "evidence" seized in the September raids, indictments in Chicago, Sacramento and Wichita were issued against those whom the advisers to the federal government considered the back bone of the IWW.[13] These were charged in many pages that the IWW was interfering with the war by strikes, sabotage and discouragement of conscription. The strikes were legitimate disputes not with the government but with the profiteers who were milking the government. The evidence of hostility to conscription dated from pre-war days when it, too, was not unlawful. The alleged sabotage consisted of unsupported tales as far back as 1911 by company henchmen. The defense objected that if charges were to be based on these tales, the accused should be tried in the district where the offense was alleged so that witnesses could be secured and cross-examined, and all this within a reasonable time of the commission of the alleged offenses. But this and the old literature were admitted by the court as evidence of the "frame of mind" of the IWW, and with the court conceding that these alleged acts were not within federal jurisdiction, let them go before the jury without any requirement thus that they be proved. Most of this trash got thrown out by the higher courts, but the conviction was sustained. On August 17, 1918, the Chicago jury in less than an hour reached a decision on the tons of evidence that the court conceded had been illegally seized, and the evidence it had been hearing since April 1, and on the fate of over a hundred men. Judge Landis gave fifteen men 20 years, thirty-five 10 years, thirty-three 5 years, twelve a year and a day, and the rest nominal sentences.

In Sacramento the men did not go to trial until after the war was over – when Australia was already releasing its IWW prisoners. In the long delay five of the 51 had died under bad jail conditions. The defendants decided to treat the proceedings frankly as a kangaroo court and remained silent. The results were the same as if they had lawyers to interpose overruled objections. The Wichita proceedings were even further delayed.

On these federal indictments, on Criminal Syndicalism charges and on various other pretexts arising largely out of strike activities, probably close to two thousand IWWs were arrested during this time. Further IWW stationary delegates, branch secretaries and job delegates were chased from home or job by plug-uglies and vigilantes, often with beatings and tar and feather parties. The arrests required an almost complete change in official personnel of the union, and a concentration on legal defense that led to the formation in October 1917 of a General Defense Committee to coordinate defense work nationally. It was handicapped by a general reluctance of lawyers to serve, not only because of the prejudice built by press against IWW but because of such instances as the deportation of lawyers from Klamath Falls, Ore., or from Bisbee, or Staunton, Illinois where defense counsel Metzen was tarred and feathered along with the IWW he went there to defend.[14] On October 30, *Solidarity* was denied the mails; a *Defense News Bulletin* was issued instead. Its mailing was interfered with so that distribution had to be by small bundles mailed from various places in other publications as wrapping.

In retrospect sober judgment has looked upon this period as one in which the IWW was engaged in activities that were not only legal, but positively praiseworthy, and that the lawlessness was that of the war profiteers and of their political and judicial henchmen. The positive results were improved job conditions and a growing IWW with its attention focused on "conditioning the job."

Notes:

1. Average annual membership calculated by dividing dues stamps sold in calendar year by 12; probably peak membership for any month may have been in August 1917 and comes close to 100,000.
2. For war profits, see U.S. Senate Document 259, 65th Congress, and chapter 17 of Seldes, *Iron, Blood and Profits.*
3. Jensen, *Heritage of Conflict,* pp. 480 and 422. Jensen has a detailed account of the copper strike, biased by Mine Mill contentions that IWW was imported by the mine companies!
4. *Defense News Bulletin* No. 17.

IWW defendants on their way to court, Chicago 1918

5. As quoted in Gambs' *Decline,* p. 44.
6. Correspondence with Jas. Phillips, MTW sec'y. Boston, at time.
7. Exchange of wires in *Defense News Bulletin* No. 16.
8. Foregoing paragraph digests many letters, minutes, etc., used as evidence in the Chicago trial, gathered from briefs filed with U.S. Circuit Court of Appeals, 7th District, October term 1919, docket 2721.
9. This paragraph is based on information in a manuscript by William Preston of history department, Denison University, on "The Ideology and Techniques of Repression." This author had access to Washington files for his study.
10. Account of copper strike is compiled from IWW papers of the time, Jensen's *Heritage* and correspondence with A.S. Embree and report of President's Commission.
11. Account of lumber strike from IWW papers of the time and reminiscences

in later IWW publications, and discussion with participants. Fairly good accounts by others are given in Jensen, *Labor and Lumber,* and Perlman & Taft with considerable documentation. An ironic epilog to Disque's Spruce Division and its efforts to get the lumber workers to work harder occurred through the 1930s as Hoover's economizers tried to get the Spruce Division abolished on the grounds it had been collecting its pay and doing nothing since November 1918. Borah quotation in *Congressional Record,* March 3, 1918.

12. Sources same as Footnote 9 above.

13. There is extensive literature on these cases by American Civil Liberties Unions and others. All three summarized in *N.Y. Nation* 1919 XVIII, p. 383. The cases are Haywood v. U.S. Fed. 795 (1920), Anderson v. U.S. 273 Fed. (1921) and 269 Fed. 65 (1920). W.D. Lane described Kansas City jail conditions in *Survey,* 1919, XLII, 807. Cases are summarized also by Gambs and Perlman & Taft. While Dowell's book, previously cited, concentrates on the Criminal Syndicalism cases, it is the best study so far of the psychological and economic processes involved in this effort to get the IWW. It is still hoped that a thorough Ph.D. thesis will be written on the role of the federal government and how it was induced to take that role.

14. *Defense News Bulletin* 16 – the mob was led by the District Attorney.

General Sources:

Huge wartime profits provide essential background for the period, noted in Nye Committee Report, Report 944, Senate, 74th Congress, 1st Session, and in Congressional debate on Chamberlain bill regarding lumber, *New York Times,* April 6, and June 30, 1918.

The basic study of the effort to suppress the IWW is William Preston's *Aliens and Dissenters* (Harvard Univ. Press, 1963; 2nd ed., 1994, Univ. of Illinois), based on study of government correspondence and other records; see p. 129 for proof IWW membership lists given Gompers for blacklist. Joan Jensen's *The Price of Vigilance* (Rand McNally, 1968) describes some of the unofficial terrorism against the IWW; Eldridge F. Dowell, *History of Criminal Syndicalism Legislation* (John Hopkins, 1939; reprinted 1970) focuses on state action; Rob Hanson, *With Drops of Blood* (Signature, 1999) is an annotated compilation of government documents on its persecution of the IWW from 1912-1923. Robert C. Sims, "Idaho Criminal Syndicalism Act" (*Labor History,* 1974) explores motivations, and its surviving ban on slow-downs; David Wagaman, "'Rausch Mit': The IWW in Nebraska During World War I," in Conlin, *At the Point of Production;* Dorothy B. Schmidt, "Sedition in the State of Washington," (M.A. thesis, Washington State, 1940); Woodrow Whitten, "Criminal Syndicalism and the Law in California," *American Philosophical Transactions,* 1969.

For IWW attitude toward the war see Kornbluh, 316-348; James O'Brien, "Wobblies and Draftees: the IWW's Wartime Dilemma" (*Radical America,*

Sept.-Oct. 1967). For Rockford draft resistance, see John Burns, "IWW in Illinois During WWI" (MA thesis, Western Illinois Univ., 1972).

The Chicago indictment is quoted in its entirety in *Labor History,* Fall 1970; Philip Taft summarizes the trial in Winter 1972 issue; Michael Johnson, "IWW and Wilsonian Democracy," *Science and Society,* Summer 1964; an out-of-print pamphlet, "The Silent Defense," discusses the Sacramento trial; on Wichita indictment, Clayton Koppes, "The Kansas Trial of the IWW, 1917-1919," *Labor History,* Summer 1975, and "The IWW and County Jail Reform 1915-1920," *Kansas Historical Quarterly,* Spring 1975; Earl Bruce White, "The United States v. C.W. Anderson et al.: The Wichita Case 1917-1919," in Conlin, *At the Point of Production;* Nigel Sellars' *Oil, Wheat and Wobblies* discusses Oklahoma trials. Stewart Bird and Peter Robilotta's play, *The Wobblies: The U.S. vs. Wm. D. Haywood et al.,* (Smyrna Press, 1980) is based on the Chicago trial. Ellen Doree Rosen's *A Wobbly Life* (Wayne State Univ. Press, 2004) documents the devastating effect of the repression on IWW organizer E.F. Doree and his family.

For IWW wartime organizing in agriculture, Carl F. Reuss, "The Farm Labor Problem in Washington 1917-1918" (*Pacific Northwest Quarterly,* October 1943); Thorstein Veblen, "Using the IWW to Harvest Grain," *Journal of Political Economy,* December 1932; and agricultural references in chapters 7 and 8.

For lumber, see Tyler; Benjamin G. Rader's "The Montana Lumber Strike of 1917" (*Pacific Northwest Quarterly,* May 1967) draws on district forester reports to acquit IWW of sabotage; Robert Herrin, "Great Lumber Strikes in Northern Idaho" (MA thesis, Northern Illinois, 1967).

On copper, John H. Lundquist and James Fraser, "A Sociological Interpretation of the Bisbee Deportation," *Pacific Historical Review,* November 1968; May and November 1972 issues of *American West* for pro-company account of Bisbee and insider rejoinder; Gerald Ronning, "I belong in this world: Native Americanisms and the western Industrial Workers of the World" (Ph. D. dissertation, Univ. of Colorado, 2002) has much on Bisbee, Butte and Frank Little; Rob Hanson, *The Great Bisbee IWW Deportation* (Signature Press, 1996) reprints many documents; Mike Byrnes and Les Rickey, *The Truth about the Lynching of Frank Little* (Old Butte Publishing, 2003); *Labor History* (Winter 1972) includes Philip Taft on Bisbee aftermath and white-wash trials, and Lindquist account of Jerome deportation in Arizona and the West, Autumn 1969; Arnon Gutfield, "The Speculator Disaster" (*Arizona and the West,* Spring 1969) and "Murder of Frank Little" (*Labor History,* Spring 1969), implying Anaconda used the IWW to hamper AFL organizing, a notion discredited by Brissenden's evidence on the rustling card in *American Economic Review,* December 1920.

10. Revolution Around the Corner

The First World War ended in a wave of revolutions that brought great hopes for those who wanted the world to be different, great fears for those who wanted it to remain the same, and great problems for those who wanted it not only different but better. These are the hopes, fears, and problems that characterize the age in which we still live.

News of the March and November revolutions in Russia was welcome to the IWW. Revolts in Austria and Germany brought the war to a halt; in January workers in the Ruhr seized the industries in which they worked; in March Karolyi peacefully handed Hungary over to a Communist regime; Britain and France had strikes for workers' control and for "Hands Off Russia"; with all this the term "revolution" lost its customary overtone of distance. Capitalists believed revolution imminent, feared it, legislated against it and bought books on how to keep workers happy. Workers too favored change, but most held hopes in the vague promises of wartime politicians for a "world fit for heroes to live in." A minority in the labor movement believed world social revolution a possibility that needed only some nurturing, with a bit of conspiracy and the properly formulated theses. This minority consisted typically of those who conversed (or debated) mostly with other members of the same minority and who thus dived "in a miasmata of their own effulgences." Those whose manner of living kept them in steady contact with the general run of workers were not so prone to let hopes distort their perceptions. This was the situation with most of the IWW, but a few managed to acquire the view of the self-appointed "militant minority" and to do such harm as the forces of repression had not been able to do, with results not fully apparent until 1923-24.[1]

No major consequence of the revolutionary upheaval in Europe appeared in America until 1919. Not until late summer was the divisive effect of the Russian revolution upon the general anti-capitalist movement evident. A new bogeyman was replacing the IWW as a newspaper stereotype, and the left wing was playing with Soviet terms, running strikes under Workers' Soldiers' and Sailors' Councils in Seattle, Butte and Toledo – or trying to.

The Seattle General Strike of February 6th to 11th, 1919, was an AFL strike, but many held it showed IWW influence, the more so as

The Arlington, Washington IWW hall.

under wartime conditions many IWWs had become "two-card men" active in Seattle AFL circles. The purpose of the strike was to back up the 25,000 metal trades workers in the shipyards against a Macy award that cut wages. It was a marvel of orderliness, with the Central Labor Council officially responsible, but in the background this Workmen's Soldiers and Sailors' Council. (The business group later boasted it had its man there too, drafting a constitution fit to send any man to jail who signed it.) It was abruptly ended by threat of invading international officers to revoke the charters of the participating unions. In the open shop reaction that followed, both the Socialist Party and Equity Press, where the *Industrial Worker* was printed, were raided; also 31 members of the IWW were arrested and charged with trying to overthrow the government by participating in the strike. That the rank and file of the unions favored the strike was shown by its orderliness, its completeness and the fact that all local officials were re-elected.[2]

Butte followed with a general strike two days later, February 8th. It was precipitated by announcement of a dollar a day cut on the 7th. To cope with craft disunity that had wrecked the 1917 strike, it was necessary to create some inter-union body. In the Soviet fad this was called a Workers' and Soldiers' Council; its veteran members wore part of their military uniform. The IWW Metal Mine Workers furnished a large part of the strikers and also delegates to this Council. To give the crafts an excuse to stay home, for lack of transportation, they picketed the streetcar barns. When the strike was on for a few days the Silver Bow Trades & Labor Council ordered all members to join the strike, but international officers were soon on hand to threaten revocation of charters. This broke the strike. The pay cut was put across temporarily, but soon put back to the $5.85 rate again by resistance action on the job.[3]

(In 1919 Metal Mine Workers Industrial Union 800 had an average annual membership of 8,000 roughly divided into 2,500 in the Great Lakes iron district and 5,500 in the copper district; there was considerable turnover, for with about the same membership through the year, there were about 6,000 initiations.) It struck again in August in Butte in support of the AFL crafts, and at Oatman, Arizona, for a 6 hour day and a dollar an hour. They had the mines tight, but the Moyer union signed an agreement for a 50 cent increase with the proviso that no member of the IWW be hired.[4]

Another "soviet" formed in Toledo gave the IWW its first disillusionment with this phenomenon. Early in May workers at the Ford plate glass factory walked out and joined the IWW. Overland workers followed, and soon the Autolite, bringing the total on strike to 13,000. To unify it all the left wing formed a Soldiers and Sailors' Council. The IWW learned that the funds raised for this body for strike relief went instead to pay for printing its revolutionary propaganda. The IWW didn't object so much to the lurid phrases, but it did object to the tapping of the strike funds, and the strike appears to have fallen apart.[5]

The 11th Convention of the IWW met May 5th to 16th, 1919. It was the first convention since 1916. The financial statement for the intervening 31 months showed per capita income of $77,968.18, which, at 7 1/2 cents per dues stamp, indicates an average membership during those 31 hectic months of about 33,500. The current membership was figured at 35,000. Defense activities had required major expenditures: $101,808.54 for lawyers' fees; $29,603.43 for relief of prisoners and their families; and $8,985.13 for witness fees. The IWW press had two English weeklies and an English-language monthly magazine, seven weeklies and two monthlies in other languages, and the Finnish daily. About this time there was considerable recruitment in Chicago and cities east, much of it "language branches" formed for propaganda and social activities and pride in "redness" rather than for conditioning the job. In an effort to ensure an industrial focus this 11th Convention eliminated the Recruiting Unions. Soon, however, it was found necessary to make other provisions for the membership of those who wanted one big union but for whom local industrial unions did not exist. Subsequent constitutional changes set up a General Recruiting Union with the intent of generating industrial locals and eventually new national industrial unions.

Through the summer of 1919 the IWW carried on in harvest field and lumber camp despite the additional harassment of the anti-red frenzy of 1919. The Agricultural Workers had an average annual membership for the year of about 4,000 but recruited about twice that number, 3,039 of them in August alone. Its techniques made it the most unstable part of the IWW, engaged in the selling of union cards rather than in the organization of men. Its spring and fall conventions were newsworthy. Mayor Short of Sioux City announced he would open the spring convention with an address of welcome; citizens met to protest and he read them the constitution. The mayor and other citizens, including a government agent and his stenographer attended; after the mayor's speech all outsiders left except the agent and his steno, and for two days the 103 members conducted their affairs in peace. Then the sheriff closed the hall. The convention moved to the corner of 4th and Jennings and completed their convention in front of a large and interested audience who joined in closing it with the singing of "Solidarity Forever," the government agent and his steno not participating. The boys found Sioux City such an interesting place they set their fall convention for it too. Haywood was out on bond and was scheduled to attend it and speak on the street. Permission was denied, so he addressed a largely hostile crowd of about 5,000 from the windows of the hall, and soon had them with him. The indignant editor of the *Tribune* ran his car back and forth through the crowd until the chief of police arrested him. (This was about the only instance in the year of the law favoring the IWW; arrests were as numerous as in 1918, with the Criminal Syndicalism laws providing the new technique.)[6]

The lumber workers were the sturdiest industrial union in the IWW with an average annual membership of close to 20,000 through 1919. During the year they initiated 8,800 new members, but about half of this represented growth, not replacement of others dropping out. In the northwest it had from a third to a half of the lumberjacks organized and about a sixth of the mill workers. It had no competition except the dying 4 L's, which retained some membership in the mill towns. A spring strike on the river drives got the same bedding gains for this work as had been won already in the camps. In October a generalized wave of strikes in the short logs against adding the cost of blankets to the board bill ended with return to work and winning again by job action. The strike had two novel demands: release of all class war prisoners and withdrawal of troops from Russia. In the Great Lakes area, small walkouts and job action won some minor improvements in camp conditions and maintained a fair degree of organization. When a mob attacked the district office of the lumber workers in Superior, Wisconsin, those inside let the mob see that they were armed, and there was no further trouble. In Centralia, Washington, the lynching fever of the business class was not stopped by similar action, but following these two examples of resistance, raiding of halls was checked.

When the Armistice Day parade, November 11, 1919, stopped in front of the IWW hall in Centralia, there was no doubt what the intent was. Once before on April 20, 1918, a parade had stopped at the IWW hall and demolished it, the banker taking the secretary's desk. In June of 1919 a Citizens' Protective League was talking of driving the IWW out of town, and a blind IWW newsboy had been kidnapped, taken out of town and told not to come back at the risk of his life. A ways and means committee of the Citizens' Protective League was elected to attend to the details of driving the IWW out of Centralia, and it was common talk that the Armistice Day parade would be used for this purpose. IWW lumberjacks consulted a local attorney, Elmer Smith, who told them they had a legal right to protect their hall by arms. On November 7 it was announced that the parade would march to Third and Turner and return – that is, march to the corner past the IWW hall, turn and march past it again. That left no doubts. When the parade came, the postmaster and ex-Mayor McCleary were each carrying a coil of rope, conspicuously prepared for a lynching bee. Paraders broke out after the turn of the line of march, and when they broke through the door of the IWW hall, IWW members shot and killed three of the attackers. Then the mob surged in, beat and arrested the defendants, except one, Wesley Everest, a returned soldier, who went out the back of the hall, holding the mob at a distance

The Centralia hall after the mob attack.

with his automatic as he retreated toward the Chehalis River. There he offered to surrender to any officer of the law, but not to the mob. Dale Hubbard, son of the banker who had taken the IWW desk in the 1918 raid, stepped out to take him; Everest shot and killed. Then his revolver jammed and the mob had him. They beat him, rammed a rifle butt down his throat, and threw his bleeding body in the center of the jail where his fellow workers, locked in cells, could see him but do nothing for him. That night the mayor and city electrician shut off all lights in the city and the businessmen opened the jail, took Everest out to lynch him, cutting off his genitals before they did so.[7]

A reign of terror followed in the region. It was open season on Wobblies. When the defenders of the hall were brought to trial on a charge of conspiracy to murder, troops surrounded the courthouse at Montesano. The evidence clearly established that the conspiracy was that of the businessmen to drive out the IWW with a threat of lynching and with the probability of an actual lynching such as they did indisputably perpetrate, and that the first shot was fired after the invasion of the hall. A Seattle labor jury, sent by the AFL to witness the trial, judged the men completely innocent. The jurors found them guilty of the impossible charge of second degree murder on a conspiracy indictment. Later affidavits from the jurors declare that this verdict was wrung from them by intimidation, and fear what the business class could do to them in the community where they had their homes. Elmer Smith, the lawyer who had advised them, was acquitted and spent most of his time until his death in 1930 in efforts to obtain their release, but his efforts and the findings of church and other bodies left the governors unmoved; probably because to recognize the men's innocence was to recognize the guilt of the American Legion and the business men. Lumber Workers Industrial Union survived the terrorism and remained a sturdy organization until 1925 when it was rendered ineffective by dissension and the "gyppo" system.

At this period the program of revolutionary industrial unionism was growing internationally by extensions of the IWW and the birth of similar movements with which the IWW had friendly relations. In Canada, where the rather small IWW had been repressed during the war by orders-in-council, a similar movement, the One Big Union, swept the western area largely because the conservative leaders refused to join the western bodies in protests against these orders-in-council which suspended civil rights for radicals.[8] They proposed a reorganization of the Canadian labor movement on an industrial basis, were turned down, and formed the OBU, originally representing substantially all labor from Port Arthur west. The Winnipeg General Strike, though arising out of disputes antecedent to the OBU, brought it great publicity as it was headed by the active spirits in the new movement. These men were convicted of trying to overthrow the government on the grounds that permitting milk deliveries was assuming governmental powers. The loss of their chief spokesmen occurred at a time when AFL officials were threatening that bodies with the old treasuries would take over existing contracts and bar OBU men from their jobs, and the OBU was reduced to a few occupational groups, in mining, streetcar transportation, lumber and the railroad shops. In the lumber industries of the Great Lakes and coast areas, an interchange of IWW and OBU cards was arranged, and these lumber workers eventually joined the IWW in 1924 after the OBU had further declined with pro-communists shifting it from an industrial to a geographical or mass basis. The Canadian OBU persisted for years in Winnipeg, and even had branches in the United States trying in San Francisco to build an industrial union in the building trades and also in eastern textiles; its paper the *OBU Bulletin* for years was a sort of *Reader's Digest* of the left-wing and liberal press sustained by a betting pool rather popular because of its honest conduct, but eventually declared illegal.

In Latin America the Marine Transport Workers had established a branch in Buenos Aires with its own paper in November of 1919, and in December IWW administrations were started in Mexico and Chile. Through the summer of 1920 the Chilean union conducted a three-month strike to prevent the export of cereals from the country at a time when this export was producing famine, and famine prices and profits. The profiteers retaliated on July 4 with a raid at Santiago, starting a reign of terror against the IWW and other unions that lasted for years, the favorite punishment being to send the men to stony islands off the coast where not a blade of grass grew, and tell them to build their Utopia there. On June 2, 1921, the IWW hall at Tampico, Mexico, was raided, and the IWW called a general strike in the area which won them the right to have their hall.[9]

In Great Britain wartime attacks on union standards had resulted in a militant Shop Steward movement; in January 1920 this body resolved to link itself to the IWW, and at the 12th IWW Convention, May 1920, arrangements were made for the interchange of cards. But the major international question was Moscow. The IWW had been invited to join the Third International and to send a delegation to its Second Congress in the Kremlin, July 19 to August 7, 1920. The IWW did not attend, but its General Executive Board, very friendly to the general idea, had set up a committee to arrange for contact with the various revolutionary movements around the world. The Second Congress adopted the 21 points as conditions of affiliation, and set up a provisional body to found an international of red trade unions, to convene January 1921. To this the IWW was again invited and sent delegates. A preliminary caucus of syndicalist bodies was held in Berlin in December 1920 and it aimed at a union international based on the class struggle and free from political party domination. When the Red Trade Union international met eventually in Moscow in 1921, both the IWW delegate and the delegate from the Canadian OBU reported that it was a body to manipulate unions at Kremlin dictates and not a union body at all. By referendum the IWW turned down all of the various proposals, though with a remarkably small vote that gave only slight negative majorities. The three questions were a bit confusing and the entire ballot later declared void. It appears to indicate a refusal to be dominated by Communists and at the same time a reluctance not to participate in a gesture of left-wing unity.

IWW relations with the communists slowly but steadily shifted from an original comradely disagreement to open hostility. When the American Communist and Communist Labor parties were born out of the splintering of the Socialist Party Convention in Chicago in 1919, the IWW, though friendly to the Socialists too, allowed them temporary use of one of their local halls. In the eyes of reaction, IWW and anarchist and communist were all alike, and in the mass arrests especially around New Years 1920 in the deportation delirium, hundreds of IWWs were included in the roundups in Chicago, Detroit, Cleveland and elsewhere.[10] The Wobs ridiculed the early spouting about "mass action" especially in the sense of armed insurrection, pointing out that if military superiority was to be achieved, those looking for dimes to keep their organizations alive might take a peek at the combined federal, state, municipal and private corporation arms budgets before adopting that policy in place of the sure bet of workers' industrial solidarity. Lenin's doctrine of scrapping the left wing unions to facilitate capture of the trade unions was not acceptable to the IWW, nor the Communist demand that it appoint the editors for IWW publications. Their maneuvers inside the IWW eventually ended Wobbly tolerance for them. Philadelphia became the end of any brotherly love.

There the Marine Transport Workers struck on May 26 for a 20 cents an hour increase. They had good support from other unions, Marine Firemen refusing to provide steam for scabs, but the strike continued through all of June 1920 to July 10. The stevedores wanted to settle on foreign trade only; the shipping board wanted the men to go back on the promise of whatever terms the ILA negotiated in New York, but the IWW insisted on settling for all, and on July 10 marched back to all docks, including some that had previously escaped organization, with all workers wearing the button to assure complete job control. It was a union the communists could not maneuver, but early in August they spread talk that the IWW in Philadelphia was loading arms for Wrangel to use against the Soviet government. In August the General Executive Board ordered the Philadelphia local suspended. The local insisted no arms were loaded for Wrangel and asked for some proof, some record of the shipment, but none was forthcoming, though the rumor persisted. This charge dismissed, the local was kept suspended on the grounds that it charged a $25.00 assessment actually as initiation fee in disguise. (The constitution of the time required universal rates for all industrial unions, with initiation fee of $1.00, but this active local needed a strike treasury.) It was not until a

IWWs reporting for Leavenworth prison when their appeal was denied.

new General Executive Board was elected, less sensitive to communist approval, that the Philadelphia local was reinstated. Actually on all coasts the IWW was stopping shipments to the interventionists, even where it did not have job control.[11]

Other events moved the IWW in the same direction. The repression of the Kronstadt revolt in Russia, the role of the communists during the seizure of industries by Italian workers in September 1920, and their division of the Italian labor movement the following winter and spring into two sections fighting on the streets against each other – all such events made the IWW realize that no matter how "left" the Communists might be, they were still politicians, primarily concerned with getting and holding the power to rule.[12] In April 1921 those out on bail on the espionage indictments had to start serving their sentences. The Court of Appeals had thrown out the first and second counts of the indictment (interfering with the execution of the Espionage Act and Selective Service Acts, and injuring those employers who were supplying the government), but sustaining the charges of conspiring to deter men from registering and to bring about insubordination in the army. This did not reduce sentences. Of the 46 out on bond, Haywood and eight others did not show up; they had been spirited away to Russia. The communists said they would make good the bond losses, but never did, though publicly announcing that Haywood went to Russia on orders of the Communist Party.[13] It soon became plain that the communists in the IWW were operating under instructions to wreck it.

The discussion did help clarify IWW thinking. It became recognized that putsches and insurrections cannot achieve industrial democracy in a complexly industrialized country. IWW periodicals began to put their emphasis on technical articles and descriptions of industrial processes and avoidable wastes. The chief damage done by the Communists to the IWW was the cultivation of the notion of a militant minority, priding itself on its revolutionary consciousness and holding in contempt the mere "union consciousness" of the majority of members. This was to show itself in the lumber strike of September 1923 and later, and do irreparable harm.

Notes:

1. For events of time, see Borkenau, *World Communism.*

2. Seattle General Strike: see Crook, *The General Strike,* for accounts of this and other major general strikes, and W. I. Fisher in *New Solidarity* No. 16. Perlman & Taft v. IV, p. 440 et seq. *Nation* 108-487.

3. Butte strike: see *New Solidarity,* issues 15 and 16, and for a record of the scheming on the employer side, a stenographic record published in *Industrial Pioneer,* August 1926. Another bitter strike was fought by the IWW in Butte in April 1920, turned into a job action strike by the massacre of pickets on Anaconda Road April 21. (See *OBU Monthly,* June 1920.)

4. Oatman strike: *New Solidarity,* No. 45.

5. Toledo strike: *New Solidarity,* No. 29.

6. Spring AWO Convention: *New Solidarity,* No. 5.

7. Most complete account is Chaplin's *Centralia Conspiracy.* See also Jensen, *Labor and Lumber* for affidavits of jurors given in mid-thirties.

8. For circumstances giving rise to OBU, see Logan, *History of Trade Union Organization in Canada,* University of Chicago Press.

9. *Solidarity,* No. 137.

10. Fully described by Louis F. Post (Assistant Secretary of Labor) in *The Deportation Delirium of 1920,* Kerr & Co.

11. Facts on Philadelphia most clearly given in pamphlet issued by MTW No. 8. It was not reinstated until October 1921.

12. Communist maneuvering most thoroughly documented in Borkenau's *World Communism.*

13. Chaplin's *Wobbly* gives details of efforts to induce communists to pay for the loss on bond-jumping.

General Sources:

Harvey O'Connor's *Revolution in Seattle* (Monthly Review Press, 1964) gives details of the Seattle strike. The *Butte Daily Bulletin* of the time is a repository of both local history and all news that cheered labor leftists, giving much space to left organizations for veterans. For anti-labor purposes in launching American Legion see series in *Nation* July 7-28, 1921, and William Gellerman's *American Legion as Educator,* 1937. The Toledo Ford strike is detailed in Wortman, pp. 101-109; for Sioux City see Taft, "Mayor Short and the AWO," *Labor History,* Spring 1966.

Tom Copeland's *The Centralia Tragedy of 1919: Elmer Smith and the Wobblies* (Univ. of Washington Press, 1993) is the best account. See also John McClelland, *Wobbly War: The Centralia Story* (Washington State Historical Society, 1987); Kornbluh reprints Anna Louise Strong's biographies of the four defendants, pp. 271-74; Ralph Chaplin's *The Centralia Conspiracy* (IWW, 1920, reprinted 1973) conveys the full horror on the attack on the IWW hall, the lynching of Wesley Everest, and the subsequent frame-up trial; Ray Gunn wrote on defendant Ray Becker in the April 1968 *Pacific Northwest Quarterly;* the March 17, 1950, *Industrial Worker* has Becker's obituary; Esther Barnett Goffinet's "My Father Eugene Barnett Deserves A Long Overdue Pardon" (*Labor's Heritage* 10[4], 1999-2000, pp. 34-40) has excerpts from letters during his 11 years in prison; Wm. Friedland and Archie Green publish annotated excerpts from FW Barnett's memoirs in *Columbia* 11 (1997, pp. 10-17).

The best sources on Winnipeg are Norman Penner's (ed.) *Winnipeg 1919: The Strikers' Own History of the Winnipeg General Strike* (James Lewis & Samuel, 1973) and David Jay Bercuson's *Confrontation at Winnipeg: Labour, Industrial Relations, and the General Strike* (McGill-Queen's University Press, 1974). In *Canadian Historical Review* (June 1970) Bercuson argues that the strike was prolonged out of bureaucratic fear of the radical implications of industrial union structure. For IWW activities in Canadian timber, see J. Peter Campbell, "The Cult of Spontaneity: Finnish-Canadian Bushworkers and the Industrial Workers of the World in Northern Ontario, 1919-1934," *Labour,* 1998, pp. 117-146.

For Latin America, Peter De Shazzo and Robert J. Halstead have written an unpublished paper tracing the IWW in Mexico from WFM support for strikers at Canea in 1906 to the 1917-1929 efforts in Tampico. The account of IWW organizing in Chile notes successes among marine transport and construction workers from 1918 to 1924, repeated repression, and a temporary revival in 1931, and also briefly mentions IWW efforts in Peru, Ecuador and Argentina. Much of this material is incorporated in Peter DeShazo, *Urban Workers and Labor Unions in Chile, 1902-1927* (Univ. of Wisconsin Press, 1983). The most comprehensive published account addressing the IWW in Mexico is Norman Caulfield's *Mexican Workers and the State: From the Porfiriato to NAFTA* (Texas Christian Univ. Press, 1998).

Peter Cole discusses the communist role in Philadelphia MTW controversy in his 1997 dissertation, "Shaping Up and Shipping Out," and in "Quakertown Blues: Philadelphia's Longshoremen and the Decline of the IWW," *Left History* 8(2), 2003, pp. 39-70. Cole's *The Colors of the Waterfront* is forthcoming from University of Illinois Press. His *Black Wobbly: The Life and Writings of Benjamin Harrison Fletcher* is forthcoming from Charles H. Kerr.

11. Peak, Split and Recovery (1922-1929)

In the early twenties, the Marine Transport Workers progressed steadily. It had a firm basis on the Philadelphia waterfront, reinstated in October 1921, and among seamen, engine crews and stewards departments on the Atlantic Coast and the Gulf, particularly among the Spanish-speaking personnel.[1] Its expansion into Latin America and its alliance in Britain and elsewhere added to its prestige and to the service it could render its members. The AFL crafts grew increasingly disserviceable. In New York the ILA in the fall of 1920 had struck to keep up with the high cost of living, and its officials, lauded by the press, had broken their own strike.[2] In 1921 the seamen fought cuts in base rate and overtime that took about half their pay, but the dictatorial action of the president of the Marine Engineers pulled out his craft and broke the strike.[3] After that strike an effort was made on West Coast to form a federation of the various crafts, but Furuseth, head of the Seamen's Union, fought it from fear that landside workers would have too much to say, and even accused the editor of his *Journal* of being pro-Wobbly for supporting such an idea. Furuseth developed an anti-IWW mania, charging in Congress that the shipowners were coddling the IWW to disrupt the AFL.[4] He induced the 1923 AFL Convention in Portland to authorize an investigation of the IWW on these charges. The IWW wired the convention it would help it investigate, but the challenge was not accepted.[5]

Back of all this was the actual growth of the MTW. The IWW actively participated in all maritime strikes as good union men and won increasing esteem from their fellow workers. Where it could not aim at job control, it recruited the staunchest unionists in all classifications, so that MTW membership became a mark of prestige. Its *Maritime Worker* published news of the industry and propaganda for its immediate needs.

In Portland, Ore., the ILA and MTW struck jointly on April 23, 1922, when employers announced that hiring would be through their new "Fink Hall," instead of by the union list system which had worked fairly. The Shipping Board induced the ILA to work its vessels, though this meant going through their own picket line. MTW held a meeting for all strikers and the decision was that all would go through unless ILA quit doing so. The ILA settled for the right to have their man stationed in the Fink Hall. The IWW began a program of job action that brought it considerable growth. In October there was talk of a joint MTW and ILA strike, voted down at ILA meeting by a narrow margin of 215 to 200. The employers association tried to bribe the ILA with an agreement providing that no IWW would be hired; the ILA did not sign it, and the strike was on. Some scabs were obtained, but the vessels they loaded made more trouble for their owners when Australian workers refused to unload them. The right to be a Wobbly was thus safeguarded in Portland.[6]

During that same month unsuccessful efforts were made to drive the MTW from Philadelphia and Hoboken. In the former the issues were a blacklist imposed by leading shipping companies and the 44-hour week. The MTW tied up the port from October 27 to November 19, winning its point and remaining solid on the Philadelphia waterfront until 1925. (Its disappearance then seems to have come from the dissatisfaction of its chief personnel over interference by the general organization, though there was little of this after its reinstatement in 1921, and disappointment with the 1924 split in the IWW; this situation, coupled with a threat that vessels would be unloaded at nearby ports where ILA was in control, induced the secretary, Baker, and others to take their following into the ILA.) In Hoboken, N.J., in October 1922, repeated attacks by thugs, who MTW said were hired by ILA, also failed to drive them out. In February 1923, the Mobile, Ala., police ordered IWW to take their sign down; the 14 members in the hall held a meeting, decided not to, and went to jail. Others opened up and soon joined them, until they won out. But this sort of fight was eclipsed by the May Day strike.

The General Executive Board had recommended that where members felt they could strike effectively on May 1, 1923, they should do so, primarily to demand the release of all class war prisoners, but also for appropriate economic demands. Many were still in jail on wartime indictments; the number convicted under Criminal Syndicalism laws particularly in California was growing; the Centralia victims were in jail, and a number, such as Mooney and McNamara out of labor trials not connected with IWW. Protest strikes occurred in northwest lumber, on many construction jobs and elsewhere, but nowhere with such effectiveness as in the maritime industry. San Pedro, port of Los Angeles, was tied up tight, as was Aberdeen and, on the east coast, New York, Baltimore, Philadelphia, Mobile and Galveston. In most of these

The piano was all that survived of the San Pedro IWW hall after the June 14, 1924, raid that hospitalized several children with severe burns.

ports it was a short protest strike but won pay boosts of 15 percent. In San Pedro it developed into a lengthy free speech fight on Liberty Hill. It broke out again July 12 when 27 members, many of them seamen, were convicted of Criminal Syndicalism after a long trial in which they defended themselves to enjoy the freedom of saying what they wanted to. This was a five-day protest strike in which all shipping in the port was tied up.

The free speech fight in San Pedro was the last such large scale effort by IWW. Various liberals joined the fight, and Upton Sinclair got arrested for reading the Declaration of Independence. Stockades were built and filled with speakers; it was hopeless to arrest the hundreds who joined in mass singing of IWW songs. Young fellows on roof tops made speeches while cops chased them as in movie comedies.[7] In June of the following year, the morale of the upper crust was shown by a raid on the San Pedro IWW hall during a social evening; men and women were beaten; young children were scalded in a coffee cauldron; the place was demolished, and five members were taken out into the desert and tarred and feathered.[8] Light on all this was given by Captain Plummer of the police in the following statement:

"Somebody has been making holy asses of us policemen. Last summer at the time of the harbor strike I went to see old man Hammond. He told me to take a bunch of my men, arm them with clubs, go up on Liberty Hill and break the heads of the Wobblies. I replied that if we did that, they would burn down his lumber piles. 'They will do

Philadelphia MTW hall, circa 1924.

it anyhow,' he answered. But they didn't. Not an overt act have they committed. The police who raided the IWW hall in San Pedro recently did commit an overt act however. In fact we policemen have been made the tools of the big business interests who want to run things. I'm ashamed of myself for consenting to do their dirty work. The big fellows in this town can do anything they like and get away with it, but the workers can't even think what they want to think without being thrown in jail."[9]

The Marine Transport Workers reached their peak of influence in 1923. In such a field, organization can grow to a sizeable minority on the conviction that there should be the better unionism that it offers; after a certain point, it must forge ahead to replace the unionism it has criticized, or its new adherents lose hope and drop out. The MTW could not cross the gap; it was left once more a small minority championing the cause of direct action and industrial solidarity, but completely unable by 1926 to give any support to the British General Strike, or to prevent the shipments of American coal that broke the miners' strike. (Coal from Europe was effectively stopped by unionists.) Its solid core continued and was able in 1934 to put up a good fight once more.

In railroad transportation the IWW has had similar ups and downs, recruiting significant minorities of "two card men" from time to time in the hopes of building the industrial solidarity that all railroad workers realize they have needed. One such wave was in the years following World War I. Their activity prompted Attorney General Daugherty during the 1922 railroad shopmen's strike[10] to charge that the IWW was preparing to take over transportation and the government. Secretary Carlson of the Railroad Workers' Industrial Union issued a statement that IWW members in all crafts were backing the shopmen, and that the IWW was quite willing to run railroads or any other industry, but didn't want to bother with the government because they could not see that it was in any way useful.[11] Up to the 1924 split there was considerable growth of this Industrial Union particularly among the shopmen in western divisions, though also among train crews.

Despite the persistent strike demand for release of class war prisoners, the IWW of this period aimed deliberately at practicality. A favorite cartoon of the time depicted the sundry radicalisms as pointing at the stars, while the IWW was pointing to the industries, shouting "Organize." A pamphlet of the Construction Workers Industrial Union 310 centered on "Immediate Demands and Ultimate Aims," its argument that only by the unionism that could win immediate demands could workers develop the capacity to achieve the ultimate aim of Industrial Democracy. The outstanding orator of the IWW, James P. Thompson, persistently argued against the theory that a working class beaten down enough would some day turn to revolt with these contentions: the worse off the workers were, the more docile, and the more likely to settle for a bowl of soup; the working class was changing from the lot of the man with the hoe, to the man with education, technical training, organization and self-respect; and a working class lacking the organized competence to maintain decent job conditions certainly lacked the power to take over industry or the competence to run it. The IWW press emphasized similar teachings; its magazines were given largely to articles on industrial techniques; it started an Industrial Encyclopedia of booklets each giving the history of a major industry, and emphasizing its capital integration and the need for modernized unionism in it.

The construction workers of this period were especially engaged in a campaign to improve job conditions, for safety and better living. The large construction projects of the time were built mostly by single men, housed in camp until they made their "stake," then back to a sojourn on the skidroad, and another job. The IWW had largely established free fee or hire on the job, and in many places the jobseeker could stay overnight and clean up before rustling the next camp. Perhaps more effective than the numerous strikes was the less publicized practice of systematizing the quitting. Three weeks was about average stay; if some quit from one to five days earlier than they had planned, and others a few days later, this meant a sizeable number would quit at the same time; without strike, their complaints about job conditions were effective, and usually a job delegate recruited new members out of these men practicing painless unionism. But to raise wages took the consent of absentee management and usually required a strike.

In April 1922 camps of Guthrie and Grant Smith, along the Great Northern, were struck for a pay boost, better conditions and uniform 8 hour day. The men returned May 28 with subcontractors still working their men 10 hours. Mess halls were induced to refuse meals at the hours this schedule required, and soon the general contractor posted notices of a nickel pay boost and 8-hour day for all subcontractors. Strike victories on the Cazadero power project in Oregon and on the Skaggit Tunnel job in Washington soon followed, winning a 50 cent minimum, free blankets and waterproof clothing.

In November two large projects were struck in California, the Hetch Hetchy which was to furnish water for San Francisco, and the Edison power and irrigation project at Big Creek, up in the mountains from Fresno. The Hetch Hetchy strike grew out of organization in some of the camps; the men walked out almost 100 percent, but scattered so that non-strikers were needed for picketing, and picketing was important because of the large number of operations under various subcontractors and various names, and it was the time of year when many of America's most ragged and rugged individualists were heading for "sunny Cal" with "wrinkles in their bellies and flat broke." Because of difficulties maintaining a picket line, the strike was called off December 2nd, with no direct gains; the union had to operate on the job with new faces after the strike, and even mail got opened in company offices.

On the Edison job a major grievance was the cold "nose-bag" at mid-shift in the tunnels when the men wanted a hot lunch. On November 13 a job delegate was fired, and the men in his camp walked out with him. Meeting other IWWs, some of them from Agricultural Workers 110, in Fresno, resulted in a call to strike all camps on the project. All the lower camps came out by the 18th and 3,500 strikers staged the largest meeting Fresno had seen in the Opera House. News got to the upper camps, snowbound, through the press, and the men had to improvise skis and snowshoes to get out. The demands were $6 per day in tunnels and $7 for shaft men; 50 cents increase for all other labor; 8 hours portal to portal; two men on all machines; hot meals and other improvements. The strike petered out like the one on Hetch Hetchy. Calling it actually deprived the former strike of the manpower necessary to make it effective. The late arrivals from the upper camps were indignant about how it had been called. It was called off Dec. 22, a total loss. Some of the 310 members claimed it would not have been called if it hadn't been for the irresponsibility of the 110 "strawcats" in the valley, that such strikes should be called only by a conference of delegates from the various camps.

Many of the strikers from both jobs, no longer likely to be hired on these major projects, went to work for the Warren Construction Co. on a job out of Fresno. On January 3, 1923, they struck for reinstatement of a discharged IWW cook, enforcement of sanitary laws, $4.00 for 8 hours and no discrimination. The company settled, posting a notice of agreement to these terms. A second strike followed January 21 on the complaint that company did not live up to its agreement, and additional demands were made, including the right to hold an Open Forum every Wednesday night in camp. There was some dissatisfaction by those who preferred fewer strikes to interfere with the process of making a stake, and this second strike was never definitely settled. The various protest strikes on construction jobs May 1, 1923, increased this apprehension of many construction hands. The problem was actually to enforce IWW teachings of rank-and-file control against the maneuvers of a professed militant minority.

The major demonstration of this injudiciousness of the "jawsmiths" occurred in the northwest woods. The Lumber Workers' Industrial Union had been strong enough to prevent any appreciable reduction of standards in the Harding "return to normalcy" depression, and the extensive construction work of the era made a firm market for lumber. The IWW had the field to itself: the AFL Timberworkers' last battle had been fought at Klamath Falls in 1922, and it surrendered its charter in March 1923.[12] These standards had been kept by innumerable small job actions. The employers now found a divisive force: the gyppo system, or piece work. They brought it in with a sugar coating, letting men earn three and four times as much as they would make at hourly rates, but wiser heads knew this was to get it going: the need to settle prices for each operation would bring individual bargaining, and eventually less pay for more work. It worked out that way in the later twenties after the union had lost its strength. Opinions among IWW members on how to cope with this differed. The general sentiment was that no Wobbly would work gyppo. Many, who took little part except to pay dues and strike with the rest, felt it foolish to pass up big money. A few who knew their economics suggested that given these circumstances of a money-hungry majority, and the current high rates offered for piecework, the judicious thing was for the union to allow it on the proviso that rates be set for each operation by collective bargaining and kept so high that unit costs would exceed those resulting from hourly rate. The outcome was that those who worked gyppo dropped out of the union.

Even more critical was the difference of opinion on the rather haphazard strike policy that had been developing in other industries. May 1, 1923, brought an orderly four-day protest strike; a longer strike might have broken ranks. There was talk of a September strike but delegates from the camps in conference warned against it, that it might play into the employers' hands. However the "militant minority" who seemed to have talked to each other more than to the men on the job, felt it must be called to demand release of class war prisoners and had a strike call distributed by airplane, the leaflets fluttering down into one surprised camp after another. The men came out solidly and later made an orderly return to work; but confidence in the union as their instrument was greatly weakened.

This strike was memorable for a sideline activity: the "dehorn squad." This was the prohibition era; but there were bootleggers, and in the Seattle area in particular the "smilo joints." Knowing that alcohol and strikes don't mix well, that "you can't fight booze and the boss at the same time," the dehorn squads told the smilo joints to close up for the duration of the strike. Those that didn't were closed by Carrie Nation direct action or the threat of it. The daily papers felt they must approve the resultant sobriety of the strike, and could hardly object to union enforcement of the prohibition law, but felt obliged to denounce such lawlessness just the same, and many of the dehorn squads were thrown in the clink by police who had been tolerating and perhaps profiting from the smilo joints. The IWW was concerned only that booze should not disrupt the strike; it did not champion prohibition, but ridiculed intemperance and did induce most of its members, recruited from a hard-drinking lot, to maintain customary sobriety.[13]

Metal Mine Workers won a strike in Bingham Canyon in September 1922 and at the same time in Butte, getting a 50 cents increase. This was the last IWW strike there, though a skeleton membership was maintained in Butte into the fifties, and considerable organizing effort was made in Butte during the twenties. Company intimidation and the rustling card system make a partial explanation; but since these cards could be obtained easily enough for soapboxers to ridicule the system by tossing them out to the crowd beneath the nose of company gunmen who were the most assured audience, it seems that failure to maintain a union came chiefly because somehow those who favored it figured it hopeless.

An effort was made to organize the oil fields of the southwest early in 1922. Organizers Erwin and Hickey were given 90-day vagrancy sentences. Attorney Mulkes went to Shreveport to defend them, was kidnapped from his hotel and so badly beaten he had to go to hospital. The American Civil Liberties Union, finding it could not secure an attorney, asked the American Bar Association to provide one, but none accepted the challenge. The Oil Workers Industrial Union sent in more delegates. A number were arrested at Eldorado, Arkansas, and Attorney Julian went to their defense. He was jailed with his clients. In court he won freedom for them and himself. Outside the courthouse they were met by a Ku Klux Klan mob; Julian drew his revolver and he and his clients left unmolested.[14]

Metal and Machinery Workers Industrial Union 440, without strikes or attempting to bargain, kept up a steady growth in the early twenties in Chicago, Detroit and other eastern areas, working chiefly on a propaganda and social activity basis. In the harvest fields I.U. 110 kept selling "red ducats": 15,217 in 1923, 9,219 in 1924, and 8,507 in 1925, though the average annual membership for these same years was 6,483, 4,503, and 4,175.

Apart from MTW activities in eastern ports, IWW efforts were largely concentrated in the areas of greatest repression, particularly California where Criminal Syndicalism prosecutions came in a steady flow. To speed up the effort to jail the whole IWW, Judge Busick issued an injunction again all members so that they could be prosecuted without offering evidence to show that the IWW was in any way unlawful. To prosecute under Criminal Syndicalism statute it was necessary to show membership – regularly stipulated by the defendants – and to make some showing that the IWW practiced or preached sabotage, overthrow of government or other unlawful divertisements.

This requirement was filled by two professional witnesses whose credibility could not have been high with any jury; their evidence was a formality to warrant convictions obtained by appeal to prejudice. Judge Busick became notorious also for his practice of arresting the defense witnesses who established their membership in order to qualify their competence to testify. The continued prosecutions, frequently appealed, resulted in stricter requirements for the prosecution and in a growing community perception that the IWW was a commendable rather than a vicious organization.

By 1924, in California alone 317 members had been indicted under Criminal Syndicalism and 140 convicted. Sentences were 114 years, with prison board handing out a customary four-year sentence, which with good time off made three calendar years. Over a hundred of the 140 were in San Quentin at one time and they continued their habit of collective action. If one was thrown in the dungeon for some breach of discipline, all struck and were thrown there too. Since the San Quentin bunch consisted largely of the job conditioning members, they soon set up machinery for reaching such decisions by majority vote instead of being precipitated into them by a minority. Many used their time for education, reviewing and going beyond their school work and taking correspondence courses, several for the mathematics of navigation; they also all bought books on social and labor issues and had a library of their own of close to a thousand volumes, which they kept circulating even though this, like decisions on organization issues, had to be done under guards' eyes during lineups for meals, etc.

Even though the big split of 1924 occurred during this time, and some prisoners were on one side or the other, goodwill and friendliness resulted from these organized procedures, and as they came out they sought to heal the breach. (In contrast, the men in Leavenworth were largely top officers, speakers, and writers whom the job delegates often considered somewhat like prima donnas; the enmities that developed among them are generally considered the major source of the disastrous split of 1924.) The fact that the IWW grew from the war years to the 1924 split, and that this disaster occurred when these leaders were released, does not fit in with the conclusion of Perlman and Taft and other historians that the decline of the IWW was due to the loss of its leadership by imprisonment. The collective action of the IWWs in San Quentin, by attracting attention to routine bad conditions, resulted in a great improvement in the diet.[15]

The IWW split wide open in 1924. On the surface the issue was over the degree of centralization, but its causes lay deeper; personal rancors developed in Leavenworth, especially over the issue of accepting conditional pardons, found vent in it; dissatisfaction with the haphazard strike policy and the associated fear of lumber and construction workers that the "strawcats" were trying to lead them around by the nose also underlay it. The immediate circumstance leading to it was the reorganization of the general administration in 1923, so that it consisted of general secretary, general organizer and the chairman of the general organization committee of each industrial union. A rule that GEB sessions could be called by a two-thirds vote led to a situation where some said a two-thirds vote had called one and others said no and both had arguable cases. Two IWWs as a result competed for survival, one getting its name Four Trey because it moved from 1001 Madison Street to 3333 W. Belmont, Chicago (this being the body that exists to the present day), and the other body because of its "Emergency Program," dubbed the EPs. The EP was the smaller, but most members dropped out the middle.[16] Whatever its explanation, most IWW old-timers consider this 1924 split definitely the worst thing that ever happened to it. Considering how the IWW had gone ahead to this event in years when the AFL was declining, it seems possible that if the split had been avoided, and even more had the underlying factors been avoided, the IWW might have retained stability in the lumber industry and achieved it at least in general construction, metal mining and marine transport. As it was the woods went unorganized and gyppo; the only construction strike in the '20s after the split was one at Natron cutoff. It showed its vitality only in new fields, particularly coal mining.

The first large IWW coal strike was in Alberta, Canada, where the miners, fighting UMWA check-off since it did not actually represent them, had gone into the Canadian One Big Union. In 1924 the lumber workers and coal miners of the OBU switched affiliation to the IWW. They struck in November 1925 for abolition of this taxation without representation; companies offered a 10 percent increase if they would continue to accept the check-off; this was refused as a bribe.

In Colorado the coal miners were unorganized. A. S. Embree, who had formerly been an active organizer among metal miners, settled in southern Colorado after his release from a criminal syndicalism sentence in Idaho, and slowly built the skeleton of a coal miners' union

The Trinidad, Colorado, IWW hall, after the milia torched it.

among the veterans of the fight of 1914 and their sons. Progress was inconspicuous up to the Sacco-Vanzetti protest demonstrations of August 1927. The IWW had joined in the worldwide protest, and pulled one-day protest strikes where it could, but the outstanding response was among the miners of southern Colorado. Of the 12,000 miners in Colorado, of whom about half were employed by Colorado Fuel & Iron, the 6,000 in the south struck almost to a man on August 21, and stayed out three days to assure no discrimination. Organization grew faster, and on September 8 a conference was held at Aguilar to formulate economic demands. Colorado law required 30-day notice before a strike and this notice was given at that time. The State Industrial Commission said the notice must be given by the miners, not by the IWW. The IWW suggested that the Commission check on whether it represented the men by holding meetings at each mine and taking a vote. The commission declined the proposal, and though the strike was postponed to October 18 in efforts to meet the requirements of legality, the Commission held the strike outlaw, and the strikers fair prey for the mounted police who could harass any gathering of them as unlawful. Demands were a daily wage of $7.50, check-weighmen, payment for "dead work" and recognition of pit committees and the miners' organization. Technically this was not the IWW, but the organization of all miners who would agree to stand by these demands whether IWW or not.

There are three coal fields in Colorado; this was the first time all three had been struck together. To assure completeness a caravan of singing miners left Lafayette in the north and trekked to Walsenburg by November 4th, leaving the habit of singing "Solidarity Forever" behind them. The open enemy was the state police. Strike meetings were harassed by them and by low-flying planes zooming close to the heads of the miners and their families who also attended. This hazard was least if the meeting were held near a mine tipple, and various mine owners were not as ferocious as their uniformed watchdogs. One such customary spot for meetings was the Columbine Mine of the Rocky Mountain Fuel Co. There on November 21 the state police turned machine guns on the miners, killing six and wounding many. On January 12 the hall at Walsenburg was raided and Chavez and Martinez killed. But these were only the murders in a campaign of terrorism.

Companies eventually offered a dollar a day increase in the south and 50 cents in the north, bringing the scale to the second highest, and on February 19 the miners voted to return to work. Following the strike came elections of pit committees and check-weighmen and procedure for grievances. White cards of the striking miners had been issued during the dispute with IWW cards only to a minority. It was a significant victory and all considered it an IWW strike, for UMWA did not participate, but little unionism came out of it, though efforts continued into the early thirties and a number of locals were maintained which assured election of check-weighmen and pit committees. This situation seems to have grown out of the strike arrangements with little actual union recruiting. It was later found that some officers of the union were planning during the strike to form a new miners body out of the Colorado miners, the Kansas followers of Howatt and dissatisfied miners elsewhere such as those who followed the communist line in Pennsylvania and those who were to step over the traces in Illinois a few years later. Suits against Governor Adams and Louis Scherf, head of the police and who personally gave the order to shoot at Columbine, were lodged and dragged along to 1932 to claim damages for the widow of George Eastenes and other victims; but the court turned thumbs down.

A major organizing drive followed in 1929 in the Illinois coal fields where miners were under UMWA check-off, but chafing under it and divided as Fishwick men, Lewis men and what not. The communists, who had switched from their no left wing union program, attempted to horn in also. The IWW secured a considerable two-card membership around Benld and Collinsville. When the communist National Miners union announced a statewide strike for Dec. 9, 1929, it had no following among the Illinois miners, but precipitated a strike at Taylorville by putting out a picket line which brought in the militia. The miners there struck only to demand removal of the troops. The National Miners then picked out a mine where the IWW had about a third of the miners as two-card men, and picketed there, saying it was part of a statewide strike. The miners struck for the day to ascertain what the facts were, and voted with only one dissenting vote to return to work the next day. This led to communist accusations of scabbing by the IWW. Batteries of speakers were brought by IWW into the Illinois coal fields and a sizeable membership built up. In the many cornered fight in 1932 the IWW withdrew its organizers to avoid a situation where, no matter what they did, they would be cats-paws for one or another of the warring factions. They left the miners with ideals how a union should be run and advised them to try to make whatever union they found themselves in live as close as possible to those ideals.

Temporary success came among the gypsum miners employed by U. S. Gypsum Company in the vicinity of Oakfield, N.Y. They struck in February against a cut from 51 to 45 cents a ton and settled on April 26 for an increase to 75 cents a ton. A local of I.U. 210 was established, but despite the victory and repeated efforts to maintain organization, the local died. The crutch of a contract might have made for stability, but the IWW expected grown-up men, as their columnist T-Bone Slim said, to be big enough to pay their own dues without a check-off. The repeated allegation that the IWW did not try to maintain organization after a strike is certainly not true of any of its strikes during the twenties, if it is true of its strikes at any time.

Notes:
1. For this reason, activities are more fully chronicled in *Solidaridad* and *Cultura Obrera* than in English-language publications.
2. Perlman & Taft, Vol. IV, p. 452.
3. Ibid. p. 495.
4. Gambs, op. cit., p. 138; *Congressional Record,* Vol. 62, pp. 2124 and 4500,

and West in *Survey,* Oct. 14, 1923.

5. Wire given in *Solidarity,* Nov. 8, 1923.

6. *Solidarity,* Nos. 218-219, and pamphlet containing affidavits issued by Portland Branch MTW.

7. From accounts of the time, *Solidarity,* No. 238 et seq. Descriptions are given by Upton Sinclair in his novel *Oil,* and his play "Singing Jailbirds."

8. *Industrial Worker,* June 25, 1924; detailed account and photos in pamphlet "The Blood Stained Trail," issued by *Industrial Worker* but not officially approved by IWW because of various inaccuracies; it does however contain much valuable material supplementary to this history.

9. Quoted in letter from Clinton J. Taft of ACLU who heard the statement; in Gambs, op. cit., pp. 49-50.

10. See *New York Times,* Aug. 16, 22 and 23, 1922.

11. Given in *Solidarity,* 1930; for strike situation see Perlman & Taft, 519.

12. Jensen, *Labor and Lumber.*

13. This "dehorn" activity written in various papers at time; *Seattle Star,* Sept. 7, 1923, *Union Record,* Sept. 6, and denounced by H.L. Mencken at time as puritanism.

14. *Solidarity,* Nos. 168-177

15. Most complete account of Criminal Syndicalism is in Dowell's scholarly *History of Criminal Syndicalism Legislation,* Johns Hopkins University, 1939. Much of the Wobbly library in San Quentin was sent to Work Peoples College, Duluth, and used there as it was a residential labor school controlled by IWW, chiefly supported by its Finnish members; some was still in use in 1955, dog-eared, in San Quentin.

16. The EP started the *Industrial Unionist* in Portland in April 1925, ceasing publication June 1926; later issuing the *New Unionist* in Los Angeles, which appeared off and on to 1931 as the last gesture of a union that had died.

Other sources for items not given: IWW press of the time and personal knowledge of events; Colorado strike described in "25 Years of Industrial Unionism" and fairly adequately in Gambs.

General Sources:

For maritime, see Giles Brown, "West Coast Phase of the Maritime Strike of 1921," *Pacific Historical Review,* 1950, pp. 385-396, for free speech angle of the San Pedro 1923 strike see his "Politics of Confrontation," *PHR* November 1969. On this strike, Louise and Richard Perry give 25 pages in their *History of the Los Angeles Labor Movement* (Univ. of California Press, 1963), treating the strike as a disturbance of the labor movement. Dublin Dan's verses, "The Portland Revolution," in various editions of IWW songbook, depicts IWW enthusiasm of the 1922 events. Jon Bekken, "Marine Transport Workers IU 510 (IWW): Direct Action Unionism," *Libertarian Labor Review* 18 (Summer 1995, pp. 12-25) offers the broadest overview of IWW organizing in maritime. Peter Cole's dissertation (forthcoming as a book from University of Illinois press) on the Philadelphia MTW is the definitive study of the IWW's longest-lived example of job control; his "Quakertown Blues: Philadelphia's Longshoremen and the Decline of the IWW" (*Left History* 8(2), 2003, pp. 39-70) focuses on the intersection of race and class.

Don Lescohier, "IWW in Wheat Harvest" (*Harpers*, August 1923) reports on a 1922 trip by this economist and his staff living the life of the harvester; Greg Hall's *Harvest Wobblies* and Nigel Sellars' *Oil, Wheat and Wobblies* discuss the decline of the Agricultural Workers Industrial Union in the 1920s. On IWW job conditioning efforts in timber, see E.B. Mittleman's articles in *Quarterly Journal of Economics*, June and December 1923.

The trial involving attorney Harold Mulkes is reported in the Jan. 15, 1922, *New York Times*; on criminal syndicalism cases in California, see Woodrow Whitten, *American Philosophical Transactions* (1969, pp. 1071); Fred Thompson discusses his experience in *Fellow Worker* (Charles H. Kerr, 1993, pp. 55-59); Kansas' criminal syndicalism was overturned by the U.S. Supreme Court as unconstitutional in 1927 in Fiske v. Kansas (247 U.S. 380), the first known case in U.S. history where a criminal conviction was overturned by the court on free speech grounds. Harold Fiske had been arrested in July 1923 and charged with signing up three workers into the IWW.

On the 1924 Emergency Program split, Jon Bekken's "A Note from Labor History: The IWW's Emergency Program Split" (*Anarcho-Syndicalist Review* 27 [1999, pp. 23-24]) and Gambs' book are the only readily available sources. Fred Thompson's *Fellow Worker* discusses the split, pp. 59-62; as do Thomas McEnroe, "IWW Theories, Organization Problems and Appeals as Revealed in Industrial Worker (Ph.D. Dissertation, Univ. of Minnesota, 1960); Leland W. Robinson, "Social Movement Organizations in Decline: A Case Study of the IWW (Ph.D. Dissertation, Northwestern Univ., 1974); a contemporary rank-and-file voice was class war prisoner Jon MacRae's song "To Fan the Flames of Court Respect: James Rowan Forever," excerpted in Kornbluh, p. 350. The *Industrial Unionist* was reissued in a facsimile edition in 1968, and is available in several libraries.

The Colorado strike is the subject of Lowell May and Richard Myers (eds.), *Slaughter in Serene: The Columbine Coal Strike Reader* (Bread and Roses, 2005); Charles Bayard, "The 1927-1928 Colorado Coal Strike," *Pacific Historical Review* (1963, pp. 235-250); Donald McClurg, "The Colorado Coal Strike of 1927 – Tactical Leadership of the IWW," *Labor History*, Winter 1963, pp. 68-92; Ronald McMahan, "'Rang-U-Tang': The IWW and the 1927 Colorado Coal Strike," in Conlin, *At the Point of Production*. An opera dealing with the fatal shooting of six strikers on Nov. 21, 1927, "Columbine" (music by Mary Davis, libretto by Joanna Sampson) was produced at Boulder, Colorado Civic Opera, April 1973.

12. The Stimulus of Depression (1930-1940)

The stock market crashed in October 1929, as accurately predicted by the *Industrial Worker.* Constriction of business activity, layoffs, wage cuts and the Big Depression followed, just as the IWW right along had been saying was the certain consequence of the increasing exploitation of labor. The IWW had no doubt what labor should do: resist all wage cuts to make them expensive; organize the jobless so that they would no longer menace those who still had jobs, while these fought to cut the workday and raise real hourly rates; back all demands with the determination that if employers did not employ, the working class could dispense with their disservices and establish planned abundance.

The IWW made a tremendous propaganda effort. Its effects cannot be measured, but the outstanding fact of the thirties remains this: For the first time a labor movement, instead of shrinking in a depression, grew as never before. This turn from abjectness preceded Roosevelt and the Blue Eagle. AFL propaganda of the early thirties was craft union echoing of the assurance that business was sound. The various radical propagandas focused on political issues. The healthy change in labor attitudes can thus largely be attributed to the millions of pieces of IWW literature, straight to the point, issued at factories or where the unemployed gathered, and to the IWW soapboxers who held meetings daily at factory gates and at street corners in the evening, establishing regular schedules in even out-of-the-way places that they had to reach by boxcars or hitchhiking.

This propaganda effort was constructive, educational, and put on by flat-broke members of a flat-broke union. The IWW had never recovered from the 1924 split. It lost its building and printing plant into which it had sunk all its resources. To economize, in 1929 it replaced its various Industrial Union offices with a Clearing House run by its general secretary. Even so, the general secretary taking office in November 1932 found $29.00 cash all told with which to pay back wages, run the office, and pay accumulated printing bills and the industrial union funds that had been loaned to the General Office. Within a year it was all in the black again, but with less than a thousand dollars to run on. The campaign among miners in Illinois had, like that in Colorado, meant expenses instead of income, and in May 1930 it was thrust willy nilly into the Harlan, Kentucky, fight.

Harlan had been UMWA territory to 1924; after that a faithful few held the charter. Some IWW literature falling by chance among these miners as they faced 10 percent cuts led them to write the IWW for information, and to organize themselves into I.U. 220. Their local charter was in the mail when headlines told of the battle of Harlan and of the arrest of over a score of miners charged with murder. The IWW General Defense Committee undertook impartially the defense of members and non-members. Its field representatives were beaten up, and so were visiting journalists. Communists nosed in but got no following. Illinois miners and Colorado miners responded to appeals for help. The picture developed in the courts was very different from that originally given in the papers; many were acquitted, all saved from the death penalty, and the last were released in 1941.[1]

In February 1931 the IWW stirred up its own members and sympathizers to greater activity with a leaflet "Bread Lines or Picket Lines," very widely distributed. This urged that the unemployed organize either in IWW or out of it, so that they could assure those still working that they would not scab; and then, by demonstrations outside plants that cut pay or worked longer than normal days, promote action to abate the depression. In execution the program became much modified: the unemployed helped picket in strikes called independently of this program; it was approximated among jobseekers at out-of-town construction jobs, for example Cle Ellum, and the Portland Unemployed Union did assure success to a small loggers' strike. These Unemployed Unions were formed to provide housing and food for footloose jobless members while they carried on IWW agitation. The UU at 2005 W. Harrison, Chicago, held meetings outdoors nightly throughout the city, sold over a thousand IWW papers a week and many pamphlets, solicited their own food in the large markets, and defrayed rent etc. from proceeds of social affairs. A similar venture in New York made publicity even out of its move from E. 10th Street to larger quarters at 133 W. 14th, and accommodated personnel for an organization drive in eastern industrial centers that did much educational work though it secured few members. In Seattle the less spectacular 6 Hour Committee did its most effective work through influence in other unions to demand shorter workdays. The Portland UU beside housing soapboxers and leaflet peddlers, managed to provide the food for the unorganized lumber workers at Biex Logging when

Harlan County mine strike; Evarts, Kentucky, 1931.

they struck and won them a 25 percent pay boost. The chief result of this agitation everywhere was that the morale of the unemployed became such that workers dared to strike.

Construction Workers Industrial Union 310 was active through these "threadbare thirties." It set out to organize among the jobseekers at Boulder Dam in April 1931. Those who were union minded were welcome at the Wobbly jungles just outside the reservation while they waited to rustle jobs. On the reservation 11 were arrested for promoting the union on July 15. On August 7 a wage cut of a dollar a day was announced. IWW speakers rallied the men as they came off shift and got 1,400 to assemble at the cookhouse. On the 9th the Biex Six Companies tried to deport the strike committee in locked trucks, but the Federal Marshall set them free. Jobseekers and local merchants favored the strike, and even its 6 hour day demand. On the 12th Young of the Reclamation Bureau ordered all strikers off the reservation. The IWW called the strike off so they could remain, but insisted their demands still stood.

Boulder Dam was a speed-up job, rushed ahead of schedule, where state safety laws were daily violated and where men collapsed from gas. By October 1932, when I.U. 310 held its convention in Las Vegas,

127 workers on the job had been killed. By that time a prolonged free press fight had convinced the Bureau that it might as well abide by the Bill of Rights, after repeated arrests and deportations of men selling the *Industrial Worker.* The final effort of the IWW on the job was made August 16, 1933, in desperation as all suspected of IWW sympathy were being fired. Those not yet fired passed handbills in the mess hall; those already fired tried to rally the men to demand safety, 6 hour day and no discrimination, but the majority went to work and there was no strike. This is the only instance known of the IWW attempting a strike and none developing. It occurred on a government project among bulldozed workers fearful of the loss of a job, in the daze of the New Deal, and working for a dollar a day less than the low of the Hoover era.

Near Cle Ellum, Washington, 250 men were working for the Lahar Construction Co. on an irrigation dam for 30 cents an hour. As many again waited around town or in the jungles for a job – these were the days when any freight train might have 300 free riders. IWW members sounded out men on the job, in the jungles and the merchants in the towns nearby; there was agreement that if the men struck for a dime more an hour, the unemployed would not take their jobs, and the merchants would provide beans and bacon. The company saw the situation and granted the dime boost in a short strike May 11, 1932. The job was 100 percent organized. A second strike in October raised the rate to 45 cents with walk to work on the company time instead of on one's own.

Other major efforts by this I.U. 310 were made to organize the Mississippi Bridge job near New Orleans (summer of 1933); the Los Angeles Aqueduct, where organizers had to demand jury trials to stop arrests for vagrancy; the Fort Peck job in Montana, where it won a $15 boost for commissary workers; the New York Water Tunnel and among WPA workers. Only on the WPA jobs did it win managerial recognition, but on all these it recruited men and agitated for better conditions and achieved them.

The days of the old harvest drives were over, but Agricultural Workers I.U. 110 fought battles for families of "fruit glommers" in Yakima in 1933 and in Watsonville, Calif., in 1939. The Yakima skirmish started with a strike of 200 hop pickers in May. Some had been earning as little as 75 cents for 10 hours. Picket lines were crashed by ranchers' cars; one picket was run over and many arrested. On June 3 the strike ended with a 50 percent increase in piece rates. The IWW stayed active in Yakima, solidifying "homeguards" and migratories for action in successive crops. Strikes were on again in August; on the 25th over a hundred were put in a stockade. Mike Capelik, a disabled veteran who represented the General Defense Committee, visited the jail and was held for the convenience of a vigilante mob who drove him 40 miles away, beat him and covered him with glue. The trial of arrested pickets was postponed to December. The Yakima Central Labor Council elected its own labor jury to keep an eye on proceedings; all were released on the 17th of December. The IWW local organization in Yakima persisted for several years without further strikes, but holding socials and lectures through winter months.

The major IWW efforts of this period were made in New York, Philadelphia, Detroit and particularly Cleveland. In New York the Marine Transport Workers, at a time when seamen's unionism was at ebb tide, started off the decade with a spectacular meeting of the 1,700 crew members aboard the Leviathan, then the world's largest vessel, April 9, 1930. No major waterfront action occurred, despite steady organizing, until the strike of 1934, though there was a victorious fight for the right to speak at Coenties Slip and repeated squabbles with the Muscovite Marine Workers League. A branch of the MTW had been started at Stettin, Germany, in 1929, and it became part of the anti-Hitler underground, with the MTW getting its supplies of the thinnest paper, ink, etc. ashore to it; eventually contact was lost. A local of Building Workers I.U. 330 was started in New York in 1930; agitation among cafeteria workers was stepped up when an attractive hall noted for its class struggle murals was opened on Fifth Avenue; the good start in this field was undone by conniving between AFL and Communist racketeers.[2] A local of Municipal Transport Workers for bus and subway employees was also launched and later a campaign among apartment house janitors, called superintendents in New York's provincial dialect.

In Philadelphia, as the ILA agreement neared expiration in September 1930, Wobbly speakers addressed longshoremen from Richmond to Point Breeze on the grievances endured since they had left IWW in 1925, but the ILA won. During the Cuban general strike of 1933, IWW picketed to stop the unloading of scab-loaded sugar. That year a drive started among stonemasons, largely Italian, building suburban homes. Rates were far below AFL building trade scale, and competition so

New York Wobblies displaying signs for a shorter-hours rally.

keen among the petty employers that rates could be raised only a trifle at a time by repeated short strikes progressing into 1936, by which time I.U. 330 had organized the quarry workers too. In this campaign the IWW found it was impeded by its anti-Mussolini propaganda, featured especially in its *Il Proletario*; many of these workers believed Mussolini was trying to get them a syndicalist commonwealth, and pointed to his labor head, Edmondo Rossoni, a former MTW-IWW organizer who first turned to Italian nationalism from his American experience with the additional exploitation Italian workers here suffered under the padrone system.[3] Among other groups the IWW won a 25 percent boost at Denston Felt & Hair Co. with the provision that all should hire through IWW hall, but subsequent indifference developed. During 1933-34 at the RCA Camden plant, noonday speeches, leaflets, and house-to-house visiting rallied a sizeable membership, but not enough to win the plant.

Successes were scored on a smaller scale: Women who knitted at home for Mrs. Franklin's Shops, Inc., raised their rates by a third. In the swank suburbs there were pockets of African-Americans who did the laundry, mowed the lawns and tended the golf greens. These organized and glowed with pride when organizer James Price refused to meet the links committee in their clubhouse unless the strike committee came along too. To save hall rent, they held their IWW meetings in a church they had recently built and of whose congregation they were the majority. Their first meeting in the church was opened with a few words of prayer by a venerable deacon who thanked the Lord that though He had not blest these men and women with the good things of life, He had given them the good sense to organize and go after them. A drive among the private enterprise garbage crews was stopped by hoodlumism.

The Marine Transport Workers put up some hard fights and lost some good men. In the early thirties it held forth the demand of the 4 watch system, and the restoration of the old Shipping Board manning and wage scale; in the later thirties, as competitive unions split maritime labor asunder, its main concern was mutual respect for all picket lines and solidarity in all strikes. In the Gulf in the early thirties only Lykes Brothers paid the old scale of $62.50 for AB's (able-bodied seamen) but cut that to $50 for time in port. Other lines paid rates even slimmer, down to Luckenbach's low of $33 a month. As of early 1933, the ILA had longshoremen on Atlantic and Gulf coasts and the port of Tacoma; San Francisco longshoremen had been in an employer-dominated "blue card" association since 1921, but organized an ILA local that year; on the east coast the old Seamen's Union was as good as dead; Great Lakes and Inland waterways were unorganized; on West Coast the Sailors' Union of Pacific retained some life.[4]

On May 1, 1934, the ILA struck the Gulf ports. Originally to support them so that crews would not furnish steam or assist scabs, the MTW issued leaflets urging crews to back the longshoremen and suggesting they go after demands for themselves. The outcome was packed meetings in IWW halls to demand the old Shipping Board scale. Lykes promptly agreed to end its port pay cut. With the longshoremen back and victorious, the MTW called off its strike May 31 with the intent of calling quickies on the various lines paying less than Lykes. This was a hectic waterfront month: the big west coast strike had started May 9 with the Frisco longshoremen, followed by other unions and the development for a few years of Maritime Federation of the Pacific; the IWW hall in San Francisco was raided during the big strike, and later the City agreed to pay $100 damages. During this time in Baltimore the IWW tied up the West Eldarado, the first time in nine years that an American ship on foreign run had been held up.

Results for IWW on east and west coasts were quite different. On the Atlantic the surprise action of the MTW led the moss-grown ISU to secure contracts from 28 lines on the assurance that it would keep "irresponsible agitators" from shipping. The Communists, who had changed their Marine Workers League into a Maritime Workers Industrial Union, attempted a protest strike against these contracts; when it flopped, they switched back to boring from within. On the West Coast, at first the MTW found cooperation with the SUP fairly easy out of a joint fondness for "quickies" and an aversion to the political maneuvers of the clique around Bridges. This West Coast militancy and sense of solidarity irritated the resurrected ISU, and as it was nominally the parent organization for the SUP, it revoked this west coast charter at its February 1936 convention. It was perhaps even more irritated because West Coast rates were higher. On March 2, 1936, the ISU crew of the SS California struck in San Pedro to demand West Coast rates; Madame Perkins phoned that the issue would be settled when it got back east; on arrival in New York the crew was fired with the blessings of the ISU. Protest strikes under Curran that followed were the conception of the National Maritime Union. On Sept. 12, 1936, the IWW tied up the SS San Jose in Philadelphia as it was carrying explosives to Franco; the New York ISU sent a crew to board it unwittingly in midstream.

When the SUP contract expired Sept. 30, 1936, union-minded seamen on Atlantic and Gulf wanted to grab the opportunity to achieve equality with the west coast and whatever it gained anew, and thus strengthen it. Instead the ISU hired scabs in the Great Lakes area in an attempt to break the West Coast strike, as its own members refused to scab. The ISU was hampering solidarity action wherever it could. One of its fink-herders shot IWW member John Kane as Kane stopped him from taking off with the Marine Firemen's records in Houston. MTW and SUP pickets tied up all Pacific vessels as they reached eastern ports; in so doing another IWW seaman, Blackie Hyman, was shot in Philadelphia. MTW members fought through the east coast strike called off on tankers Dec. 31, and sought to keep cargo and passenger vessels still hot after that, but the fight deteriorated into political conniving in Washington, and the birth of NMU. This development in turn soon brought about a waterfront "cold war" in which Lundeberg of SUP and Curran of NMU each brought their membership to heel with the threat that the other union would steal their jobs: thus Curran got acceptance of unfavorable contracts, and Lundberg, as a trade for ILA support in jurisdictional squabbles, got members to OK return to the "union" in 1938 that had hired scabs to use against them in 1936 – it changed its name from Int'l Seamen's Union to Seafarers Int'l Union.

Next imposition on the corralled but disunited seamen was the Copeland Continuous Discharge or Fink Book. The MTW tried to rally the growing list of maritime unions to refuse to accept this. Two MTW members even obtained a court order requiring Philadelphia shipping master not to demand the fink book as a condition for shipment. (One of them Harry Owens, a soapboxer who helped in various campaigns when not at sea, soon after was killed in Spanish Civil War, where he again found politicians exploiting the needs of labor to put themselves in the saddle.) There followed the U.S. Maritime Commission "Fink Hall" to put an end to shipping through union halls; SUP and MTW pickets prevented its use while Curran and the communists tried to make a grab by telling NMU members to ship through it; NMU rank and file was so disgusted that the Muscovites had to pack NMU meetings with furriers to keep control. At the end of the decade the MTW was the same minority arguing for basic unionism as at the beginning, but stronger and sturdier, only now surrounded by workers under contract.

Metal and Machinery Workers Industrial Union 440 almost organized the auto industry of Detroit, flopped, then achieved for the IWW a hitherto unparalleled stability in Cleveland. In Detroit in 1932 the IWW had a small but solid basis of seasoned members with extensive contacts who had moved into a good hall at 3747 Woodward capable of accommodating a thousand, where socials, lectures, dances, plays, etc. kept up a good attendance. Through 1932 it engaged in extensive general propaganda, soapboxing, leaflet passing, recruiting additional members. In January 1933, the local labor temper changed: a series of strikes which the IWW did not call, but in which it participated, changed the local picture. First the 600 tool and die makers at Briggs Vernor plant struck on January 11; Motor Products on January 20; 6,000 production workers at Briggs Manufacturing on January 23, the next day the Vernor plant came out in support of these newcomers; Murray Body January 27. These were all strikes against wage cuts. On February 7 men at Hudson Body struck for a pay boost. At the largest of these, the Briggs strike, organizer Frank Cedervall made daily pep talks but without mentioning his IWW connections. Soon various groups sought to get control of the strike, and the IWW opened a branch office near the struck plants and started recruiting members from strikers and from the industry generally. Its prime argument was industrial solidarity, as opposed to William Green's "Tentative Plan" for federal unions which the various crafts would soon dismember.

Through the summer of 1933 the IWW in Detroit passed out an estimated two million pieces of paper specially mimeographed for the situations where they were distributed, beside large quantities of printed general appeals; this kept an organization crew busy at every change of shift; at lunch periods they staged meetings at the plants; in spare time they cranked the mimeograph or made house-to-house visits. In addition there were daily radio programs over WEXL which, though aimed at auto workers, brought the start of a railroad workers campaign.

The first IWW action of the season was among metal finishers at Briggs Highland Park plant. Wobblies were a minority among them, but they struck on second shift for a 10 percent pay boost, sitting down to get it. After shift they came to IWW hall and organized for action at 6 a.m., and won the 10 percent for several departments. With growth of a skeleton membership in every major plant, the IWW moved to a larger hall on Sproat Street, a lavish front for the growing union; in the kitchen back of it, the organizers survived on bread and beans and slept on benches. The drive centered on the Murray Body plant with the unfortunate result that the dribble of recruits swelled into significant numbers only on the eve of layoffs due to changeover in body designs. Men who joined the union and were laid off within a week felt it was discrimination, especially as departments were thinned out rather than closed down; since it was these men, and not the non-unionists, who came to the union hall, the same interpretation gained ground there. A meeting of men from all departments decided to send in a committee the next day to ask for rotation of work during changeover.

Management insisted there was no discrimination and that rotation was unworkable; the committee asked for acceptance in principle, each department to work it out so that the men available under the plan were those technically competent for the work on hand. Management felt it was going far in receiving a committee without knowing to what extent it represented the men, and would make no commitment beyond the declaration that it intended no discrimination. The committee went to their nearby branch hall and by a ballot, with only one negative vote, decided to pull the plant. It needed only a signal from the street for members inside to blow whistles, shut off power, and bring the whole force to a vacant lot for speeches. The strike started September 27 with enthusiasm, but since there was no urgent need for more men than supervision with a few favorites could provide, the strike was doomed to fritter away and was called off November 12. In retrospect it was later felt that had the committee used the sudden strike at 11 a.m. as a rally to show the men were behind the rotation plan, and sent them back at noon the union could have given some protection to the men, gained prestige in other plants, and even used the laid-off men as part-time organizers to develop the already started membership in most other plants in the city.

The loss of the Murray strike was the loss of the campaign in Detroit. Early in it, the big hall and the radio program were dropped. A block system to provide pickets and contact with those who didn't show up was an economy measure that foreshadowed the wartime "share-the-ride" system. Through the strike, but on a reduced scale, organizing efforts continued at other plants; and after it house-to-house visiting centered on the Murray recruits; yet all but a few of the newly won members dropped out and new recruits became rare. The IWW in Detroit was left with most of its members the unswerving Finns and Hungarians who had constituted its backbone in 1930. But the new members were activists who planted a seed in the American labor movement: the sit-down. Some of the Murray metal finishers moved to Hudson Body and there in Dept. 3760 they pulled such sit-downs as they had used at Briggs Highland Park, but this time with little cards that the IWW mimeographed reading "Sit Down and Watch Your Pay Go Up." The men did as the cards said and their pay did go up, in five successive increases during February and March 1934. (Frank Ellis, IWW, had sparked a stay-in at Hormel in November 1933; the first Akron sit-down was in June 1934; a sit-down wave came in 1937.) Job action with similar techniques (primarily designed to show the IWW was inside the plant rather than outside it) won improvements at Budd Wheel and cleaned up the spray booth even at the lost Murray Body plant.

These slight successes put the union in no shape to seize the opportunities presented by 1934, when throughout the auto industry there was hope for a general strike and growing suspicion of the AFL and its domineering policy of appointing disliked personnel and its threat of craft division. In the spring 230,000 workers were finding that "hope deferred maketh the heart sick," and accepted the General Motors representation plan. Self-critical Wobs contemplated what they might have been able to do had they not lost all their eggs in one Murray Body basket. In later years, with some revival of the IWW in the area, they consoled themselves that whatever commendable distinctions Detroit unionism showed could be attributed to the unflagging propaganda efforts of 1933-34.

Meanwhile preliminary spadework for an organization campaign had been done in Cleveland with much leaflet passing and noonday speaking by Jim Corrigan, an old anarchist who never let a dogma interfere with his sense of humor. (During the Sacco-Vanzetti protest of 1927 when a scheduled demonstration was forbidden, he had loaded all the banners and signs on a wagon, hitched up the most decrepit nag he could find, and meandered down Euclid Avenue, tying up traffic, explaining in extenso and loudly to all interfering policemen that since the demonstration was forbidden he had to take the signs away to hide them.) The *Bermunkas* office on Buckeye Road was near a number of small plants and for a while the IWW concentrated on these smaller units, keeping that office continuously open for those who called in response to meetings in front of shops or leaflets. The Cedervalls and other organizers gradually shifted from Detroit and a wide campaign was on again for I.U. 440. A total of twenty plants got organized in the process, most of them medium size, some of them lost soon after organizing, but out of this process continuous bargaining through the IWW continued at most of them from 1934 to 1950, when the union still lived on – and does to this day – but felt obliged under Taft-Hartley requirements and IWW refusal to sign affidavits to disaffiliate.

First in the series (omitting a victory at Ferro Foundry in 1933 that resulted in no permanent union) was the enameling division of Ohio Foundry in April 1934. Next was Accurate Parts with a two-hour strike on April 28. At Draper Steel Barrel, a few enthusiasts for the new union got alarmed at the formation of an inside union, struck and got a promise of no company promotion and recognition of the committee to process grievances of union members. Two small metal container plants, Perfection Metal Container and Permold, followed. On June 7, collision with the company union at Draper led to a strike that lasted to Sept. 10. During it, word came that orders were shifted to a plant at Niles near Youngstown; a caravan of strikers went there, found it organized in AFL and got the men to demand of management that no struck work be accepted. AFL officials in Cleveland were not so union minded and took the company union under their wing. The Regional Labor Board offered a no discrimination settlement; I.U. 440 proposed a return to work on promise that a Labor Board election would be held and the winner would get a 100 percent union shop; the IWW won by a narrow majority of 93-75. Unionism grew solid in the plant, even after it was taken over by Jones & Laughlin, and members there brought in additional plants later.

While the three-month strike was in process at Draper, noonday talks continued at two of the city's larger plants, American Stove, maker of Magic Chef ranges, and National Screw, a major auto industry supplier. On June 14 the committee was recognized to act for its members at American Stove. Organization grew at Cleveland Wire Spring. On October 1, a three-day strike won recognition at Republic Brass. (All of these victories were accompanied by wage increases, considered at the moment more important than recognition.) At Cleveland Wire Spring there was trouble with the company union and a strike was voted October 23 against the best judgment of the organizers. This became the first in a series of concurrent bitter fights that almost wrecked the new union; hired thugs attacked pickets and injunctions restrained the number of pickets; many were arrested for telling scabs what they thought of them; fights developed near the homes of scabs, and the strike dragged on through the winter. Before it was over the IWW was involved in two larger strikes, that of the charwomen at a group of the largest downtown buildings, including Terminal Tower, and at National Screw.

The charwomen's strike required a picket line long enough to circle the several blocks the buildings occupied, and members off shift helped fill it out. Their banners asked if $2.50 was too much to ask for scrubbing floors at night. Public sympathy was with them, and the antics of Captain Savage of the police force led all papers to deride his frequent arrest of the charwomen. The manager was a Regional Labor Board member, and one picket sign read: "Snead is on the NRA. He hauls scabs here every day."

Mysterious cars intimidated the women by following them home; the Cedervall brothers were waylaid New Years Eve as they left the hall where they stacked the picket signs, and badly beaten. The AFL attempted to make a settlement without asking strikers or union. About the same time papers carried a scare headline about dynamite being found in the ventilating system of the Terminal Tower, the first of a series eventually depicting the IWW as terrorists. The strike dragged on through the winter.

On February 8, 1935, the men at the most recently and only partially organized plant, National Screw, struck also, though the char-women's strike and that at Cleveland Wire Spring was more than the union could handle. It had been encouraging in January to add more small brass shops to the union list, Cochran and Holland Trolley, recognition at Dill Manufacturing, maker of most of the nation's tire valves, and recognition at National Screw with the promise of a 10 cent boost for its 1,350 employees. Later National Screw claimed it had made no such promise and the men struck. When they had been out a few days and collected their pay, it contained a five cent boost. It was suggested to the strike committee that they consider accepting this as a temporary settlement, go back with their more than doubled membership, and look for more later; but the committee felt it should hold out for the whole dime. Now that prohibition was over former bootleg gangsters were on hand to beat pickets and break picket lines; the strike grew weaker with increasing violence. Stench bombs were thrown in the IWW office; one that didn't break there was returned through the head gangster's window the same way, and the gangsters were out to get the IWW. The hall was now protected, and organizers at night moved with others a distance behind them; but papers began carrying stories of bomb outrages at loyal workers' homes. Mystified IWW officers checked and found repeatedly that those living at these addresses were not involved in any dispute. A member arrested for a picket line altercation got thrown in with a character who evidently believed the papers and started discussing rates for various window breakings and bombings, and indicating that plate glass suppliers, some building trades officials and those interested in what brand beer certain taverns served, all had a pool for such services.

Anyway, there was extensive vandalism and the IWW got the blame. Police raided the home of Mike Lindway, master mechanic at National Screw, and an enthusiastic unionist, without a search warrant or witnesses and claimed to discover an arsenal there. Lindway was convicted. To sustain the conviction the Ohio Supreme Court had to over-rule both the Appellate Court and its own previous decisions, to deny that federal search and seizure provisions applied to Ohio. Frank Cedervall was arrested on the charge of threatening the secretary of the company union. The prosecution had a large number of witnesses to the alleged threat. Attorney Wolfe moved that they be separated. Thus they could not hear the cross examination of their predecessors. One after the other repeated their story letter perfect in

IWW logger, picketing struck Idaho lumber camps, 1931.

a singsong but all disagreed on cross examination about the weather, whether they were standing and the defendant sitting, or vice versa and all other relevant circumstances. Soon the jury was smiling and tapping a rhythm to their sing song, and acquitted the organizer. Over 200 were arrested during the strike, with many jury trials, but the only convictions were Lindway and Bart Dudek, who had escorted his fiancé through the thugs with a revolver in his car.

But legal victories did not win strikes. All three had to be called off, the AFL accepting the Cleveland Wire Spring. The blow would have knocked out the IWW as the Murray strike did in Detroit, had it not been for solid organization in various other shops. Within a year it was as effective as before, winning new shops and new gains in old ones. But meanwhile the IWW spotlight shifted to the woods of Idaho and elsewhere.

The Lumber Workers had been hit hardest of all industrial unions by the 1924 split. It recovered slowly to a peak in 1936 and declined again. It helped in the unorganized Grays Harbor strike of 1932 and acquired a few members afterwards there, but when the AFL Timberworkers campaigned and struck in 1935, it could play only second fiddle in the long log region of its greatest historic triumphs. It staged a serious campaign in the short log country east of the hump. Organizers went through camp after camp in the white pine country, getting meetings going after supper before the office force could prevent it, talking union and distributing a straw ballot to determine what demands the men favored and whether they wanted IWW to represent them. During the traditional July 4 shutdown, meetings were held in all central towns, and by September 70 delegates or voluntary organizers on the job were recruiting a sizeable membership in Idaho. The 120 "covered wagon," actually a truck used by part of the organization crew, carried a mimeograph to issue bulletins, and headed through Oregon to Klamath Falls, then, after the AFL strike, up the coast to the Seattle District, where it found many wishing it had been the IWW in the woods instead of this non-benefit wing of the Carpenters.

In March 1936 near Pierce, Idaho, where the flume system is used to get the logs down, the movie "Come and Get It" was being shot, and the Wobs used the occasion to raise the pay a dollar a day. A strike at Elk River raised the rate for the drive to $5 and another in May wound it up with $6.00. On June 29, when logging was in full swing, a complete walkout cleared the Weyerhaeuser and other camps. Along the St. Manes small employers settled promptly, but the big fight continued. Early in August, plug-uglies opened fire as a truckload of 15 unarmed pickets went near Fromelt camp, wounding several so badly they were crippled for the rest of their lives, and three died within two years. (Later the 10 thugs were tried and fined at the rate of $500 each.) Martial law was declared August 3. The situation became quiet; the Guard at one side of the road near each camp, the seven permitted pickets at the other, listening to the sounds of saws and hammers improving camp facilities. The strike was called off without seeking recognition, but a 10 percent boost was obtained. In a few years it was

CIO territory, with an IWW organizing crew carrying on from camp to camp just the same as in 1932.

In Michigan the IWW had built almost complete organization in several camps. When the AFL struck the area, demanding union shop, the IWWs all struck too, with no effort to protect their hold on their own camps. NLRB action to do this was suggested, but they didn't want to mess around with politicians. There and in the west, despite hard organization and fighting and propaganda, even using Tacoma radio station KNO, the Lumber Workers ended the decade as they had entered it.

Two railroad campaigns occurred in the thirties. In Detroit those involved were train crews. They were content to build slowly while maintaining their old unions, but quit their active grievance work in the Brotherhoods. Thus when they were accused of the inevitable infraction of the multitude of rules, the grievance machinery was in the hands of those who would be glad to see them fired. They retained their jobs by legal pressure, but the campaign was strangled. During 1937 to 1939, a campaign among the hundred extra gangs surfacing approximately 2,000 miles of track on the Northern Pacific and Milwaukee roads was attempted. Conditions were improved, but wages would have taken system strikes, and adequate strength for this was never achieved at any one time.

Among WPA workers in the late thirties I.U. 310 built many branches. The strongest was in Oakland where the branch was recognized for processing all grievances in Contra Costa and Alameda Counties. In Missoula a 310 branch was built, and toward Christmas of 1937 the women on a WPA sewing project staged a sympathetic sit-down. Students leaving Work Peoples College in 1937 started several branches in Minnesota. In April 1938 the WPA workers around Watsonville, Calif., organized, won free transportation, which was the current irritant, and the branch soon had a fruit pickers strike to handle. The 150 Filipino workers involved first asked CIO then AFL to do it for them, but both wanted cash on the line, so the IWW arranged their picketing and relief, won their strike, but retained no members from it, though the Watsonville branch was active to late in the forties. In Detroit, in 1938, where the IWW was campaigning on Great Lakes and organizing restaurant workers, a WPA branch won recognition of a committee to represent all workers though elected in the IWW hall, also the right to make up for time lost due to weather or sickness. At

Bloomfield, N.J., a 310 WPA local won pay for hours the men were required on the job but not assigned to work. At Olympia, Washington, they won a dispute so they could build a fire to keep warm.

In the later thirties the revived I.U. 440 in Cleveland won new plants at American Brass, Superior Carbon, Globe Steel Barrel and Independent Register. It was anxious to get a number of the drum plants organized as its best chance to apply industrial rather than shop structure unionism; for organizers were already noticing that the shop-wide union, like the company union, led to the use of "we" to mean management and men, when even a craft union used it to mean those engaged in the same work. American Stove gave it two major issues: the need to organize in Lorain where one division had been moved during the National Screw strike, and the first occasion for a signed contract. This latter need grew from the fact that the company union which 440 had been steadily battling, joined the CIO, and sought recognition. Though the IWW constitution still forbade time agreements, the Cleveland union signed one, containing the provision that no struck work would be accepted. This stirred up hostilities between jobbites and radicals throughout the IWW; in 1938 the constitution was amended to permit the practice.

In the Lorain campaign the company signed with the CIO over IWW protests; I.U. 440 struck to enforce an election; it was a draw; the runoff was moved up and the CIO squeaked through. During the campaign, the Wobs got members at Steel Stamping in Lorain. The company lawyer, a son-in-law of William Green, induced the AFL to sign a contract over the protests of members of the Trades Council, even though AFL had no members in the plant. IWW demanded NLRB election and won two to one. But hard battles in an unfriendly town eventually lost the plant.

As Europe went to war and the New Deal went in for peace-time military training, the IWW was among the first to negotiate accumulation of seniority during this enforced service. In November 1940 an 11-day strike at American Stove ended with the trading of a demand for a closed shop for the settlement of an accumulation of grievances. This was what the bargaining committee wanted, for they saw that a closed shop (unless accompanied by hiring through the union) ends up in the company personnel office eventually selecting the membership for the union. Instead they preferred a sieve system through which those who didn't care for the union got dropped by not fighting for them when they got into trouble.

This record is one of industrial action; but the chief efforts of the IWW were largely propagandist. Even much of its job conditioning was done through minorities on jobs where other unions had a check-off. The prime IWW concern was the large problem of a misemployed society drifting toward totalitarianism and war. It noted how government intervention was centralizing union functions in Washington, and unions becoming dependent on government props. It held up the ideal of job democracy, invulnerable to any such arrests as those with which Hitler had cracked the highly centralized German labor movement. Internationally it felt drawn toward the anarchist International Workingmen's Association. In 1934 a referendum carried to affiliate with it, then it was pointed out that this would commit the IWW to declaring for its members their religious and political attitudes which it had always left to the individual, and a new referendum reversed the decision, so the IWW did not affiliate. During the Spanish Civil War it had an assessment for the support of the CNT, and friendly relations with IWA persist.

In Canada the IWW through the thirties had a similar history on a smaller scale. Because of customs difficulties, a separate Canadian Administration was established in 1931. Extensive unemployed agitation in the early years led to the imprisonment of organizer George McAdams and others at Sioux Lookout. In the later thirties, organization work was undertaken in Newfoundland and the Maritime provinces. Dairy workers at Ritchies Dairy in Toronto won a boost and a union work stabilization plan. A fishermen's local was established at McDiarmid, Ontario in June 1939 and the 1939 Canadian Convention got considerable newspaper publicity with pictures of the eastern delegation detraining from boxcars. The Chilean Administration of the IWW, long repressed, came to life again in the mid-thirties. The world over, serious labor journals discussed the IWW as a solution to problems otherwise insoluble.

Looking back in 1940 at the commemoration of its first 35 years, the *Industrial Worker* observed: "Today we see government agencies certifying the IWW as the collective bargaining agency for those workers logical enough to demand it. In post-war years we saw the same government sending hundreds of our members to jail for insisting upon the IWW as their bargaining agency. The IWW has proven itself able to carry on equally well in either circumstance."

Notes:

Most material for this chapter from IWW press of the time and personal knowledge of events. Following notes are for further information rather than documentation.

1. Pamphlet: "The Shame that is Kentucky's"; also extensive reports in *New York Times* and other periodicals; also in Perlman & Taft, or Gambs' book previously cited. IWW among Colorado coal miners elected pit committees and checkweighman into January 1933.

2. New York situation described, without IWW angle, in Lens' *Right, Left and Center.*

3. For more on Rossoni see "Black International" series in *Industrial Worker,* March 4, 1950. Another IWW turned fascist was Harold Lloyd Varney. Fascism has been described as a synthesis of syndicalism and nationalism.

4. Best account of maritime affairs through thirties is Taft in *Political Science Quarterly* for June 1939. Accounts also in Madison's *American Labor Leaders* (Harpers, 1950), Yellen's *Labor Struggles* and similar books.

General Sources:

Gambs briefly describes IWW involvement in Harlan, Kentucky. In 1972 Appalachian Movement Press reprinted E. J. Costello's 1931 pamphlet, "The Shame That Is Kentucky's." Herbert Mahler's papers on the defense effort are at the Tamiment Institute at New York University. On efforts to organize in Yakima, James Newbill, "Yakima and the Wobblies, 1910-1936," in Conlin, *At The Point of Production*; Lichtman papers at University of Washington, Seattle; article by Cletus Daniel in *Pacific Northwest Quarterly,* October 1974.

The Boulder Canyon strike is discussed in Guy Louis Rocha, "The IWW and the Boulder Canyon Project," in Conlin, *At the Point of Production.* The chief study of the Metal and Machinery Workers is Roy Wortman's "The IWW in Ohio"; Robinson's dissertation includes extensive discussion of the contract question. On the IWW in Canada, Gary Jewell's account appeared as a supplement to the *Industrial Worker* (May 1975), and was subsequently issued as a pamphlet, *The IWW in Canada.* Mark Leier's *Where the Fraser River Flows* does not carry its story past the 1920s.

On the Hormel stay-in of 1933, see Larry Engelmann's article in *Labor History* (Fall 1974) and Peter Rachleff's "Organizing 'Wall to Wall': The Independent Union of All Workers," in Staughton Lynd (ed.), *"We Are All Leaders": The Alternative Unionism of the Early 1930s* (Univ. of Illinois Press, 1996).

IWW relations with the International Workers' Association (AIT) are discussed in Wayne Thorpe, "The IWW and the Search for an International Policy," *Anarcho-Syndicalist Review* 42/43, 2005, pp. 13-18. See also Matt White, "Wobblies in the Spanish Civil War," pp. 39-47. A follow-up article is scheduled for *ASR* 45, Fall 2006.

13. World War and Cold War (1941-1955)

During World War II the IWW carried on its organization activities undisturbed, and expanded its policy of gaining bargaining rights by winning NLRB elections in the maritime and metal mining industries. Peace was followed by a period of manufactured hysteria – parallel to the reaction to the great French Revolution of 1789. In this period the IWW late in 1949, largely as the victim of the cold war, the subversive list and Taft-Hartley Act, lost much of its membership, and wound up a period of expanding influence. It observed its fiftieth anniversary unable to engage in collective bargaining anywhere. It persists because its members have no doubts that the working class needs the sort of organization it has been striving these many years to build, today more urgently than ever.

The story of U. S. Vanadium's operations at Bishop, California, typifies the period. During the summer of 1941 job delegates for Metal Mine Workers Industrial Union 210 of the IWW, by old-fashioned recruiting, organized this camp high in the mountains solidly and directly negotiated a 13 percent pay boost. In December a meeting in Bishop pondered what to do if someone wouldn't join. As reported in *Industrial Worker* of Dec. 6, "After some discussion it was decided that anyone refusing to line up will be told to state his reasons in a speech before the membership, now a body of 300 workers. The membership will then weigh the reasons given and decide the status of such new worker. The members are anxiously waiting to hear the speech of Objector No. 1." This union security program worked well.

Soon the union had a discriminatory discharge case to handle. Clarence Dahl, of its Organization Committee, working at the Bishop mine took a trip to Darwin, 125 miles away, where the same union was involved in a strike at a mine. Returning over mountain roads in winter, he was late for his shift and was fired. Management refused to discuss his reinstatement. The next evening at the mess hall top management for this U.S. Steel subsidiary announced a wage increase but warned that any strike would be dealt with by law and order. The union took the case to NLRB and Dahl was reinstated with back pay, in January. Next month a hearing was held to arrange for an NLRB election. So far I.U. 210 was the only union concerned. It had been concerned only with the mine, but now that the question of bargaining unit shaped up, it decided March 12 the mill should be in same unit. This led AFL Operating Engineers to hold a meeting at the Legion Hall and seek members, but got none. Immediately the company's eastern legal staff filed a brief with NLRB asking for dismissal of the election on the grounds that the IWW was not a union within the meaning of the Act. In May the NLRB held further hearings on the company contention and the desire of AFL to carve out a unit of 75 men. A new election was scheduled and postponed on request of the company. Meanwhile the IWW organized workers in local taverns and restaurants and soon Foodstuff Workers lU. 640 and I.U. 210 opened a joint hall. On August 7 the local *Inyo Register* carried a story, "Angry citizens voice protest against IWW with talk of vigilante action." The two unions issued a leaflet explaining their aims to the community and nothing adverse occurred. In the election the IWW won 231 votes to 55 in Group A, the mine, and lost 35 IWW to 41 Operating Engineers, with 6 no union votes in Group B. In the run-off the AFL won Group B.

The wartime wage and manpower freeze transferred much collective bargaining away from the job. I.U. 210 demanded an increase and argued that to require men to stay permanently at this high altitude warranted pay above what the War Labor Board permitted. The argument dragged on and in October 1943 the local accepted a 50 cent compromise to clear the way for new demands, for the "gumpets," as the *Industrial Worker* called the growing host of government functionaries, would not process new demands until the old case could be marked settled, tied up in red tape and stored away. The same request was made by UMWA for a similarly situated mine of the same company at Rifle, Colorado, but appears to have been settled for a check-off instead.[1]

In 1944 the company wanted a tunnel and contracted the work to Morrison Knudsen. The contractor hired 37 local men of whom 30 had IWW cards, then contended that under his area-wide agreement with AFL they must all take out AFL cards. IWW insisted to NLRB that Section 7(a) of the Labor Relations Act gave these men the right to choose their union and did not permit the contractor to choose their union in advance for them – but the NLRB didn't see it that way. I.U. 210 decided to sign a contract covering the mine, the first contract outside of those made by Metal & Machinery Workers. Soon operations died down and toward the close of the contract no union crew was on the spot to administer it with effectiveness. Work opened up and Mine, Mill & Smelter Workers won an election. Later in June 1952 the UMWA won over Mine-Mill by getting workers to vote "No Union," since UMWA had not signed the non-communist affidavits that had been signed by Mine-Mill, commonly considered "communist-dominated."

Marine Transport Workers I.U. 510 carried on with increased effectiveness. Its activities in the Gulf centered from desirable facilities in a new building in Houston technically owned by a seamen's club, because the IWW, ever since its printing plant fiasco in the twenties, had avoided real estate. It held on to its straight principles during the ideological and jurisdictional fights of the maritime unions, and during the about faces of the "gumpets" who went from from drinking vodka with the Muscovites to wanting to bomb them. During the Finno-Russian war, the MTW backed the SUP proposal of an embargo on material for Russia, but refused to join it in whooping it up for war. War and post war experiences made many seamen favorable toward IWW views: tanker crews knew of oil trans-shipped to Germany by way of Franco at the Canary Islands; all whose work took them to the waterfront knew that top brass blaming the disaster of the Battle of the Bulge on union action in American plants were frauds, for they knew that the docks were always fully loaded with materiel; others saw food dumped in the Pireaus while Greeks were starving within sight of it, so as to save free enterprise in its distribution; others saw the same in Shanghai and the black market in operation; still others brought home troops from Italy and Germany who had seen fascist cliques restored to power in town after town, and the insurgent administrations ousted. IWW views on world affairs no longer shocked such men.

In 1941 a new attempt was made to deport Bridges. A new law provided for deportation for previous membership in organizations seeking to overthrow the government or alter it by unconstitutional means. In his 1939 case Bridges had recalled a short membership in the MTW about 1920. The Department of Justice now contended that his membership in the IWW was membership in an organization that sought by strikes and economic and industrial pressures to alter the form of government to One Big Union. The IWW provided witnesses for Bridges defense and its attorney filed a brief as "friend of the court." Judge Sears eventually issued his decision that Bridges was deportable, but made it plain that this was not on account of his past IWW membership, for his examination of the record and literature of

The Houston MTW hall remained active into the early 1960s.

the organization showed that the IWW was not such an organization as the Department of Justice contended. The case went up through the courts and eventually in 1945 the United States Supreme Court decided that Bridges was not deportable, incidentally thereby affirming the view that the IWW was not engaged in the alleged activities. The previous Supreme Court decision in the Fiske case, finding the purposes of the IWW lawful, had been based on the Preamble only; this decision was based on all that the prosecution could gather to give the IWW a bad name.[2]

The increasing activity of the IWW on waterfronts and elsewhere toward the close of war led the observant *Business Week* to note in a feature on the union in its issue of January 6, 1945: "The IWW shows signs of life. In the metal shops of Cleveland, the vanadium mines of California, the copper diggings of Butte, on the waterfront of San Diego, New Orleans and New York, the dead past is stirring and men are carrying red cards."[3]

With war over, the quarrels between right and left waterfront unions were intensified in reflection of the growing cold war. Through the big maritime strikes of 1946, embittered with jurisdictional disputes, MTW secured observance of its slogan "Respect All Picket Lines." When the 510 conference met in Houston on Sept. 16 it received telegraphic and other greetings from unions on all sides thanking the IWW for its willing cooperation in a strike that won $27.50 per month on all coasts.[4]

In 1946 the IWW had chartered a British Administration which was also active along its waterfront, and during the 1947 "outlaw" British seamen's strike, it backed the rebels. Here the MTW circulated the information the British Administration provided about this fight against an Establishment Scheme that benefited a few but left most worse off. In 1948 when the SUP sent its members through Bridges' picket lines, solidarity in the maritime industry deteriorated. In 1949 any MTW enthusiasm for the SUP cooled further when the SUP-SIU flew scabs to break the strike of the Canadian seamen on the grounds that their union was communist-dominated. The IWW did not dispute this allegation, but held both here and in Britain that scabbery was no way to undermine communist influence. Even the staid Canadian Trades and Labor Congress took the same stand and informed the SIU that although it had expelled the Canadian Seamen, it could not invite the SIU to affiliate on account of its policy of "replacements" i.e. scabs, in this strike. The MTW did endorse the repeatedly proposed boycott of Panamanian vessels, actually American vessels flying the Panama flag to escape American unions, wages, manning scales and safety inspection. These repeated attempts were always fouled by union contracts and Taft-Hartley.

The MTW'S own organizing activities were confined to the towing industry through the extensive inland channels on Gulf Coast, first in 1946 among crews working for the Galveston & Houston Towing Co. In 1947 it won an NLRB election on the Gulf Barge and Towing, with MTW getting all the votes, and in November on the Pasadena and Lynchberg ferries. It incidentally did a service to the "ancient mariners" of Snug Harbor, a foundation kept up by income from an old farm now in the center of New York's highest priced real estate. Late in 1948 the aged seamen there had been required to turn over to the institution all assets and claims so that they had no spending money. An account of this petty meanness in the *Industrial Worker* Jan. 22, 1949, and later examination of the terms on which the foundation rested, resulted in rescinding these impositions.[5]

Several of the smaller shops organized by Metal & Machinery Workers I.U. 440 in Cleveland went out of business during the war and others were lost to the union through sudden changes of plant personnel. It acquired one "war-baby," Federal Aircraft, where the contract had the unusual provision that no worker could be fired without the approval of the shop committee. The American Stove plant was largely converted to aircraft production, and the union changed from a departmental to a plant-wide seniority system. It wanted rates as high as paid in aircraft plants elsewhere, but War Labor Board insisted that area rates applied. A slowdown developed, followed by a walkout in May 1943. The War Labor Board, finding a union that boasted it had given no "no-strike pledge," considered the union viewpoint and allowed readjustments retroactive to Jan. 18. The expanding work brought many new people into the plant, usually from CIO plants. Most found the IWW a welcome difference, but a few wondered if it was patriotic. All new members were given the regular IWW dues book, with the Preamble up front, and some of these new workers questioned the propriety of its language. A pressure developed in the Cleveland branch to change the Preamble or even sever IWW connections. Explanations of the meaning of the preamble and improved personal relations between the general organization and the branch soon led the branch to hearty participation in IWW affairs.

The members in these shops relished job action tactics. As American Stove expanded its work force, more time clocks were needed, but the company said it was difficult to obtain them in wartime. One night all went home without punching. The additional clocks needed were installed the next day. A canteen service supplied coffee, sandwiches etc., and workers could get a pickup there whenever they wanted one. Management figured this led to a waste of time and ruled that this service would be available only during the 10-minute rest period. Committee induced them to try it out first in one department. When the experiment was made, all maintenance, repair and other crews who had an excuse for coming there were on hand, and those who ordinarily brought a lunch and thermos bottle left them home that day. The committee and management had an appointment to examine the safety conditions in another department that morning, but the committee led the way through the new experiment just at rest period. Management saw a line at the canteen, went on to investigate the safety complaint, returned and the line was still there. It quit its attempt to confine coffee-and to the rest period. Such methods proved effective for many grievances and were thoroughly enjoyed. Freedom to engage in such methods was one of their strong ties to the IWW.

In a nearby plant of American Steel & Wire, the United Steel Workers had their customary multiple step grievance procedure. Under it grievances were regularly shoved up one step until they finally accumulated at the end where they were to be settled far away by legal minds who knew nothing of the conditions that produced the grievance. Local 1519 USW stopped work to demand a settlement of these grievances. The United Steelworkers removed the elected officials of the local and appointed in their place men who had been snowed under in the preceding election as the workers looked on them as "company men." The International representatives also told the custodian of the hall not to let the rebels use it. Men in the plant asked I.U. 440 for advice. The IWW rented the hall for the rebels to use and told the men that this combination of check-off and rule by those they had defeated in an election was the same issue of taxation without representation as led to the American revolution. It was pointed out that the law in Section 7(a) definitely assured them to the right of representatives of their own choosing; but that the Board had taken this to mean that they had chosen the Steelworkers as an international along with any such impositions it might order. I.U. 440 recommended that they raise this issue to NLRB, pointing out that the basic provision of 7(a) outweighed any procedure the NLRB had set up under other sections. The IWW local prepared such an argument on their behalf, avoiding making it an inter-union dispute. No answer was given but the locally elected officials were restored to office. Very soon after, however, the leading militants were given new draft status and had to leave the plant for the armed forces.[6]

The IWW shop committees had found it desirable to take charge of the "share-the-ride" system for the transport of the expanded working forces. The streetcar system of Cleveland was municipally owned. The streetcar workers wanted a boost and were confident from a comparison with rates in other cities that if the city would submit the issue to arbitration, this comparison would get them a boost. But the city held that it was beneath its dignity to submit its labor relations to arbitration. Thus the streetcar men threatened to strike in May 1944. This created an embarrassment for the IWW shop committees, for to handle the "share-the-ride" might impair the effectiveness of the strike. I.U. 440 wrote a letter to the streetcar union expressing this reason for its concern, supporting the men's bid for arbitration, and suggesting that they put the responsibility for any break of streetcar service squarely where it belonged by offering to work during the dispute but collect no fares. A copy of the letter was given to the newspapers and *Cleveland Press* front-paged it in an early noon edition. At barns and elsewhere streetcar workers discussed the idea and supported it, even with telegrams. That afternoon the City Council decided that after all it could submit to arbitration. It did and the men got their boost. (After the war this same tactic was developed in Japan.)

It was an era of endless regulations, interpretations thereof, executive orders and a growing body of case decisions that had to be digested by unionists if they were to administer contracts effectively in their members' best interests. Most unions had legal staffs for this, and a lawyers' view percolated to top officers who advised field representatives how to explain to shop committees what little they could do under this heap of regulations. The IWW could afford no legal staff, so it studied these papers with a workman's eyes to figure how either to use them or get around them. Summaries were given to shop committees and as these men met with committees in CIO and AFL plants quite often, more copies were wanted. Thus a *Labor Newsletter* was issued monthly by the Cleveland Branch, digesting new angles in labor law and giving tips on what could be done about it. It got about a two thousand circulation chiefly among shop committee members of different unions around the country, and tended to make them much less dependent upon their International and its representatives for advice. It was an IWW bid to build more organized self-reliance at shop level,

IWW headquarters in 1946. L to R: Alice Westman, Walter Westman, Charles Velsek, Jennie Velsek, Fred Thompson and John Russell.

rather than to recruit members.

The IWW was much concerned with the developing pattern of unionism and alarmed at its tolerance of government trespass and its solicitation of such intervention. During the manpower freeze the *Industrial Worker* ridiculed the Statements of Availability required for a change of jobs as "Certificates of Manumission." (In non-IWW shops they were frequently obtained by wearing a large IWW button to work.) When Sewell Avery was carried out of Montgomery Ward offices, the *Industrial Worker* did not join in the general glee of the labor press, but pointed out that it was part of the drift to give unions the status of public institutions, and thus deprive them of their rights as voluntary associations. The fate of the Roman guilds under like circumstances was pointed out. The growth of fringe benefits under the wage freeze was noted also as a means of tying workers to one employer, generating a new industrial serfdom with virtual adscription to the job, as our ancestors had been adscripted to the soil. (For this reason it approved any such effort as that of UAW in Toledo to pool pension funds on an area basis.)

The IWW was probably the only union to welcome the U.S. Supreme Court decision in the Elgin Joliet and Eastern Railway case. Employees whose claims for premium pay had been sacrificed by the Brotherhoods in a general settlement of many grievances had gone to court as individuals and won their case; the company defense was that it had settled these claims with the Brotherhoods. The top court decision was that the Brotherhoods were free to contract for more than the worker could claim, but not for less than he could claim as a contractual right from his employer. The IWW thought this a good one-way valve protection against the frequent complaints of "being sold down the river," but CIO and AFL sought a re-hearing on the ground that this upset all their bargaining functions; the decision was re-affirmed but with the additional dodge added that if application for membership forms contained an agreement to accept the settlements the International made, the workers signing these applications could not avail themselves of this decision. The IWW urged its members in other unions to resist the adoption of this dodge. When the Supreme Court ruled that the UMWA must not even by beck or nod approve a strike, the IWW press said this decision offered up the working class to the employing class on the terms of a forced sale, and observed that this, like all anti-labor decisions, was premised on the extensive "rights" given to unions, confirming Gompers' dictum that when the government gives, it can take away, and take away even more than it has given.

Though the 1946 General Convention was expected to provide a collision over contract policy, it turned out quite amicably. It was settled there that "No agreement made by any part of the IWW shall provide for a check-off of union dues by the employer, or obligate the members of the union to do work that would aid in breaking any strike." The opposition to the check-off was stated in another resolution: "It transfers to management an important function of the union. It takes from the hands of the dues payers their control over their own organization. It tends to make union officials more concerned with the good will of the company than with the good will of the members." On the developing cold war it took this position: "That we look upon the Communist Party and its fledglings as a major menace to the working class, and that the interests of world peace can best be served by labor movements that clearly represent the interests of labor and not the interests of any political state; and that we consider that the foolishness of the communists can best be exposed by assuring them complete civil liberty."

Though the Cleveland branch was the largest local organization of the IWW, it was not so important as a financial prop as it was as evidence that the IWW ideals of on-the-job militancy and industrial solidarity could actually work. In this way it contributed appreciably to the growing influence of the IWW in early post-war years. With a stoppage that the IWW insisted was a lock-out at the Jones & Laughlin barrel plant in 1946 and negotiations in other plants during these reconversion days, it kept rates at least "ahead of the neighbors." It encouraged the formation of inter-union bodies, such as stove worker councils, and copper and brass councils, and participated in them actively. In 1946 it organized the Schrimer-Dornbirer pump company; was sued under the War Labor Disputes Act for striking, but won a 45 cents boost and dismissal of the suit. In February 1950 it organized the Coleman-Peterson wire plant, but in November of that year the entire branch withdrew from the IWW over the Taft-Hartley affidavit issue.

This loss of its largest local organization is best understood from a consideration of IWW propaganda through this period and the reaction to it in various quarters. The IWW felt that the labor movement was veering in a disastrous direction, growing into a big business of labor brokerage, suppressing the organized self-reliance that is the yeast of unionism, and becoming increasingly a pawn of government in both internal and world relations. The *Industrial Worker* during this time pointed to many evidences of the inadequacy of this large labor movement: Since a strike is most readily won when supplies of material and orders for finished products are both large, strikes got in each other's road for lack of coordination; for example, creating a steel shortage reduces incentive to settle with auto workers. It was plain that top management maneuvered the timing of bargaining to set a pattern for all with the union in the weakest bargaining position – often weakened by attacks from other unions in labor's reflection of the cold war. If there were to be patterns for all, there should either be a union for all, or means of joint strategy judiciously selecting the order in which different industries went to battle, and supporting those so engaged. It was an era of shortages, and full employment, and thus if more green paper was given, to workers, but no workers switched over to producing the extra goods that workers wanted to buy with their increases, the effect was simply to offer more green paper for the same quantity of goods. The IWW pointed out that a wage demand, if stated in physical terms, is a demand that either unemployed workers be hired to produce these extra goods, or that employed workers be allocated to their production. It urged therefore that a coordinated labor movement, maintaining full employment, would find it necessary to bargain for increases in these terms demanding a voice in the allocation of resources and the decision about what is to be produced. These IWW arguments were frequently reflected in other labor papers, for example as "economic union" versus "organic union" by the AFL *Butcher Workman.*[7]

This painful lack of coordination was plainest in the acceptance of the Taft-Hartley Act which all unions denounced. The IWW objected to the act chiefly on the grounds that it initiated a system of unionism by permit, such that the terms of permit could be made into terms that guaranteed harmless and useless unions (as recent developments in South Africa could prove); that it is up to unions to keep free from political domination, not a job for the politicians themselves; that the ban on sympathetic strikes and secondary boycotts, constituted an order to scab. Otherwise the act provided much amusement for the IWW, particularly the prospects, when an employer did not want to deal with the union, of arranging for each individual worker to insist upon processing the collective grievance on company time, though it might take days and weeks to do so. The IWW held that all that was necessary to defeat Taft-Hartley was for no union to sign its affidavits or seek NLRB service under its terms. This was the general sentiment of the labor movement, but first the Machinists, then one union after another, each claiming it needed NLRB service because of some union threatening to raid it, signed up, until only the UMWA, the ITU and the IWW were outside the Taft-Hartley pale.

The IWW felt that this acceptance of Taft-Hartley was due to the decreasing democracy of the unions, and that the officers accepting it were not as actually opposed to it as they purported to be. For remedy the IWW sought to stimulate on local levels both inter-union solidarity and the demand for democracy.

A comparison of newspaper situations in Chicago and Seattle illustrates what can be done by insistence on inter-union solidarity. In Chicago when the ITU struck the newspapers, they published regularly for many months of strike from photoengravings of copy set up in Varitype. Newspaper trucks carried banners screaming: "21 Loyal AFL

Unions Bring You Today's Paper." In Seattle a Labor Defense Council of active unionists, including many with IWW cards, told newspaper publishers when they made similar plans that Seattle labor would not sink to the Chicago level and the papers would be faced with the same picket lines of lumberjacks and longshoremen and other workers as won the Guild strike in the '30s. The publishers backed down. Later in 1950 in New York where there was some IWW influence among the trades involved, inter-union solidarity had a similar effect. The IWW "two-card" members have been able to avert many obnoxious jurisdictional disputes and to secure local union cooperation.

The *Industrial Worker* devoted considerable space to supporting the contentions of local unions against the usurpations of their internationals, as the San Francisco Machinists, the St. Louis Distribution Workers and the Roofers of Baltimore, but particularly Local 104 of the Boilermakers in Seattle, where a technical side-issue, the local paper, seemed to be an actual major concern. The issue was over whether the local could set its own salaries, technically, but actually the entire issue of union democracy was involved. Eventually the courts gave decisions substantially the same as the IWW contentions. The local was happy but the AFL was so alarmed that it had its general counsel Joseph Padway seek a reconsideration of the case as impairing the capacities of the internationals.

It was at this time that Tom Clark put the IWW on the "subversive list" as the newspapers customarily call the entire long list of organizations compiled originally as a guide to suitability for federal employment. The long list is divided into groups which Clark described as being "mutually exclusive," and only one of these is headed "subversive." The IWW was not placed under this heading but in the category of organizations seeking to alter the form of government by unconstitutional means. The IWW at once protested this classification both on the grounds that it was contrary to fact and that it was reached without the due process of enabling the IWW to confront its accusers or present argument or evidence. It has been pointed out that this listing conflicts with judicial determinations of the IWW aims and character, both in the Fiske and Bridges cases already mentioned. The Department has repeatedly been asked: what are the grounds, what form of government is the IWW alleged to prefer, and why refuse to tell it what the government believes it does or aims to do that is unlawful; but the answer is regularly that "Executive Order 9835

The Oakland IWW hall was a center of Wobbly efforts to organize industrial solidarity in the railroad industry in the 1940s.

contains no authority for a hearing or a disclosing of the bases upon which a designation is made." This irresponsible attitude has increasingly alarmed many conservatives and even awakened some "gliberals" to the constitutional dangers involved.

The IWW is in the dark as to why it is listed. It notes that to list it the Department must either overrule court decisions as to its character as late as 1945, or base its case on some novel policy instituted between 1945 and May 1949 when it was listed; and it can detect no such novel policy. Opinion in IWW circles runs that if it had been listed simply on the basis of newspaper bogyman repute, it would have been listed at the beginning of this practice; thus the time of the listing leads to the suspicion that it was listed as a favor to some labor skate on whose toes the IWW had stepped in its efforts for greater union democracy. As a result the IWW has the distinction of being the only union that must pay an income tax and whose members cannot occupy federal housing projects. This, it contends, is penalizing it and its members without due process, but it has found no way to make the government obey the law. [The government dissolved the list in 1974, thereby ending this situation.]

A New York law relating to public schools provided a sort of hearing before the Board of Regents of New York University in July 1949. When the IWW was notified to present its case, it requested the Regents to try to have Tom Clark there to defend his listing, or at least to tell them on what grounds he had listed the IWW, so that it would have something more or less specific to answer. According to the *Ithaca Journal* of July 8, 1949, Clark told the Regents that of the seven or more score organizations he had listed, there were five that he "was sure were subversive." Tom Clark did not appear to defend himself. The IWW pointed out that his statement about being sure of only five after listing over 150 indicated a gross carelessness with the reputation of others and would make him an incredible witness if he appeared. (The statement was also in contradiction of Clark's own statement about the six categories being "mutually exclusive.")

The IWW went ahead with its class-struggle program. In Cleveland it succeeded in winning two new shops. When the city observed its Sesquicentennial, the unions and management of many plants staged a big labor-management celebration in the Municipal Auditorium. The IWW was approached and agreed to participate, if it was free to put up its own display. The result was that it had the only booth with a union rather than a brotherly love motif. Typical IWW slogans decorated the booth; it distributed its newly revised "One Big Union" pamphlet and a special issue of the *Industrial Worker* telling the history of the working class of Cleveland. (This seems to be the first instance of the labor history of a city.) In the railroad industry, somewhat neglected by the IWW since its Detroit campaigns in the mid-thirties and the extra gang efforts somewhat later, the IWW made renewed efforts in 1944, issuing a monthly *Railroad Worker,* widely distributed through railroad yards across the country, and again in 1948 to 1950 concentrating on Southern Pacific and Western Pacific crews with activities centered in Oakland. For this campaign it issued several leaflets, a railroad workers' pamphlet, and the *Industrial Worker* ran a series of articles from July 3 to November 6, 1948, giving the most complete account of the history of railroad labor so far available.

The 1950 General Convention was stormy. Indignation at Clark's listing expressed itself in a resolution that the organization should refuse to pay any income tax so as to force a court review of Clark's irresponsible action. The Cleveland members wanted the issue of signing Taft-Hartley affidavits put to referendum. They had some support from other delegates who aimed at job control unionism, but most of the delegates were opposed to signing. The NLRB had ruled that since the IWW was One Big Union, its Industrial Unions could not sign effectively unless its general officers also signed. The decision was to submit it to referendum.

Shortly after the convention, while the referendum was still being voted upon, efforts were made by other unions to raid the IWW shops in Cleveland. It was suggested that in such a raid they ask the members to vote "No Union"; but it was felt that with considerable change of personnel, some of them very friendly to organizers in the competing unions, and with the disadvantages that competitors could allege came from being on the subversive list, it would be unusually difficult to hold their union together. The Cleveland Branch was confident that the referendum would carry to sign up, and that submission of the affidavits would require a review of the subversive listing, so what it needed was time until these events happened. It decided to withdraw from the IWW until such time as the IWW branches could avail themselves of NLRB service. It took this action November 5, 1950, and adopted a lengthy resolution explaining why it felt compelled to do so, and ending up that it would pay all per capita to that date, but withhold it thereafter. Only this conclusion was transmitted to membership, and much indignation was expressed that the Cleveland branch was attempting to coerce the rest of the organization. Outside of Cleveland, the vote on the Taft-Hartley issue was two to one against signing, but if the Cleveland votes were counted it would have swung the decision to require signing. The ballot committee contended that since they had withdrawn, their votes could not be counted. Those taking the opposite view contended that if the members were in good standing when they voted, the votes must be counted, the same as a dead man's vote would be counted. The consensus of branch minutes around the country was not to count the votes. Thus the Cleveland branch was lost. In May 1955 it joined the MESA, with which the IWW and it had been friendly especially as it took a critical attitude toward capitalism, and later MESA joined CIO. With the 1955 merger of CIO and AFL this Cleveland body will have boxed the compass of collective bargaining agencies.

The loss of the Cleveland membership also checked a possible reorganization of class struggle unionism. There were a number of industries in which either Communists or fellow travelers had taken a leading hand, and had twisted unionism to suit party purposes. They had been tolerated by the rank and file, not out of sympathy for Communism, but because in most instances the alternative was to back bootlickers. The Mine, Mill and Smelter Workers offered such an example; a communist hard-rock miner is a rare bird indeed, but even such a hostile compilation of the evidence as Jensen's *Nonferrous Metal Industry Unionism 1932-1954* makes it plain that the metal miners' choice was militancy and progressive policies associated with the Moscow-tainted candidates, or a meekness that spelled disaster. In the United Electrical Workers and various other unions, this situation existed either in locals or generally. The IWW had been building increasing contact in such unions with active members who wanted a militant, anti-capitalist program, free from Communist or other political domination. Their pending ouster from CIO made them consider new organizational possibilities. Many such delegates to the ousting CIO Convention in Cleveland discussed possibilities with IWW members there, and a considerable correspondence was developing at the time that the Cleveland branch felt it necessary to secure access to NLRB. All plans to rescue these militants from the communists were voided by the IWW decision not to count the Cleveland ballots.

Since that time the IWW has had to confine its efforts substantially to local instances of promoting inter-union solidarity and its educational work.

The latter is no small chore. Its general arguments have been indicated already. A resolution adopted at its 1950 convention shows its slant on the major current world problems: "Kremlinism is a social tendency, an institutional development ... it cannot be shot with bullets or devastated with A-bombs. Reliance on these inappropriate means has permitted Kremlinism to stretch from where it engulfed only a sixth of the world's population to where it now engulfs a third. ... It grows only because the labor movement of the rest of the world is not effectively serving the interests and needs of labor. This is the indispensable condition for the growth of Kremlinism. The only es-

cape from it is for the labor movement to act independently of governments and capitalists and proceed to serve the interests of labor. To do
so it must advance to a social system in which essential production is
carried on for use under the direction of organized labor, for the good
of mankind. Doing this will stop Kremlin expansion. Further it will
topple Kremlinism in the areas it has already engulfed."

The occasional picket lines of the fifties have been joint protests
with other groups as at Spanish consulates in New York and Chicago, or the "Third Camp" poster walk in the Chicago loop during the
Christmas rush of 1953. There leaflets consistent with the foregoing
resolution were passed out to the crowds while posters proclaimed
"Against Both War Camps" or "Capitalism – No! – Stalinism – Never!!" The protest picketing that attracted most attention however was
that at the *New Republic* in April 1948. Its January 6th issue had carried a piece by Wallace Stegner depicting Joe Hill as a stick-up man.
The Friends of Joe Hill formed and asked that corrective information
be published; the picket line won the point. The committee engaged
in extensive research and wrote too lengthy a study for the magazine;
the *New Republic* ran a synopsis of the study and the whole document
was published in the *Industrial Worker* for Nov. 13, 1948.

Under the circumstances it has focused its attention on maintaining
its own press and occasional leafleteering. Its most noted columnist,
T-Bone Slim (Matt Valentine Huhta, an Ashtabula Finn), died in October 1942. Another columnist, John Forbes, was put in the peniten-
tiary for refusing to register, but he kept up his column of satiric verse
from behind bars. His conviction was protested even by an American
Legion group as he was a veteran, not subject to draft, but he could
not square his conscience and concede the right of the politicians to
register him. Of current union issues the *Industrial Worker* had been
particularly concerned with the longshore situation on the New York
waterfront, and has not been without influence in it.

The IWW observed its 50th anniversary with its 1955 General
Convention, representative of a scattered membership chiefly along
Atlantic, Gulf and West Coasts. It was the first convention since 1950,
and the first since the early thirties which the "no contract, dyed-in-
the-wool" Wobs completely dominated; the few who disagreed with
their views felt that to bring up any such proposal as signing Taft-
Hartley affidavits, would only constitute a futile gesture, and provoke
disunity where unity was necessary for survival. Thus it was a harmo-

nious gathering, and a remarkable one as a bridge across history: one delegate could readily recall the depression of 1893, or compare the difficulties currently faced by the IWW with those encountered by the Knights of Labor about that time; the convention installed as editor of its official organ a spry octogenarian, C. E. Payne, who had edited that paper in earlier years and had attended the first convention in 1905.

These delegates had no idea of "giving up the ghost." They had read premature obituaries of the IWW as long as they could remember – some as early as July 1906. They knew that the IWW had the stamina not only to withstand militia, prisons and plain plug-uglies, but what is harder: fond hopes shattered, sudden reverses and repeated losses of substantial memberships. The IWW had been near to extinction and pronounced dead many times before, but had always come to life again. Why give up in a world that plainly needed the sort of unionism the IWW had been championing these fifty years?

Accordingly the 1955 Convention attended to routine chores, passed a resolution clarifying its concept of revolutionary unionism, another aimed at the age-group blacklist confronting those over 45, and approved the publication of this record, on the understanding that it be not the history of the IWW, but the history of its first fifty years.

Notes:

1. *Industrial Worker,* Aug. 23, 1943.
2. Bridges' account of leaving MTW was much along the line of Furuseth's attack on J. Vance Thompson. Sears decision was summarized in press at the time, most fully in San Francisco papers.
3. The *Business Week* account of IWW was reprinted with editorial comment in *Industrial Worker* on Feb. 27, 1945.
4. The maritime situation through 1946 was summarized in *Industrial Worker* of Sept. 28, 1946 and in its end-of-year labor summary. The *Industrial Worker* of that period is an exceptionally full source of waterfront news.
5. *Industrial Worker,* July 10, 1949.
6. *Industrial Worker* carried a full account of this, including the document I.U. 440 submitted to NLRB, on Apr. 8, 1944.
7. *Butcher Workman,* May 1950.

General Sources:

The best sources for this period are the *Industrial Worker* and IWW archives, Roy Wortman's "The IWW in Ohio," and Leland Robinson's "Social Movement Organizations in Decline." Jon Bekken's "Marine Transport Workers" (cited chapter 11) carries the MTW story forward through the 1950s.

Charles H. Kerr has brought out a collection of T-Bone Slim's writings, *Juice Is Stranger Than Friction,* edited by Franklin Rosemont (2002). Kornbluh also includes some IWW writings from the era. Kerr has also reprinted the Cleveland Metal and Machinery Workers IU 440 pamphlet, "The Workers Who Built Cleveland."

Work People's College in Duluth (affiliated to the IWW from 1914 until it stopped offering classes in 1941) offered a curriculum including book keeping, economics, labor history, organizing skills, and general education for adults, as well as programs in Finnish culture and language for the children of the immigrants who built it. The College also had a theater troupe that toured the Midwest performing in Finnish community centers and labor halls. Pictured is the summer 1939 class.

14. Rebuilding the IWW (1955-1985)

The IWW entered the 1950s facing the most serious crisis in its history. The loss of the Cleveland metal shops was quickly followed by the loss of several smaller shops around the country, and a rapid collapse of membership. Although Wobblies in the maritime and timber industries, in particular, continued to maintain union halls on both coasts (as well as in Chicago and Houston), they increasingly functioned more as an agitation group within the business unions than as a union in their own right. Leland Robinson's study of IWW financial reports concluded that there were only 115 dues-paying members in 1961, as the IWW began a modest recovery.[1]

In 1957, the IWW operated halls and branches in 13 cities in the United States and Canada (including three branches of the Marine Transport Workers Industrial Union), as well as in Australia, Great Britain (where a branch of the IWW rail workers union was still active), and Sweden. But many were staffed by a handful of old-timers, and some, like the Marine Transport Workers hall in Houston, were literally falling down. Twelve years later, in 1969, the IWW listed 12 U.S. branches, few of which operated halls, two branches in Canada and committees in Australia, Great Britain and Sweden (where shipyard workers at the Kochum works in Malmö organized an IWW job branch two years later that lasted until the late 1970s). While the union still boasted many veteran members, an influx of younger members built an organization that was more visible both in the streets and on the job.

Barred from contesting NLRB representation elections in the 1950s, and no longer having enough members in any particular industry to be a real presence on job sites, Wobblies increasingly concentrated on educational and solidarity work, joining picket lines in solidarity with the civil rights movement and workers' struggles around the world, and anti-war protests. This work gradually brought the IWW to the attention of a new generation of rebellious workers, who sought to return the IWW to the job even as the organization played a larger role in the emerging New Left.

Even in the darkest days, IWW members continued to organize. In New York City, after years of modest protests and educational events, Wobblies threw themselves into an ambitious organizing drive in

1959. The campaign targeted the city's restaurant employment agencies, which charged $25 to $40 to refer workers to jobs that often paid below the minimum wage. Over the course of the campaign, an IWW hiring hall was established, thousands of bilingual leaflets were distributed to workers approaching the job shark offices, and dozens of new members signed up. The campaign had some early successes, including winning back pay for one worker by throwing up a picket line outside the restaurant where he had worked (which, ironically, turned out to be under contract with the AFL-CIO's restaurant workers union, but hired from the job sharks and cheated workers of their overtime pay). Several restaurants soon agreed to hire from the IWW hall or from the state-operated employment service. IWW members in the industry located more jobs by notifying the union whenever a position opened. But the campaign was also met with persistent police harassment of IWW leafletters outside the job sharks, organizers were subpoenaed by the Grand Jury, and the city ordered the IWW hiring hall closed as an unlicensed business. By September 1959 the drive had collapsed, as too many workers felt obliged to hire through the job sharks and the IWW was unable to effectively pressure restaurants to abandon their use.

The collapse of the campaign left the New York branch exhausted and demoralized, but suggested to the rest of the union new possibilities for organizing outside of the NLRB process. In the San Francisco Bay Area, where a handful of Wobblies had long been active in the railroad industry trying to unite workers across craft union lines, a number of younger workers joined the local IWW branch, which became increasingly active in the anti-war movement. This work brought the branch into contact with early counter-cultural movements, signing up some of the era's leading poets – the best known of whom was Alan Ginsberg – into a poets' union and, in 1963, beginning to actively reach out to students on college campuses. Berkeley Wobs launched *The Wobbly* as a magazine aimed at this younger generation. This agitation combined an emphasis on supporting labor struggles in their communities with an emerging "student syndicalism" that suggested that students could adapt Wobbly tactics to address immediate problems in their own lives, and to democratize colleges under the joint control of students, staff and faculty. These ideas influenced many in the emerging student movement, and their echoes could be seen in the Berkeley Free Speech Fight, where student radicals went about winning their right to free speech through direct action.

But while increasingly reaching out to students, the IWW's primary emphasis remained in industry. In October of 1964, the San Francisco General Recruiting Union Branch[2] organized and soon took out on strike workers at a popular coffeehouse, Cedar Alley. It was a long dispute, as the "radical" owner proved intransigent, signing a sweetheart deal with the AFL restaurant workers two months into the strike and persuading a few purported "lefties" such as folksinger Malvina Reynolds to cross the picket line. A number of IWW members were arrested on the picket line. After several months of picketing, the owner filed for bankruptcy and closed up shop.

The strike inflamed existing tensions between General Headquarters in Chicago and the San Francisco branch, which believed it had not received enough support for court and defense costs. San Francisco-based members of the General Executive Board issued a special issue of the union's *General Organization Bulletin* that was highly critical of General Secretary-Treasurer Walter Westman, who had held that position for many years. Bulletins are normally issued by the GST, and many members viewed that issue as illegitimate and rallied to Westman's defense. In an effort to calm the dispute, Westman declined to stand for re-election. However, Berkeley Wobbly Robert Rush, generally expected to win election as GST that fall (as he was the only serious candidate on the ballot), was defeated by a write-in campaign for Carl Keller, a veteran member who was then editing the *Industrial Worker.* While this exacerbated tensions in the short term, Keller worked hard to reconcile the contending factions. This was in many ways a conflict between older members of the union – many of whom had been active since the union's earliest days – and the younger members who had become the core of the IWW's most active branches. But both sides were determined to work together; on the whole, the younger members had tremendous respect for the seasoned "old-timers" who had held the IWW together, and they in turn were eager for younger members to join and take an active role in the organization.

The Chicago GMB was also growing. An IWW club was formed at Roosevelt University (a commuter college heavily attended by working-class students) that sponsored a series of well-attended educational events before college administrators barred them from campus following an event where a guest speaker burned a U.S. flag during his presentation. The new members put out a magazine, *Rebel Worker*, that combined classic IWW propaganda with surrealist illustrations, and in 1964 launched an ambitious campaign to organize a union of the unemployed. That effort had some initial success, but was soon eclipsed by a better-financed campaign by Students for a Democratic Society.

Chicago members also looked to IWW history to attempt a campaign among migrant farm workers, who they believed were one of the last remaining parts of the union's traditional constituency (as well as not being covered by the National Labor Relations Act) and so offered a promising opportunity for rebuilding the IWW on the job. IWW members fanned out into the nearby Michigan berry fields in the summer of 1964, meeting with some success and organizing a strike at Hodgman's Blueberry Farm over unsanitary living conditions. The strike was ultimately broken, but not until employers were forced to raise wages and clean up some camps.

The next year, a small team of Chicago members traveled to the Yakima Valley in Washington to support longstanding efforts by local delegate George Underwood and other Wobblies to organize the apple orchards. Even when workplace organizing had collapsed in the rest of the union in the 1950s, Washington Wobblies had continued trying to organize the apple pickers. These efforts turned back efforts to increase the size of bins (the pickers were paid by the bin) and helped maintain wage rates, but no lasting union presence was built in any of the orchards despite scattered job actions and sporadic organizing efforts that continued into the late 1980s.

Membership was now concentrated in Chicago, New York City, and the San Francisco Bay area, but the union was making inroads in other cities and maintained a modest presence overseas. With changing patterns of immigration, the IWW's foreign-language branches and publications were closing. *Bermunkas*, the IWW's Hungarian-language paper, ceased publication in 1955 – reflecting both a gradual decline in the number of Hungarian-speaking workers in the United States and uncertainty over how to respond to changing conditions in the old country – leaving only the Finnish-language daily (later weekly) *Industrialisti* to continue the legacy of the union's once-vibrant foreign-language press, until it too ended publication in October 1975.

Buoyed by growing membership, and a general trend among Canadian unionists to demand autonomy from U.S.-based unions, Canadian Wobblies voted to establish a separate administration in 1972 (the same year British Columbia's Labour Board refused to certify an IWW job branch on a construction job on the grounds that the IWW's commitment to revolutionary unionism was inconsistent with the objectives of provincial labor law), but conflicts between Eastern and Western IWW branches led to a referendum to abolish the administration two years later. Since then, Australian, British and Canadian members have regularly been elected to the IWW's General Executive Board, alongside members from the United States.

With an increasingly young membership, the IWW experimented with strategies to organize increasingly militant younger workers and to address working conditions distinct to the casual jobs and alternative workplaces many of them found themselves in. In 1967, IWW members voted to allow students not currently employed to join the IWW's Education Workers Industrial Union 620, on the theory that they were apprentices. This quickly gave rise to a number of campus-based branches and groups, particularly after a tour by veteran IWW organizer Fred Thompson. A branch with more than 100 members was formed in 1968 at the University of Waterloo, in the Canadian province of Ontario. Waterloo Wobblies did extensive strike support work in the area, began the revival of the IWW in eastern Canada, and came to exert a large measure of student control over that institution before fading away in the early 1970s. Other campus-based branches were established in Madison and Milwaukee, Wisconsin, and Ann Arbor, Michigan.

The IWW also began establishing a foothold in many of the small workers' cooperatives that had emerged as part of the counterculture. Most were operated on a shoestring, organized collectively, saw themselves as part of a broader social movement, and shared their revenues equally among all the workers. Such workers were naturally drawn to the IWW, and the union began recognizing these co-ops as job shops on the grounds that their experiments with worker self-management constituted an attempt to "build the new society in the shell of the old." Many came under Printing and Publishing House Workers IU 450, but others engaged in construction, food distribution, janitorial services, and other work. By 1970 there were more than two dozen such shops in the IWW, and the IWW union label was found on much of the movement literature circulated in North America. The number of such print shops has since declined, as some were driven out of

The Hip Products strike, Chicago 1971

business and others transformed into capitalist enterprises.

Such shops posed a number of unique challenges, as they often operated on the fringes of the economy and were organized by workers
for whom freedom from a boss was often more important than wages
or benefits. From the beginning, the IWW insisted that its union label
could not be used by any shop that undermined union conditions – a
stance that has forced it to deny use of the label to several co-ops over
the years. Other controversies arose as some co-ops became successful

enterprises, expanding well beyond the original core of workers and mutating into enterprises that proclaimed their egalitarian, cooperative vision at the same time that they subjected workers to conditions that would have made many capitalists blush. Workers in some of these enterprises organized into the IWW, waging difficult struggles to regain some level of autonomy on the job and protect themselves from exploitation, and were accused of sabotaging the community in return.

Workers at several of the "underground" papers springing up across North America also turned to the IWW, both in response to job concerns and in an effort to unite the radical labor and youth movements. Production workers at the New York-based national radical weekly *The Guardian* struck in 1969, demanding a more democratic workplace. When the "collective" refused to negotiate they joined the IWW and began publishing their own *Liberated Guardian*, which ultimately failed to attract enough subscribers to survive.

Newspaper sellers at the *San Diego Street Journal* organized the IWW-affiliated Street Vendors Free Union in 1970 to confront police harassment when the paper's publisher left them to handle a wave of arrests on their own. The union helped secure legal representation, but also organized a series of direct action campaigns that – much like the IWW free speech fights of an earlier era – flooded the areas where police were cracking down with newspaper vendors. The newspaper's staff later joined the vendors in the IWW – making the paper a solid IWW shop from editorial staff to the street sellers and the San Diego branch the IWW's largest, with more than 100 union members at its peak, until it collapsed in 1972. A growing IWW quickly became a target for police outraged by the *Street Journal's* exposes of official corruption, radical youth, the anti-war movement, and a resurgent IWW, and apoplectic when these came together.

The *Street Journal* was fairly successful in a conservative military town, with a press run of 10,000 weekly; its street vendors also distributed papers including the *Industrial Worker, Liberated Guardian* and the *Black Panther* to newspaper boxes and stores across the city. The paper served as the hub of an embattled radical movement, publishing special sections edited by Chicanos, remnants of the Black Panthers (which had been smashed by local police), feminists and radical GIs. The San Diego IWW and *Street Journal* were subjected to regular police raids, fire bombings, government harassment of landlords and other tactics that the fledgling branch was ultimately unable to withstand.[3] Nonetheless, the IWW was seen as a unifying force, organizing hundreds of people in a Fall 1970 march against police harassment of the radical community.

The IWW's resurgence, and its growing connections with the antiwar and student movements, led to renewed repression against the union in several cities. The French-language *La Presse Populaire du Montreal*, whose workers had joined the IWW, was shut down in October 1970 by a joint police/army raid during the Federal occupation of Quebec under the War Measures Act; one member was arrested and held for a month along with hundreds of others suspected of supporting the separatist FLQ. Wobblies working at the *San Diego Street Journal* were shot at and firebombed by a paramilitary organization later proved to be working with the FBI. In 1971 California's Criminal Syndicalism law was invoked against IWW members Ricardo Gonzalves and David Rico and a non-member for an item published in *El Barrio*, but those charges were dropped after the U.S. Supreme Court found the law unconstitutional. (Prosecutors elsewhere in the state had made the mistake of attempting to apply it to unionists not members of the IWW.) And two IWW members were killed overseas by military regimes: Chicago Wobbly Frank Terrugi was machine gunned to death by the Pinochet regime during the 1973 Chilean military coup; IWW journalist Frank Gould was killed the next year by the Philippines army.

While still a small organization in the early 1970s, the IWW was increasingly active. In 1971, Colorado silver miners organized a short-lived branch but were unable to establish job control. In Chicago, warehouse workers at Hip Products who were fired during a union organizing campaign began regular picketing, winning back-pay settlements after several months. Among those walking the picket line was 90-year-old Joseph Vlad, who first joined the IWW in 1913 during the Akron rubber strike. IWW members leafleted Hip-owned stores in Chicago and around the country. A strong picket line and an IWW-organized national boycott campaign crippled the hitherto-profitable company, and it closed the following year. In 1971 the IWW won its first contract since the loss of the Cleveland job branches at Chicago's Three-Penny Cinema following a short strike, but workers quit en masse a few months later when management decided to convert the once-popular cinema into a porn house. The following year 32 Wob-

Nicholas Steelink, who did time under California's Criminal Syndicalism law in the 1920s, walking the picket line at Park International in 1972.

blies struck Park International and International Wood Products in Long Beach, California, May 3, 1972, hoping for a quick victory as Park was behind on a large order and workers lacked the resources to hold out long. The strike was officially called over unfair labor practices which had been filed with the NLRB over harassment of union supporters, and when the boss proved intransigient the workers decided to return to work after two weeks pending a National Labor Relations Board representation election. However, the boss talked to each worker, telling them that they would not get their jobs back unless they agreed not to testify in the NLRB proceedings. That, of course, was illegal, and a number of workers refused and were fired. Others agreed, trusting the Board to protect their rights. After the Board's typical delays, which gave the boss more time to intimidate workers, the NLRB rejected the unfair labor practice charges. By the time a representation election was finally held, most workers still on the job were scabs and new hires brought in with the help of the Laborer's union and the Veterans Administration.

This increasing activity brought the IWW to the attention of the U.S. Labor Department, which notified the IWW that it was required to file annual reports disclosing names of union officers and financial information already published monthly, in greater detail, in the union's *General Organization Bulletin.* IWW officials began filing the reports in 1973, arousing concern from many members who feared that submitting the form could be interpreted as an agreement to abide by other obnoxious provisions of the Landrum-Griffin and Taft-Hartley acts, such as those prohibiting solidarity strikes and refusal to handle struck goods and restricting who could hold union office. After heated debate, a majority voted in a membership referendum to file the forms in order to have access to the NLRB and its ostensible protections, and to avoid possible prosecution. With the end of the Attorney General's subversive list in 1974, the IWW regained its tax-exempt status and once again had equal legal standing with other unions.

A number of organizing campaigns followed, but little success came of the dozens of drives that relied on NLRB representation election procedures or turned to the Board for protection against the bosses' union-busting. Such campaigns in the mid-1970s included drives at a Milwaukee grocery store, a Boston nursing home, a Pennsylvania chemical plant (the company destroyed the IWW's majority by merging the facility into a much larger shop), and fast-food and other restaurants across the country, including branches of such major outfits as McDonald's, Roy Rogers, Kentucky Fried Chicken and Pizza Hut. IWW organizers were able to sign up a majority of the workers in several of these shops with little difficulty. But in each case, legal maneuvering by the bosses and NLRB led to long delays during which normal turn-over, harassment of union supporters and hiring of anti-union employees led to defeat. When Milwaukee Wobblies organized a majority of workers at a Shop-Rite grocery store, the AFL's Retail Clerks union intervened – delaying the process and confusing some workers. The IWW defeated the AFL union in the initial NLRB election, but by the time the final election was held, firings and high turn-over meant that only 17 of the original 42 workers who sought IWW recognition were still on the job, and the shop remained non-union. More successful was a strike by nearly 200 student part-time workers at the University of Wisconsin at Milwaukee, who won their demands but were unable to build a permanent union organization.

The fast food campaigns were part of IWW efforts to target workers in small, high-turnover shops, who the union believed would be more likely to embrace the IWW's militant, direct action tactics. Wobblies in State College, Penn., waged a sustained organizing campaign, which began with a survey of students at Pennsylvania State University (who both patronized and worked at many of the college town's fast food joints) asking about working conditions on their jobs, identifying a number of disgruntled workers in the process. The IWW established contacts in nearly 20 area restaurants, prompting owners to pool their resources to hire a union-busting law firm. A majority of workers at a Kentucky Fried Chicken outlet signed up in 1973, striking Nov. 8 when management refused union recognition. KFC closed up shop rather than recognize the union. The IWW also signed up a majority at a local Roy Rogers, but were unable to hold on through the usual delays and turnover to win an NLRB election. In Pittsburgh, IWW organizers signed up workers at four Winky's restaurants, resulting in a one-vote loss in an NLRB election at one restaurant, the loss of another to HERE raiding, and several firings and other retaliation that led to several unfair labor practice charges.

Other fast food campaigns took place in Chicago and Arkadelphia, Arkansas. In 1972, a series of actions against a Portland, Oregon, Winchell's doughnut operation, coupled with picketing up and down the West Coast, won back pay for a fired union supporter and an agreement to pay overtime and provide paid breaks (as required by state law), but no lasting union presence.

Portland Wobblies also organized workers at Albina Day Care in 1973, winning a number of demands including the firing of the center's autocratic director, before succumbing to threats of defunding. Portland Wobs launched other campaigns at a brass plating plant (where 14 union supporters were fired), the Portland Medical Center (in a campaign sparked by massive lay-offs and workers' dissatisfaction with arbitrary and incompetent management) and the West Side School, and opened a union hall in Portland's skid row district to challenge the day labor agencies and agricultural hiring halls. And in 1974, the IWW mounted a campaign to organize workers in Guam's tour bus industry – signing up several members but unable to secure a strong enough base to successfully tackle conditions on the job.

When workers at Mid-America Machinery in Virden, Illinois, were locked out July 26, 1977 (the day after they decided to join the IWW), they turned to the Board for protection. The Unfair Labor Practice charges did get workers, who reconditioned road construction equipment, back on the job July 30, but that initial victory proved the start of a long war of attrition in which workers were fired, harassed into quitting, or injured on the job by the unsafe conditions that led them to organize in the first place. In June 1978, the NLRB ordered Mid-America to recognize the union and reinstate the first worker to be fired, but owner Larry Jabusch refused to comply. In frustration, the last IWW member left on the job decided to strike. The IWW set up picket lines at the plant, and dispatched flying pickets as far south as Arkansas to confront the boss wherever he tried to sell his equipment. The strike proved expensive to all sides. Virden was some 300 miles from the nearest IWW branch, making it difficult to reinforce picket lines. After losing a lawsuit against the union, Jabusch took refuge from his creditors in bankruptcy court; only in 1980 did the NLRB finally force him to agree to recognize the union, reinstate the workers (all of whom had long since found better jobs), and negotiate with the IWW. Several workers did receive substantial back pay, but the bargaining order proved useless as there were no union supporters left on the job.[4]

The Virden strike was the culmination of a Chicago branch campaign aimed at moving beyond haphazard efforts to organize any shop where they came into contact with dissatisfied workers in favor of developing an industrial campaign where the union could build a long-term, stable base. The branch formed the IU 440 Metal Workers Organizing Committee in 1974 after its research determined that there were hundreds of small, non-union shops in the region engaged in the manufacture and finishing of metal products. IWW members from around the country joined the local committee, seeking jobs in those shops in order to build the union from the inside. Quickly learning that many of these shops operated with cavalier disregard for workers' lives, the organizing committee researched and published *A Metal Workers Guide to Health and Safety on the Job,* which outlined a number of common hazards and offered suggestions on how to address them. But while the committee had some successes in agitating around specific issues, work in the industry was drying up and the small shops the committee had targeted proved to be virulently anti-union, often preferring to close up shop rather than deal with a union. For Chicago members, the campaign also pointed to the dangers of working through the NLRB and the courts, with the long delays endemic to these procedures, and the importance of building a strong base in the community in order to support industrial action. But the Chicago branch (which also had a promising drive under way among health care workers) nearly collapsed in the aftermath of the Virden strike, and those lessons were not taken up by the rest of the union – which for many years continued to focus on organizing small and mid-sized businesses, working to develop strategies to win recognition despite

IWW members from around the country joined the 1981 Solidarity Day march called to protest the Reagan Administration's union-busting.

the inadequacy of NLRB "protections" and winning a number of usually short-lived contracts.

Throughout the decade many workers came to the IWW for help organizing their jobs, although the union often had difficulty building branches stable enough to secure lasting job control. Construction workers at New Mexico's Rio Grande Conservancy District joined the IWW in 1977, but were unable to overcome the retaliatory firing of three IWW supporters. A promising drive among public-service workers in Santa Cruz, California, in the Spring of 1977 won substantial pay hikes, shorter hours and a grievance procedure at several workplaces, and a majority of workers at five shops joining up. Workers at the Santa Cruz Law Center won a medical and dental plan, and bus washers with the transit system had signed up every worker before the state labor board ordered them into another union from which they had previously been barred. But within a year internal fights led to the collapse of the job branches and the drive – representatives sent by the IWW General Administration were unable to salvage the situation. More successful, and longer-lasting, was IWW organizing in the Detroit-Ann Arbor area. In Fall 1977, IWW members began to broaden their contacts through educationals, strike support, and leafleting. The next summer organizers began to line up bookstore workers in Ann Arbor. At one store, Charing Cross, Wobblies demanded recognition and were refused. A strike and lockout followed, and after nine days a settlement was reached including union recognition, wage and benefit increases, and seniority rights in rehiring.

IWW organizers at the University Cellar bookstore – a co-op bookstore with an increasingly hierarchical management serving University of Michigan students – then began signing up fellow workers. Union recognition was gained in January 1979. During the course of negotiations, job actions increased in order to defend working conditions and pressure management to settle. Wobblies struck in August, just before the store's busiest season, and after two and a half days won most of their demands. The contract contained some modest wage and benefit gains, but most importantly limited management's "right" to manage the works. The agreement also upheld the workers' right to strike and to honor other workers' picket lines. Subsequent contracts at this 80-worker shop added protections governing the implementation of new technology, the right to refuse unsafe work or to handle scab goods, prohibiting discrimination against workers with AIDS (in what is believed to be the first such provision negotiated by any union), and restricting subcontracting.

The U-Cellar victory formed a base for ongoing IWW organizing drives in the area, particularly among smaller shops where workers are often the most exploited. Leopold Bloom's – a local eatery – was signed up, as were workers at Innovative Wordprocessors (an Ann Arbor printing concern soon closed by the IRS for not paying its taxes) and workers at a branch of a local bank (who quickly went out on a disastrous strike). In 1982, warehouse workers at the People's Wherehouse (owned by the Michigan Federation of Cooperatives), confronting a management assault on working conditions, joined the IWW. A campaign of direct action and a threatened strike won an acceptable contract two years later. These fellow workers faced a management as fiercely anti-union as any in the country, which used a "cooperativist" ideology to justify wholesale assaults on working conditions and wages. (Finally, in 1992, the Federation sold the operation to an out-of-state competitor and laid off the entire work force.) The branch also waged campaigns among staff for a local alternative newspaper, at a few local print shops, and among clerical and other workers at the University of Michigan. Many of these employers preferred to go out of business during lengthy strikes than to accept demands for decent wages and working conditions. Nonetheless, the Ann Arbor/Detroit IWW grew to about 150 members in the mid-1980s with an active presence in eight shops, before bankers cut off the University Cellar's line of credit, forcing it to close and throwing nearly 80 IWW members onto unemployment lines in the midst of a deep recession.

Across the U.S. and Canada, IWW groups and branches also engaged in a wide variety of agitational, educational and solidarity work. To cite just a few examples, in the 1970s the Tacoma/Olympia Branch sponsored an educational series on Demystifying the Economy, the Madison branch sponsored forums on the development of the American labor movement and the Boston Branch organized a series of "Films of Labor and Struggle." In Sweden, IWW members successfully managed the boycott of California lettuce to support farm workers; Wobblies did similar work across the United States, leading to scores of arrests and a Feb. 5, 1976, incident where the offices the union shared with the United Farm Workers in Stockton, California, were shot up. In the 1980s, the Vancouver branch sponsored a series of programs on union ideas and what happened to them under the title "Put Some Pork On Your Fork," the Chicago Branch sponsored programs on subjects such as the fight for a shorter work week and union struggles in South Africa, and the Detroit/Ann Arbor Branch sponsored educationals on the struggles of Polish and Filipino workers and a well-attended May Day celebration featuring Wobbly musicians and veteran IWW organizer and soap-boxer Frank Cedervall. IWW members have long been the backbone of an ambitious series of May Day celebrations in Madison, Wisconsin, and beginning in the 1980s have done much to revive May Day activities across the continent.

Nor have efforts to build greater international solidarity taken a back seat. The IWW has always recognized that the working class is international. With the growing importance of transnational corporations enabling bosses to shift production from one continent to another to escape strikes and unions, the IWW issued a pamphlet, "World Labor Needs A Union," in the 1960s, and worked to strengthen its ties with like-minded unions around the world. IWW branches regularly picketed Spanish tourist offices and consulates in support of imprisoned members of the outlawed National Confederation of Labor (CNT) in the 1960s and 1970s. After Franco's death, the IWW cosponsored a 1976 tour by veteran European syndicalist Augustine Souchy to raise funds for the CNT, organized a 1978 tour of Canada and the United States by CNT organizer Miguel Mesa, and issued a special assessment to help the CNT re-establish itself at the end of the Franco regime.

The IWW's re-activated General Defense Committee worked on behalf of embattled class war prisoners around the world, including efforts to assist Latin American unionists faced with death squads by bringing pressure to bear on the companies that employed them, British miners who lost their jobs during the 1984-85 miners strike, Native American activists such as Leonard Peltier, and South African unionists facing treason charges. Small IWW branches were also re-established in Australia and England in the 1970s, which have continued to the present day. The IWW participated in a 1975 international conference hosted by Central Organization of Swedish Workers (SAC), organized a 1986 international labor conference in Chicago, and established a series of committees charged with coordinating international solidarity campaigns.

The IWW remained active on the cultural front as well. Wobbly artists across the country have produced posters suitable for art exhibitions as well as for plastering on local construction walls commemorating labor struggles, promoting the need for world labor solidarity, and suggesting that direct action is the only way for workers to stop the bosses from killing them on the job. Several musicians – particularly folksingers, but in more recent years also a number of punk and alternative bands – have carried IWW red cards, including Bruce "Utah" Phillips, who regales audiences with tales of the IWW's struggles and the need for workers to organize and dump the bosses off our backs. In 1976, IWW members picketed a popular Chicago nightclub, Kingston Mines, forcing it to pay Wobbly musicians their agreed-upon fee. That victory inspired many other musicians to look into the union. A 1976 Entertainment Workers conference launched an effort to organize the industry, preparing a standard contract for performers and gathering and disseminating information on bookings and conditions. These efforts failed to draw more than a handful of musicians into the IWW, but sparked similar efforts by groups such as Hey Rube! and Songs of Freedom And Struggle (SASSAFRAS).

While the IWW retained a strong base in the Detroit/Ann Arbor area, the 1980s proved more difficult organizing terrain elsewhere. A major campaign at the Sather Cookie Company in Round Lake, Minnesota, was abandoned after the UFCW intervened, persuading many workers that it had a better chance of winning a contract. In Houston, Arkansas, IWW members set up picket lines at Castle Industries mobile home manufacturing plants after management began firing union supporters, but were defeated. Fed up with long overtime, miserable wages, and their boss's promises that the job would get better "by-and-by," truck drivers at Keller Fish in East Northport, New York, joined the IWW in 1984. When the boss threatened to fire union supporters and to move out of state, if necessary, to avoid unionization, workers struck – quickly bringing business to a standstill. After trying to operate with scabs for several months (and seeing IWW pickets follow the scab fish to its final destination), Keller made good on his threats with the blessings of the NLRB.

In 1984, IWW organizers returned to central Washington's apple orchards, agitating over the indiscriminate use of pesticides, poor working conditions, and low pay. Organizers returned the next two years, nailing down better conditions and some pay increases but failing to gain a stable presence among the migratory (and increasingly immigrant) work force. In nearby Everson, an IWW campaign made some headway among a group of 60 workers at the Mount Baker Mushroom Farm. But the only organizing victory in the early 1980s was the organization of the People's Wherehouse workers in 1983.

The 1980s hit many workers hard, and several IWW branches set out to organize the unemployed. In Vancouver, British Columbia, IWW members helped turn out unemployed workers to bolster picket lines throughout the area, shut down a local job shark who was selling bogus job lists to the unemployed for as much as $50, and worked with the Organization of Unemployed Workers to launch a campaign for free bus service for the unemployed and those on fixed incomes. Hundreds of bus riders presented "UnFare Cards" during the summer of 1985 in lieu of paying, in a campaign that had tacit support from the drivers' union. (Earlier the Vancouver branch had received an enormous boost when local business union leaders called off a threatened general strike, placing their class collaboration out in the open for all to see. IWW branches in several cities carried out similar activities.) In South Carolina, local Wobblies prepared a pamphlet showing how a shorter work week would reduce unemployment, and was winnable to boot. Bellingham Wobs ran for several months (until they lost their space) in 1983 a soup kitchen and center for the unemployed, and issued a leaflet for the unemployed that was reprinted and distributed to unemployed workers across the country.

An old IWW motto holds that "In every strike the IWW is on the side of the workers." Wherever Wobblies are to be found, they have always been found on picket lines and organizing strike support. And there were plenty of strikes, and plenty of hard-pressed workers, to support in the 1980s. The newly formed Southeast Alaska General Membership Branch was active in forming a network of unions throughout the state for mutual aid and solidarity in 1984, and worked closely with dissidents working to reform the mob-ridden Laborers' union. In New York City, the IWW was especially active in assisting rank-and-file Teamsters confronted with corrupt or unresponsive officials to pursue their strikes and fight for union democracy. In an era when many branches found it increasingly difficult to organize workers into the IWW, and in which the labor movement was under wholesale attack, many branches focused their efforts on supporting broader workers' struggles, bolstering picket lines, and trying to encourage their fellow workers to recognize the fundamental principle than an injury to one is an injury to all.

In the meantime, a long series of defeated campaigns forced the IWW to confront the question of how it could function as a revolutionary industrial union in a labor relations regime designed to defuse workers' struggles and divert them into bureaucratized, legalistic channels. IWW members learned through decades of bitter experience that the National Labor Relations Board did not protect workers' rights in any meaningful way. Firings and harassment of union activists were illegal, but even where unions won an Unfair Labor Practice charge, the boss was only required to make token back pay payments and post a notice promising to respect workers' rights in the future. In the meantime, years had passed and union supporters had given up in despair.

More critically, the NLRB process left little room for direct action, for workers coming together to address their grievances, and unsuccessful campaigns often left vulnerable groups of union supporters in their wake who needed union support as much as they ever had. As early as 1973, *Industrial Worker* editor Patrick Murfin wrote of the need to return to "true unionism": "We may have to abandon certain practices and tactics which may be fine for business-union organizing but are out of place for a class-conscious union. Organize direct action on the job. You do not need a majority in all cases to act by example...

A union is a collectivity of workers moving together, not a bureaucracy or a piece of paper declaring legitimacy."[5]

Members continued to grapple with these issues in the years that followed, striving to develop an organizing strategy that could obtain immediate results while remaning true to IWW traditions. Convinced that the union's Industrial Organizing Committee – established a decade before – was too committed to an NLRB-centered approach and was increasingly operating as a faction within the union, IWW members voted to abolish it in 1984 and began discussions of alternative organizing strategies and conceptions of unionization that began to reshape the union's approach.

Although the union's 75th anniversary had passed with little fanfare, in 1985 the IWW marked its 80th anniversary with a travelling exhibit of IWW art curated by Wobbly artist and former *Industrial Worker* editor Carlos Cortez, the first in what has become a series of annual labor history calendars featuring Wobbly graphics and world labor dates, a West Coast conference on the IWW and alternative unionism held in Vancouver, and showings across the United States of the new documentary film "The Wobblies," accompanied by union literature and speakers. The anniversary was noted by articles in newspapers such as the *New York Times* and the *Wall Street Journal* and magazines around the world. The *Industrial Worker*'s editorial on the anniversary noted:

"The IWW is 80 years young this summer... Over the years many forces have attempted to destroy it. Bosses, trade-union bureaucrats, politicians of left and right; all have sought to prevent the IWW from achieving its goal of building one big union of the workers of the world. Yet the IWW has persisted... Why? Because there have been rebel workers who understand what the workers who attended that founding IWW congress in 1905 understood that only a united working class, conscious of its power and willing to use it, can emancipate itself, and all humanity, from the degradation and violence of wage slavery."[6]

Notes:

1. Leland Robinson, "Social Movement Organizations in Decline," Ph.D. Dissertation, Northwestern University, 1974.

2. In the 1960s, the IWW began chartering General Membership Branches directly rather than through the General Recruiting Union, which was formally abolished by referendum in 1968. The GMBs quickly became the union's primary organizational form, although a handful of industrial union branches were organized in the 1970s (and more in later decades) as conditions allowed.

3. Arthur J. Miller discusses this campaign of repression in his unpublished memoir, excerpts from which were published in *Anarcho-Syndicalist Review* #42/43, 2005; extensive documents have been released by the FBI under the Freedom of Information Act documenting its role in the vigilante campaign.

4. The Virden campaign was covered on a monthly basis in the *Industrial Worker.* Also see Mike Hargis' account in *Nothing in Common,* and his "IWW Organizing in the 1970s."

5. Patrick Murfin, "What's Wrong with Unionism?" *Industrial Worker,* September 1973, pages 1, 4.

6. Mike Hargis, "Now More than Ever," *Industrial Worker,* June 1985, p. 2.

General Sources:

This chapter draws primarily upon *Industrial Worker* and *General Organization Bulletin* reports, Patrick Murfin's account of the 1955-1975 period in *The IWW: Its First 70 Years,* and on two articles from the *Libertarian Labor Review:* Mike Hargis, "IWW Organizing in the 1970s," *LLR* 16 (1994), pp. 15-17, and Mark Kaufmann, "A Short History of IWW Organizing in Ann Arbor 1981-1989," *LLR* 14 (1992), pp. 25-29. Oral histories in John Silvano's *Nothing in Common* (Cedar, 1999) discuss the Three Penny, International Wood Products, Kentucky Fried Chicken, Mid-American Metal Machinery, University Cellar and Keller Fish strikes. An as-yet unpublished memoir by IWW organizer Arthur J. Miller is the best source for information on organizing in San Diego and Long Beach in the late 1960s and early 1970s. Excerpts were published as "Rebuilding the IWW in the 1970s" in *Anarcho-Syndicalist Review* #42/43, 2005, pp. 48-52.

15. Solidarity Unionism

The IWW's largest organized shop, the University Cellar (which operated two bookstores and a warehouse near the University of Michigan), went out of business in 1986 due to bloated management and its bank's sudden refusal to renew its line of credit, costing 80 workers their jobs and the IWW its strongest evidence that workers organized into the IWW could win real gains. Although the smaller Ypsilanti-based People's Wherehouse remained an IWW shop for another six years (until it was closed by new owners in 1992), the loss of the Cellar was a major blow to the IWW in the Midwest. Southeast Michigan Wobblies continued organizing, signing up a majority of workers at a local print shop (but ultimately failing to secure an agreement) and the staff of the Ann Arbor Tenants Union, but increasingly focused their efforts on supporting other unions' struggles – most notably the Detroit newspaper strike, for which Detroit Wobblies (working with other rank-and-file unionists) launched a traveling soup kitchen that continues to support strikes and other labor efforts to this day.

IWW members continued organizing across the United States in the late 1980s and 1990s, primarily in smaller shops that were of little interest to the business unions, and had some successes. In 1989, the IWW organized the workers who pick up recycling materials from Berkeley, California, curbs, adding the predominantly immigrant workers who sort and bundle the city's recyclables in 2001. Both shops remain under IWW contract today, and were recently joined by recyclers in Austin, Texas. The IWW also had some short-lived success organizing paid canvassers and telemarketers for various non-profit organizations, especially in the Pacific Northwest. However, some of these employers proved as ruthless as any capitalist outfit. When Seattle Greenpeace phone canvassers joined the IWW in June 1988 in response to management plans to install monitoring equipment, Greenpeace responded by firing them all and closing the office. In Oregon, SANE and Oregon Fair Share recognized the IWW a few months later, but the high turn-over typical of the industry meant that the job branch did not survive into the 1990s.

The IWW also continued to be active in broader social movements throughout the era, working to bridge the chasm that increasingly divided workers from activists who should have been their natural allies. In addition to walking picket lines with increasingly embattled workers across North America, and joining in the rank-and-file anti-concessions movement that unsuccessfully tried to persuade unions to organize effective resistance, IWW members were always to be found at demonstrations against U.S. military involvement in Central America, the build-up of the military machine, and the full-scale assault against social welfare programs and the environment that characterized the Carter-Reagan era. Earth First! activist Judi Bari (a union activist who had become increasingly focused on environmental issues since moving to California's redwood forests) joined the IWW in 1987, seeking a way to overcome the deep divisions between environmentalists and workers in the timber industry that enabled the lumber barons to destroy the Northern California redwoods at the same time that they destroyed timber workers' jobs – both in the immediate sense, by shipping timber overseas for processing, and in the long run by clear-cutting forests without any thought to long-term sustainability. The IWW helped several workers seek compensation from Georgia Pacific Lumber over a PCB spill at their Fort Bragg mill, and fellow workers Gene Lawhorn and Judi Bari persuaded Earth First! to renounce tree spiking (driving nails into trees in order to make them unmillable) because it posed too great a hazard to workers' safety. Although the campaign never signed up a significant number of timber workers, it did help workers press complaints over unsafe working conditions and defused tensions in some forest communities by encouraging workers and environmentalists to talk with each other.

In 1990, Wobblies and environmental activists launched Redwood Summer, a direct action campaign that aimed to stop the clear cutting of old-growth redwood forests and force the industry to consider sustainable forestry practices. As the campaign was picking up steam, a bomb ripped through a car in which organizers Judi Bari and Darryl Cherney were traveling to a meeting, shattering Bari's pelvis. Rather than investigate the bombing, FBI agents arrested the two, chaining Bari to her hospital bed, and charged them with transporting the bomb that blew them up despite evidence of a string of death threats against Bari, and physical evidence proving that the bomb, designed to be set off by motion, had been hidden under the car seat on which Bari was sitting. The IWW helped organize a wave of international protests, and prosecutors were forced to abandon those charges. However, they never mounted a serious investigation into the bombing; a dozen years

San Francisco Wobblies picketing the End Up bar, which locked out IWW janitors in 1992 when they sought union recognition.

later, in June 2002, a federal jury ordered the FBI and Oakland police to pay $4.4 million in damages to Bari (who had since died of cancer many believe was triggered by her injuries) and Cherney. The Redwood Summer campaign continued despite the bombings, but while some stands of trees were saved, the bombing and subsequent lawsuit diverted attention from the sustained organizing needed among timber workers and a promising start at building a worker-led campaign to save the redwoods languished.[1]

The IWW also entered into an ill-fated attempt to organize prison labor at the Southwest Ohio Correctional Facility, where hundreds of prisoners were employed under sweatshop conditions and imprisoned in even more brutal conditions. The union was first contacted by inmates at the prison in 1985. Despite officials' attempts to bar the *Industrial Worker* and other union literature from the prison, 400 prison laborers ultimately signed petitions seeking IWW representation. However, prison authorities and the Ohio Labor Board refused to recognize that the prisoners were state employees in 1987, rejecting their request for union recognition and disciplining several IWW supporters. A few years later, the prison's brutal conditions led to an uprising in which inmates seized control of the institution for several days.[2]

Meanwhile, the IWW was encountering growing administrative difficulties. It was becoming increasingly difficult to find members willing to move to Chicago to serve as General Secretary-Treasurer, and an ambitious plan to build more general membership branches launched in the aftermath of the University Cellar closing proved controversial, expensive, and unsuccessful. A bitter struggle developed between the General Executive Board majority and the General Secretary-Treasurer, which ended in 1990 with the expulsion of the GEB chair (who had refused to countersign checks for rent and other operating expenses in an attempt to force the GST to cede more financial control to the Board) and a divided union. In 1991, the IWW moved its headquarters from Chicago for the first time since the union was formed. San Francisco became the site of General Headquarters for the next four years (then moving to Ypsilanti, Michigan, in 2000 to Philadelphia, and in 2006 to Cincinnati). The IWW ran substantial deficits throughout this period, running through substantial bequests received from long-time members in the mid-1980s and ultimately building up debts of some $13,000 before headquarters was relocated to Philadelphia in January 2000, in part to stem the tide of red ink and put the union on a firmer financial footing.

The San Francisco General Membership Branch was in 1991 one of the union's largest and most active, and the Redwood Summer campaign had inspired many West Coast Wobblies to launch organizing drives in their own workplaces, as well as the formation of a San Francisco-based Temp Workers Union which attempted to set up an IWW hiring hall to dump the parasites, but was unable to persuade even "progressive" agencies to break with the job sharks.

The 1990s saw a steady stream of IWW organizing drives, most of which continued to follow the model of seeking formal recognition (generally through NLRB elections) and then negotiating with the boss for a contract that would bring improved conditions – a model that grew increasingly controversial within the union as members experienced its limitations first-hand. In 1992, IWW janitors were locked-out by a San Francisco gay bar, the End Up, after demanding union recognition, prompting months of picketing that ended only after management agreed to a substantial back pay settlement. Across the country, in Allentown, Pennsylvania, Wobblies came across workers picketing outside Boulevard Bingo and offered support. The workers quickly joined the IWW and, after months of struggle (including an unsuccessful libel suit filed against IWW organizer Lenny Flank for a press release noting that the NLRB was issuing unfair labor practice charges against the bingo operators), won a contract in July 1993 providing $25,000 in back pay, union recognition, and other gains. Financially crippled by the struggle, management reneged on the agreement and closed the operation down a year later.[3]

In 1993, Wobblies in Philadelphia and Santa Cruz launched the Kinko's Co-worker/Duplication Workers Network, which published a newsletter that was faxed to Kinko's stores in the middle of the night (when managers were less likely to be around to intercept it) and established a union presence in several Kinko's outlets, but was ultimately unable to develop solid committees in more than a few stores and so could not develop the strength to sustain the company-wide campaign these workers recognized would be needed to win real gains. In Los Angeles, a revived IWW branch organized Aaron Records in 1993, but lost an NLRB election to the typical employer intimidation. The branch also organized workers at K-Jack Engineering, a manufacturer of newspaper vending machines which employed a predominantly immigrant work force, resulting in 1996 in a strike over unpaid wages that pried some funds loose but was unable to establish a lasting presence on the job. That year was a busy one for the IWW, with a strike against a small Kensington, California computer firm, Memory USA; a campaign at a Philadelphia Sears outlet that was crushed when the company fired IWW agitator Michelle Heim; an organizing campaign at two Wherehouse Entertainment outlets in northern California which won a majority at an El Cerrito store, only to be defeated by the firing of two IWW supporters and drastic cuts in work hours for the survivors; a strike by ASUC-Berkeley recycling workers in solidarity with striking teaching assistants at the campus; and a 150-day strike against Seattle's Lincoln Park Mini-Mart that ended Feb. 22, 1997, with an NLRB settlement that did not return workers to their jobs.

The most prominent of these campaigns was the Philadelphia GMB's effort to organize a Borders Books outlet that gained majority support among workers, but ultimately not enough to survive management's anti-union campaign. After the IWW was narrowly defeated in a March 1996 NLRB election, management began harassing union supporters at that store and at others where the IWW had supporters. When IWW organizing committee member Miriam Fried was fired in

IWW members outside the Center City Philadelphia store where Miriam Fried (2nd from left) was fired in a bid to crush IWW organizing efforts.

June despite glowing evaluations, Wobblies began picketing Borders stores across the country – and ultimately around the world. The first picket lines went up in Boston and Philadelphia two days after the firing; by week's end IWW branches across the United States were following suit. When Borders expanded its operations to Australia and England, IWW members in those countries organized a proper reception. Dozens of Borders stores were targeted – some on a daily basis – and while Borders refused to reinstate Fellow Worker Fried, it did back off on its harassment of union supporters around the country, leading to a number of temporarily successful campaigns by the UFCW (which currently has one Borders store under contract).[4] Chicago Wobblies, who had earlier tried to organize the local Barbara's Bookstore chain, set up an organizing committee at a local Borders but were raided by the UFCW, which won an NLRB election and a first contract, but did not survive to a second.

The picketing was the IWW's first coordinated large-scale campaign in several decades, culminating in a June 15, 1997, day of action that saw picket lines and other actions at several Borders outlets across the United States. The campaign used the IWW's developing online presence to distribute leaflets, plan coordinated picketing and other actions, and post the complete text of Borders' confidential union-busting manual, leaked to the IWW by a sympathetic worker. When the campaign began, Borders and rival Barnes & Noble were neck and neck in their struggle to dominate the retail book industry, and industry analysts generally regarded Borders as the more promising firm. But while it was unable to build a strong shop-floor presence, the IWW campaign irreparably damaged the company's reputation, and relegated Borders to a distant second place from which it has never recovered.

Wobblies were looking for ways to break out of the small, single-shop campaigns that characterized most IWW organizing in the 1970s and 1980s. Most of those campaigns had implicitly accepted an NLRB-style of unionism that relied on winning union recognition and then negotiating a formal contract for better conditions. IWW members were increasingly dissatisfied with this approach as it became clear that the National Labor Relations Act gave workers few meaningful protections, enabled employers to drag organizing campaigns out for years, and left workers who had built substantial support among their coworkers – but not enough to win recognition or a contract – with no way to defend their interests or to function as a union. Similar complaints were increasingly prominent even in the AFL-CIO, but the challenges the bureaucratized, legalistic NLRB process posed to an avowedly revolutionary union with few resources practically guaranteed that determined employers would be able to avoid unionization. For some time the IWW had been looking for alternative approaches. In May 1988 the General Executive Board approved a new edition of the *IWW Organizing Manual* that emphasized building job branches and workplace campaigns over NLRB certification; however, the *Manual* proved controversial and was withdrawn the next year. The union was without an official organizing manual for the next several years, until a new manual was developed in 1995 through union-wide discussions that stressed the need to build permanent job branches that would act union even in the absence of management recognition or majority status.

The union also began a number of attempts to build functioning industrial unions, in sectors ranging from construction to education.

Construction workers built a strong presence, publishing a column in the *Industrial Worker* in the late 1990s and building a network of rank-and-file militants in the electricians' union (particularly among the workers who traveled between major jobs) that organized job actions that gave both the bosses and the union piecards conniptions. On August 12, 1997, Wobblies led 300 workers in walking off the job in Butte, Montana, to bolster picket lines at a nearby UPS depot; this was one of a series of actions through which workers on the job – most "tramp electricians" brought in from out of town to work at below-scale wages negotiated under special "presidential" agreements meant to encourage contractors to use union work – sought to enforce union conditions and a spirit of solidarity on the job. Carpenters and others in the almost entirely nonunion residential sector explored the possibilities of establishing a union foothold in a sector characterized by cut-throat competition and fly-by-night contractors. And IWW members worked with immigrant construction workers in Austin, Texas, and Phoenix, Arizona, who were attempting to collect unpaid wages after the subcontractors who hired them skipped town – picketing open houses until the developers were forced to come through with the money.

In July 1998, construction workers in Sedro Wooley, Washington, launched a campaign at a Skagit Pacific plant that built modular housing, waging safety actions and building an organizing committee that reached majority support before management laid off the entire night shift (where union supporters were concentrated), demoralizing the surviving workers and forcing most members of the organizing committee to leave town in search of work. In May 1999, IWW members working at JeffBoat's Ohio River barge-building facility began agitating around unsafe working conditions. While the yard was officially represented by the Teamsters, that union had little presence on the job aside from its payroll deductions, and many workers found the IWW group's direct action tactics attractive. Wobblies and other workers participated in dozens of job actions, mostly over unsafe conditions, in the months leading up to negotiations for a new contract. When Teamsters leaders announced that a contract workers had voted down was going to be implemented for a year anyway, IWW members threw up an impromptu picket line April 30, 2001, pulling 800 workers out in a five-day wildcat strike that quickly shut down the shipyard. However, workers were unable to get management to negotiate, and ultimately agreed to return to work. Unfortunately, the IWW group was unable to build on the strike – management reasserted its control over working conditions and soon no Wobblies were left on the job. And in January 2002, the Hull (England) branch launched an organizing campaign among the area's 2,000-odd caravan (house trailer) builders, signing up dozens of members before the IWW campaign forced the union that had formal representation rights to begin addressing workers' concerns.

The 1990s also saw a sustained effort to build an industrial union in education, an industry where growing numbers of IWW members were employed. In a forerunner to this campaign, the IWW organized workers at a private residential school in Pittsfield, Massachusetts, in 1987, but was unable to survive staff turn-over to establish a lasting presence. Recycling workers at the University of California at Berkeley established an IWW job branch in 1989 that lasted for several years (and was the only union on campus to honor picket lines thrown up by teaching assistants when they struck for union recognition in November 1996), but were never able to gain recognition. Several workers at New College in San Francisco joined the IWW in 1991 after administrators proposed pay cuts, but the job branch collapsed when workers at the college's labor library, where IWW support was strongest, were fired. IWW members were also active in efforts to organize teaching assistants at several colleges, publishing newsletters and organizing committees that helped build union sentiment but did not lead to successful IWW campaigns. At the University of Wisconsin, Madison Wobblies organized the staff of the UW Greens Infoshop, a campus-based information and resource center that remains an IWW shop to this day despite having been forced off campus. Wobblies also worked with student workers at a Job Corps Center in Drums, Pennsylvania, who were being trained for jobs in fast food, security and telemarketing, and who worked on the center grounds as well as being leased out to local businesses. They were organizing against unsafe conditions and abusive treatment in the privately operated but government-funded residential program. (In addition to Job Corps facilities, the company also operated private prisons.) Officials routinely searched students for union literature, forcing organizers to resort to a pirate radio station and silent agitators smuggled onto the grounds. The campaign collapsed after Job Corps terminated every IWW supporter they were able to identify, and the various government agencies charged with protecting workers' rights each declined jurisdiction. An Education Workers Industrial Union Network was launched in 1991, publishing a newsletter and organizing literature for several years and working to build a stronger IWW presence in the industry. In 1997 – when the IWW had job control at the UC Berkeley recycling operation, and job branches at Stevenson College in Edinburgh and the University of Hawaii – Wobblies working in the education industry sought a charter for what would have been the union's first Industrial Union administration since the 1950s, but the General Executive Board failed to act on the petition, and soon afterwards IWW members approved a constitutional amendment raising the standards required to charter industrial unions. In Boston, an Education Workers Industrial Union Branch was chartered in 1999, and (in addition to walking picket lines in solidarity with Tufts University janitors whose jobs were subcontracted out with the connivance of the SEIU local that "represented" both them and the lower-wage subcontractor) joined with other activists in a citywide campaign to organize thousands of part-time faculty in area colleges. While the IWW was unable to establish any job branches, the campaign forced several colleges to raise pay rates and hundreds of teachers won health benefits. The IWW also participated in national conferences of the Coalition of Contingent Academic Labor, sharing equal billing on a plenary on organizing strategy with representatives of the American Association of University Professors, the American Federation of Teachers and the National Education Association, among other unions organizing in the industry, at its national conference in Boston.

In the British Isles, the IWW waged an unsuccessful campaign against privatization of research councils in 1994, and established an industrial union branch at Edinburgh's Stevenson College that, while never large, was for a couple of years able to bring together staff across a wide range of job categories, from cleaning staff to faculty, and to turn back threatened lay-offs by collecting pledges to strike if anyone's job was eliminated. At Pitzer College, in California, the IWW signed up more than a third of the faculty in 1999, but was unable to break through to majority status or to develop a stable job branch able to function as a minority union. San Francisco State University twice fired the entire staff of its Recycling Resource Center when they joined the IWW and demanded union recognition. Other education campaigns were waged in Colorado, Hawaii and Vermont; at Carleton

University, in Ottawa, the IWW organized a unit of projectionists in 2003, but a campaign among cafeteria workers there was defeated when management of the privatized facility fired union activists after a short solidarity strike.

A less successful campaign among maritime workers on the West Coast saw Wobblies join with rank-and-file activists in the International Longshore & Warehouse Union in an attempt to organize the thousands of workers working cargo as daily ("casual") hires, but not eligible for union membership.

In the San Francisco Bay ports, Wobblies organized health and safety trainings and, while not signing up large numbers of workers, re-established a reputation on the waterfront that proved valuable in later solidarity actions. When the Neptune Jade, a ship loaded by workers scabbing on locked-out Liverpool dock workers, tried to unload its cargo in Oakland, California, IWW members were a prominent part of the picket line that went up in the predawn hours of Sept. 28, 1997. Longshoremen honored that picket line for four days, before the ship pulled up anchor and headed to Vancouver and finally Japan – its scab cargo still in the holds when it was sold as scrap. (The Liverpool/Mersey dockers' struggle sparked rank-and-file solidarity actions at ports around the world, and was the subject of monthly reports in the *Industrial Worker*.) In the mid-1990s, Wobblies signed up workers on a few West Coast fishing vessels and, working with workers in the ports, made contact with workers on foreign-owned ships provisioning along the Alaskan and Washington coast. Hundreds of pieces of IWW literature were distributed; on one vessel workers responded with a "tired strike" which won shorter work shifts and other gains, but this campaign was limited by a shortage of literature and organizers able to communicate with workers in an increasingly polyglot maritime labor force.

In December 1999, IWW members threw a picket line up on a Tacoma, Washington, pier, stopping the unloading of a shipment of ore to a struck Kaiser steel mill. In a coordinated action, Earth First!ers occupied a crane for the day, dropping a banner linking Kaiser's union-busting and environmental despoliation. The action was symbolic, and the scab-destined ore was unloaded off the Sea Diamond the next day, but it nonetheless offered workers concrete evidence of other possibilities.

Another area where the IWW enjoyed some success was in the so-

Wobblies joined other labor activists picketing the Neptune Jade in solidarity with Liverpool dockers. Here, they trample copies of an anti-picketing injunction underfoot as they keep the ship tied up.   photo © David Bacon

cial service sector, where many agencies were balancing tight budgets on the backs of their workers. In 1997, the IWW successfully organized the building service staff of the Friends Center in Philadelphia, a facility housing the headquarters of the American Friends Service Committee, a child care center, a Quaker meeting house and other programs. Like many employers that present a progressive face to the public, the Friends Center proved extremely resistant to unionization, firing an IWW member during the campaign for union recognition, and dragging out negotiations for an agreement (that eliminated severe wage inequities, provided some health care benefits for part-timers, as well as giving staff more control over their scheduling) for some 18 months before finally settling. In later negotiations, workers successfully demanded the bosses keep their attorney away in order to keep talks moving.

Workers at a youth drop-in center in Venice, Florida, also went IWW in 1997, but the center's funding dried up and it was unable to continue. In February 2000 the staff of the Seattle Tenants Union lined up with the IWW, joining a long-time unit at the Ann Arbor

Tenants Union in a struggle both for better working conditions and to preserve programs that provided vital services to our fellow workers. In Melbourne, Australia, Wobblies began a continuing campaign for better conditions for street sellers of *The Big Issue*, a paper ostensibly published to benefit the homeless but which refused to provide its homeless sales staff with adequate facilities.

In Portland, Oregon, the union built majority support at social service programs run by Janus Youth Programs, the Portland Women's Crisis Line, and the Salvation Army, though the Salvation Army sky pilots quickly closed the fully funded program rather than deal with organized workers. Organizing began in 2000 at Janus, a nonprofit publicly funded outfit that operates shelters and other programs for troubled youths and their families, with a majority of workers at its Harry's Mother facility joining the next year. Wobblies used staff meetings to resolve many grievances and successfully turned back the firing (the bosses claimed these were lay-offs due to financial problems) of three union supporters through community pressure and picketing. Workers were seeking safer conditions, a say in management (the agency was steadily losing county contracts due at least in part to poor decisions), and equal pay with the county-employed agencies that referred clients to Janus and paid their workers $1.75 more an hour. By June 2001, the IWW had won recognition at four of Janus' 12 units, although agreements were reached at only two after a series of short strikes and other job actions. In October 2001, Harry's Mother workers won a series of 50 cent pay raises that narrowed shift differentials while raising pay as much as 35 percent for some workers, as well as strong language protecting workers' rights. Despite setbacks, including the death of IWW delegate Sarah Bishop in a hiking accident, the IWW continues to represent Janus workers and is working to build a union presence at other social service agencies in the region.

Staff at the Portland Women's Crisis Line won union recognition in Fall 2003, largely in response to the agency's move toward a more "professional," less grassroots, organizational structure. After a new manager was brought in, the Crisis Line workers negotiated a contract providing for a more democratic workplace, a voice in hiring decisions (including of managers), pro-rated benefits for part-time workers, and more time off, among other gains. The success of these campaigns prompted a local union-busting law firm to run an article in their newsletter warning, "The Wobblies Are Back."

In February 2003, the Boston branch won a unanimous union recognition election at a Dare Family Services unit that provided residential and support services for mentally retarded adults, successfully turning back the threatened firing of some workers and ridding the facility of a despised and incompetent manager. However, contract negotiations dragged on for nearly two years as Dare's highly paid union-busting attorney spent several sessions over the union recognition clause (she wanted the union to agree that Dare could replace union workers with nonunion staff at any time), and Boston Wobblies were unable to integrate the job branch into the union or to organize the sort of community campaign needed to pressure DARE to bargain in good faith. Frustrated by the endless talks, and with their major grievance resolved, management was able to exploit divisions among workers and persuade a majority to withdraw from the IWW in November 2004.

Each of these agencies was ostensibly independent, but received the bulk of their funding from county and state contracts as part of an ongoing process of privatizing social services. Workers in these operations are hard-squeezed, with management insisting it can't afford to pay better under its funding contracts and the funders insisting they have no control over the agencies. As social service funding continues to be cut back and privatized, workers find themselves hard pressed to preserve services with fewer workers and less support. Unionization in this sector is badly needed, but given the contract-based nature of most of these jobs it can be difficult to win substantial gains without organizing the entire sector.

Wobblies also waged a difficult struggle to win basic labor rights for "organizers" employed by the Association of Community Organizations for Reform Now and its subsidiaries – an ostensibly pro-labor outfit that requires workers to put in 55 hours or more a week in dangerous conditions and once went to court seeking the right to pay less than the minimum wage. ACORN fired IWW members in Dallas, Philadelphia (where workers struck February 8, 2001, over ACORN's treatment of union workers), Portland, Seattle (a February 26 strike turned into a lock-out when ACORN imported scabs from around the country rather than allow its workers to return), and at an ACORN Housing office in Houston, where a Wobbly was fired in May 2003 after organizing a strike against unsafe working conditions.[5] ACORN settled a number of unfair labor practice charges as a result of its vicious union-busting, and substantially raised pay for its staff across the country in order to bring its operations into compliance with minimum wage laws, but refused to bring back union workers or to negotiate with its workers (most of whom quickly flee the operation rather than be subjected to ACORN's abusive treatment). Similarly, the British social research agency SMSR fired all workers who refused to resign their IWW membership in January 2003.

While many social service agencies have proved as ruthless as any capitalist employer in fighting workers' efforts to organize, often trading on their social mission to persuade workers to endure conditions that no one would tolerate from a traditional boss, the IWW continues to score some successes in this arena. Headquarters staff at the Women's International League for Peace and Freedom were in the process of finalizing a union contract as the IWW celebrated its 100th anniversary. In 2003, members of the independent Staff Organizers Union of Pennsylvania, which represented American Federation of Teachers organizers, affiliated with the IWW, joining the staff of a Western Massachusetts United Auto Workers local (representing childcare workers, graduate employees at the University of Massachusetts, and a number of small shops) who had joined the IWW two years before. The SOUP branch later collapsed when the AFT decided to pull out of its campaign at Pennsylvania State University and withdrew resources from a much stronger campaign at the University of Pennsylvania after the NLRB overturned earlier rulings that graduate employees were entitled to union representation. The UAW-represented workers were state employees, and so not affected by the ruling, and workers there continue to lend support to other IWW organizing in the region as well as to the struggle to improve their own working conditions.

Workers at the Colorado-based Free Speech TV network, distributed over cable and satellite services, joined the IWW in 2003, entering into prolonged, but ultimately successful, negotiations for an agreement with their employer and also giving a boost to local organizing and solidarity efforts. In Austin, Texas, workers at Ecology Action joined the IWW in 2004, joining with IWW recycling workers in Berkeley four years after management broke an earlier IWW drive by firing union activists, and three years after the remaining workers got rid of their boss and took control over their scheduling.

Wobblies in the computer industry set out to build a union presence as the industry was getting off the ground. In 1993, the IWW was the second union to establish a presence on the web, as a result of the initiative of members of the San Francisco General Membership Branch. The initial web site quickly exploded into a network of rank-and-file servers, email lists and bulletin boards, giving the IWW a vibrant but sometimes quirky online presence. But while online discussions could sometimes grow heated, and conflicts often developed in the early years between advocates of open systems and those concerned with how the union might be perceived, iww.org's email lists proved indispensable in developing coordinated campaigns against national chains. When word went out over one IWW email list of Borders' firing of IWW activist Miriam Fried, picket lines quickly went up in Boston and Honolulu – sparking a union-wide campaign that spread even as Philadelphia Wobblies were meeting to develop a coordinated response. These servers relied on a core of computer-savvy volunteers to set them up and keep them running, and after a few years the IWW began consolidating its online presence in an effort to provide more reliable service and better accountability to the union as a whole. In 2005, the IWW members who maintain iww.org upgraded the IWW web sites to a dynamic, open-source content management system, placing the IWW sites technologically far ahead of most mainstream business unions.

Several computer programmers and other computer workers joined the IWW; some independent consultants who provide unions and other movement organizations with computer services, others workers who tired of the long hours (followed by long bouts of unemployment) and empty promises that too often characterize the industry. San Francisco Bay area workers formed a telecommunications and computer workers industrial union branch in 1996, and Oregon Wobblies built a solid presence among computer workers that enabled them to offer online organizing support as well as to tackle abusive employers. The IWW won recognition and a union contract at Eugene Free Net, a community-based internet service provider, in December 2002, but two years later EFN collapsed after years of skimping on technical support, transferring its remaining services to the local public utility district. In Portland, workers at a software development collective, Revolt Ltd., and a computer recycling non-profit, FreeGeek, joined the IWW, forming the backbone of an IWW organizing campaign in the industry.

In 2003, Communications, Telecommunications and Computer

Workers IU 560 members began a two-year-long (and counting) campaign to force software firm RedcellX and its owner, Troy Melquist, to pay its workers, after two Wobblies were "paid" with rubber checks. An 18-member IWW delegation confronted the deadbeat boss, getting several hundred dollars in cash out of him toward their wages, but leaving thousands of dollars unpaid. Since then, Wobblies have been pursuing this deadbeat, who has jumped from office to office in an attempt to hide from the IWW.

Although the IWW has been organizing retail outlets for decades, the mid-1990s also saw attempts to build more strategic campaigns in this sector that are beginning to have success. In response to the dramatic growth of the natural foods sector, increasingly dominated by two national chains but which is also attracting interest from the supermarket chains, IWW members have launched several campaigns to unionize this almost entirely unorganized section of a retail food industry that was once a union stronghold. The IWW has attempted to organize natural groceries in Austin, Texas; Cambridge, Massachusetts; Cincinnati, Ohio; Greensboro, North Carolina; Montpelier, Vermont; Philadelphia; Pittsburgh; Portland, Oregon; San Francisco; Santa Cruz, California; Seattle; England; and Winnipeg, Manitoba, where the IWW won certification at Harvest Collective in 1998 – the first IWW branch certified in Canada since 1919 – only to see the store closed the next year; when it re-opened as Organza Foods the new management refused to rehire any Wobblies. Edmonton Wobblies launched a living wage campaign in the late 1990s, assisting temporary workers at Statistics Canada, and campaigning along the city's popular Whyte Street retail/restaurant corridor. And the IWW took over sponsorship of the popular retailworker.com web site in summer 2003, setting up dozens of online forums where workers can discuss working conditions and seek help in organizing to address them.

In 1999, a majority of workers at Deep Roots Market in Greensboro, North Carolina, requested union recognition, but were unable to survive high turnover and the harassment of union supporters. The Seattle IWW organized clerical and support staff (the UFCW represents retail clerks and deli workers) at Madison Market in 2001, winning substantial pay hikes, health benefits and a grievance procedure after a year-long campaign that built substantial community support. That shop remains under IWW contract, providing an important West Coast anchor to IWW efforts in the retail sector. British Wobblies launched a

The IWW's South Street Workers Union marching down South Street in Philadelphia during its campaign to defend mass transit.

newsletter, *Shopfloor*, in 2001 targeting retail workers, building upon their initial success building a job branch at a Pioneer Co-op outlet (the granddaddy of the consumer cooperative movement). In Cincinnati, Ohio, the IWW was unable to prevent new owners from closing the Twin Pines natural foods distribution center, but aggressive picketing (including support from Albany, New York, members who picketed the new owners' operations there) won a much improved severance package in November 2002. Local efforts to organize the natural foods sector continued, with the IWW building strong support at a Wild Oats outlet before managers fired delegate Tom Kappas July 10, 2004, in an attempt to squelch the organizing – touching off a series of picket lines in Cincinnati and Wild Oats headquarters and stores in Colorado, and a NLRB unfair labor practice charge which is dragging through the Board's interminable process.

Nutraceutical Intl. closed a Real Food natural grocery store in San Francisco August 29, 2003, laying off 30 workers at its only profitable store in the midst of an IWW organizing drive. Two union supporters had earlier been fired for "bad attitudes." The closure, allegedly for remodeling (the NLRB upheld unfair labor practice charges that this was a mere pretext), was so sudden that workers learned of it only at closing time the night before, and newly received shipments of dairy and produce had to be tossed in the dumpster. The San Francisco Bay branch won a union agreement at Berkeley fabric store Stonemountain & Daughter in 2004, but was unable to persuade the East Bay Depot for Creative Reuse to engage in substantive negotiations despite winning an NLRB election. Instead, Depot management laid off and fired IWW supporters and harassed others into quitting, successfully destroying the union majority and plunging the Depot (which collected and resold building and other materials to artists) into a deep financial crisis.

In Portland, the IWW won recognition at the locally owned Daily Grind natural grocery but was unable to win an agreement – the owner soon closed the department where union support was strongest – and was defeated in a bitter NLRB election campaign at a Wild Oats-owned Nature's Northwest store, leading Portland Wobs to refocus their efforts on building the strong shop-floor presence which had previously won many gains. In Austin, Texas, Wobblies began picketing the FreshPlus grocery store in January 2005, after managers fired an IWW member for union organizing. Another worker was fired for briefly joining the picket line during her break, intimidating the remaining union supporters and forcing the IWW to file unfair labor practice charges with the NLRB, accompanied by continued actions at the store.

In Philadelphia, the General Membership Branch launched a campaign to organize the busy South Street corridor (a hip retail and restaurant strip) in Fall 2003, quickly establishing a strong committee in a Whole Foods store that despite pretensions to "team" spirit and cooperation, and wages somewhat better than much of the strip, is in fact ruled by managers as arbitrary and ruthless (and inept) as one could find in any grocery chain. In one early action, produce team members surrounded a manager who had been harassing a Filipino worker who had taken time off for an injury, demanding that he be returned to full-time status. When the boss explained that the budget didn't allow it, the workers offered to chip in an hour or two each, calling her bluff. This and several other direct action campaigns won many improvements, but also led management to dredge up long-forgotten absences and work rules in search of excuses to fire union supporters. Two years later, the IWW is still on the job, still holding the bosses' feet to the fire, even if many workers have been forced to seek other jobs. A district-wide grievance committee has helped workers who were being forced to work unpaid hours at the end of their shift; assisted a worker forced from her job by her boss's sexual harassment and assault; helped workers at several stores facing discipline and firings; and regularly canvasses the corridor speaking to workers about their rights. The IWW-affiliated South Street Workers Union has also organized health and tax clinics, and successfully pressured 97 corridor employers to sign on to a union letter protesting plans to slash mass transit funding (the letters were delivered to a state legislator after a spirited march down South Street on a busy Sunday afternoon). The success of this campaign encouraged the Montpelier (Vermont) Workers Union to switch its affiliation to the IWW in summer 2005, and has encouraged other IWW branches to explore the possibilities for similar campaigns in their areas. Furthest along as 2005 drew to a close was a campaign by Madison, Wisconson, Wobblies to organize the small shops and restaurants that dominate their downtown area.

Wobblies also made several forays into the restaurant industry, including a 1998 sit-down strike at Portland's Mallory Hotel; the organization three years later of a Godfather's Pizza outlet in Portland that closed almost immediately after workers demanded union recognition; and picket lines in winter 2003 at a Winnipeg café that fired an IWW member for organizing. Portland Woblies also supported four workers at Candula Café fired for striking against a pay cut in July 2004, sparking angry advertisements from the owner who apparently believed his "radical" politics gave him the right to abuse his workers.

In Hobe Sound, Florida, IWW members began regular picketing outside a local pizzeria in August 2004 in solidarity with workers whose paychecks were being withheld under the pretext that their cash drawers were short, drawing as many as 40 residents outraged by the abuse of these workers. In February 2005, Olympia Wobblies joined pizza workers on the picket line to support a strike called over worsening working conditions and the firing of two workers. The owner refused to negotiate, instead closing the shop down and later selling it to new owners who also refused to deal with the workers.

New York City Wobblies drew extensive attention for organizing at a Manhattan Starbucks against low wages, arbitrary scheduling and unsafe working conditions that caused many repetitive motion injuries. The New York branch withdrew its petition for a NLRB election after the national board decided to stall the election while it considered Starbucks' argument for a regional (rather than single-store) bar-

Stockton, California, truck drivers, meeting during their strike against Kach Trucking, February 2005.

gaining unit. However, organizing continues, with the union lining up a majority at three other Manhattan Starbucks and contacts in dozens of stores across the country. Wobblies responded to the firing and harassment of IWW supporters with an active outreach campaign to Starbucks workers and customers, and with protests as far away as Edinburgh, Scotland. The New York City baristas have reached out not only to their fellow Starbucks workers, but also to coffee farmers – demanding that the chain increase its buying of fair trade coffee beyond the current token levels.

The New York branch has also reached out to the city's immigrant workers, working with the Make The Road by Walking workers' center in Brooklyn and launching organizing campaigns among Chinese- and Spanish-speaking workers in the city's foodstuffs industry in 2005. A continuing campaign among the 300 or so workers at online grocer FreshDirect led to an unsuccessful raid by the Teamsters; on Jan. 2, 2006, predominantly Spanish-speaking IWW members held a brief walk-out at EZ Supply in North Brooklyn, chanting "rat, rat, come out of your hole" in Chinese until the boss emerged to accept a petition for union recognition.

But while the IWW was active organizing the service industries,

Chicago bike messengers during a 2005 job action against Arrow.

IWW organizers were also working with transportation workers whose working conditions and wages had taken a beating over decades of deregulation, outsourcing and casualization. West Coast Wobblies supported a series of wildcat strikes by short-haul truckers in May 2004, launching a newsletter, *Troquero,* and web site to help drivers from different transit hubs communicate. These drivers are hired by the load to haul cargo between port and rail heads and freight terminals. Once fairly well-paid work, in the 1970s shipping companies began shifting to an independent contractor model in which drivers were required to lease or own their trucks and work by the job, shifting the costs of fuel, insurance, maintenance and slack work onto the workers. Because of cut-throat competition, pay rates have remained stagnant for more than a decade, even as costs continued to rise. The situation was brought to a head in 2004 by skyrocketing fuel prices and growing wait times. (Since the shippers don't have to pay for the truckers' time, they have little incentive to schedule the work efficiently. As a result, the port and rail heads are congested, and wait times of two hours or more are common.) Although truckers won fuel bonuses and other gains by striking, many felt the need for more permanent organization, approaching the Teamsters and the IWW. In Stockton, California, more than 200 truckers – predominantly Sikh immigrants, and about three-fourths of the workforce – who haul freight to and from the rail yards there joined the IWW beginning in August 2004. Since then, the union worked to win reinstatement for several workers banished from the rail yards, and conducted two short strikes at companies that were subjecting drivers to wait times of two hours or more. However, the difficulty of extending organization to other transport hubs and the distance from the nearest IWW branch to Stockton made it difficult to build a stable IWW branch, even if the workers involved remain determined to improve their conditions.

The IWW also launched major organizing drives among bike couriers and other messengers in Chicago and Portland. In the 1990s, London-area couriers had also formed an organizing committee, continuing a long tradition of attempts to build a grassroots organization to win better working conditions. IWW bike couriers struck Portland's Transerv in October 2002 over the dismissal of a union dispatcher, after a two-year campaign organizing the city's messenger industry that foundered on NLRB procedures, high turnover, and the inability to line up the drivers and process servers also employed by the company. The Transerv strike lasted eight days, and was quickly joined by several of the workers brought in to scab. However, managers refused to negotiate with their workers, preferring to lose clients rather than treat their workers with respect or address the company's unhealthy working conditions. While the strike was not successful, it did put other companies on notice that they needed to address workers' grievances and led to improved conditions at many shops.

Working with Portland Wobblies, the Chicago General Membership Branch developed an industry-wide organizing campaign that built union committees at several messenger firms in 2004, fought the implementation of independent contractor status by several firms, and organized job actions and short strikes that won significant improvements in wages and work conditions while enabling workers to organize on their own terms rather than on a NLRB schedule. Organizing continues in both cities, and messengers in other cities have approached the IWW to discuss the possibility of bringing the IWW to their jobs as well.

IWW members are increasingly moving beyond single-shop organizing, developing industry-wide and regional campaigns that do not rely on union recognition or contracts. In the 1990s, most IWW drives continued to focus on winning recognition and contracts in single shops, even as changes in the labor relations regime made this increasingly difficult even for business unions with far more resources than the IWW. In 2001, the union launched an organizer training program, initially in order to develop practical organizing skills that would give more members the basic skills and confidence to build viable organizing campaigns. The program, which has conducted nearly a hundred sessions across Canada and the United States, soon expanded to consider issues of organizing strategy, emphasizing the pitfalls of the NLRB and contract-centered campaigns and encouraging Wobblies to carefully examine the organizing possibilities in their area and develop campaigns where the union has the capability to establish a strong job presence and make a real difference in workers' lives.

Campaigns such as Philadelphia's South Street Workers Union, the Chicago Couriers Union or the short-haul truckers' drive are part of the IWW's experiment with "solidarity unionism,"[6] a model in which workers build an ongoing, vibrant union presence on the job, even in the early stages of organizing campaigns. In many ways a return to the IWW's roots, Wobblies continue to experiment with ways to implement this approach in practice and to develop stable union structures within a strategic orientation focused on rank-and-file initiative and shop floor struggles that sometimes seem modest but implicitly raise larger issues of workers' rights to control their workplaces.

Of course, IWW members also continue to be an active presence on union picket lines. In Detroit, the IWW branch (which included many veterans of the Detroit newspaper strike) organized a soup kitchen that became a reliable presence at picket lines and union benefits. Wobblies played an active role in the fight against sweatshops and capitalist globalization, challenging activists to build active solidarity with workers in other countries.

In November 1999, the IWW had a substantial presence in Seattle protests against the World Trade Organization, helping bridge the gap between labor delegations and the most activist contingents blockading the meeting and encouraging workers to leave the AFL-sponsored march to nowhere in favor of joining the action downtown. The next year, the IWW had contingents at protests at the Democratic and Republican conventions, distributing thousands of copies of a tabloid, *Direct Action Gets the Goods,* produced for the occasion. In April 2001, Wobblies joined the successful protests against the Free Trade Area of the Americas agreement in Quebec City; and Wobblies were among the wounded in the Miami FTAA protests three years later.

In 2002, Pittsburgh Wobs launched the "No Sweatshops Bucco" campaign, targeting the Pirates' use of scab- and sweatshop-manu- factured clothing and other logo-adorned paraphernalia. After initial arrests, the campaign (which is now independent of the IWW) won the right to leaflet at the Pittsburgh stadium, and has distributed tens of thousands of leaflets and "baseball cards" calling attention to dif- ferent facets of the sweatshop system that undergirds Major League Baseball profits. They have also worked to build ties with the sweat- shop workers, particularly in Bangladesh, demanding that the Pirates keep the work where it is but negotiate with activists and workers to improve conditions. Other actions have taken place in Milwaukee (where an IWW member was arrested distributing anti-sweatshop leaflets), Phoenix and at the Baseball Hall of Fame in Cooperstown, New York, where the Upstate NY branch continues sweatshop aware- ness outreach during the baseball tourist season.

The IWW also revived its efforts to win shorter hours, as an epidem- ic of overtime and doubling up on jobs swept the United States. The Boston GMB worked with immigrant groups and others to organize a May 2002 forum on the issue, distributed 2,500 leaflets throughout the city, and organized several follow-up meetings attended by repre- sentatives of several area unions, immigrant groups, and other groups in an effort to build a broad coalition to tackle the issue. While that coalition ultimately did not come together, in the process Wobblies were invited to speak to a number of organizations – laying the foun- dation for a 2004 initiative by the Massachusetts Council of Churches that distributed information on the problem of too much work to thousands of churches. The IWW also mounted a sustained campaign against new Labor Department regulations that stripped millions of workers of their overtime protection (though millions less than ini- tially proposed), several months before the mainstream labor move- ment took any notice of the issue. In 2003, the IWW endorsed Take Back Your Time Day, an effort by religious, social service and other organizations supporting shorter work hours, publishing thousands of copies of a special tabloid, *More Time For Life!,* in conjunction with the first TBYT Day Oct. 24. Several IWW branches held events on that day, and the *Industrial Worker* continues to publish a monthly column on shorter hours struggles.

The IWW has also continued to explore ways to function as a more international organization, simultaneously trying to build the IWW outside of North America and to build closer ties to like-minded unions around the world. In May 1986, the IWW hosted an International Labor Solidarity Conference in Chicago, commemorating the 100th anniversary of the Haymarket events and the 50th anniversary of the Spanish Revolution with a conference that drew delegates from Poland (exiled Solidarnosc), Sweden (SAC), France (FA and CFDT), South Africa (SAAWU), and Japan (RSU), along with communications of support from Spain (Coordinadora) and Venezuela. In 1990, an IWW delegation participated in an international conference of revolutionary syndicalists hosted by the SAC in Malmo, Sweden, re-establishing contact with several independent unions across Europe. The San Francisco GMB organized an international conference in 1999 that drew delegations from France, Germany, Korea and Sweden. The next year, an IWW delegation participated in a May 2000 conference organized by the CNT-F in Paris, attended primarily by European syndicalists but also by a smattering from North Africa. (A distinctive feature of that conference was a series of industrial meetings which brought together unionists from different countries to discuss common problems they faced in their industries and the possibilities for international coordination and support.) And an IWW delegation also attended a 2002 labor conference hosted by the Free Workers Union of Germany (FAU).

The IWW has also built Regional Organising Committees in Australia and the British Isles, and has maintained a small group of Wobblies in Germany for several years. Shorter-lived ROCs were set up in the 1990s in Finland, New Zealand, Russia, Poland, Sierre Leone and Finland. In Sierre Leone, hundreds of diamond miners (who had learned of the IWW as a result of outreach efforts by the British Isles ROC) signed a petition seeking IWW recognition in 1988 as part of a campaign for worker-elected checkers to bring an end to rampant cheating when their pay was calculated, but the brutal carnage of civil war quickly stamped out the nascent organization. Polish Wobblies tried to pull together activists from the fragmented Solidarnosc movement to build a rank-and-file union independent of the politicians, while the Finnish group joined several demonstrations against unemployment. However, the British ROC was the most active of these international branches, with organizing drives among London couriers, the unemployed in Oxford, staff at Stevenson College, workers

New York City IWW members picketing the Amersino grocery warehouse May 1, 2006, after the firing of two union activists. The branch is in a campaign to organize Brooklyn's foodstuffs distribution industry.

at New Milton and Hampshire Co-op stores (a large UK retail operation), pharmaceutical workers, and a social research agency, SMSR, which responded to IWW organizing by firing every worker who refused to quit the union.[7]

As the IWW celebrates its 100th anniversary it is once again an international union, but, more importantly, through its International Solidarity Commission and other outreach efforts it is re-establishing direct, grassroots contact with unionists and unions around the world, working to build the kind of global labor solidarity the IWW's founders recognized was essential 100 years ago.

The IWW is also reaching out to immigrant and other alternative workers' organizations in the United States. In June 2003, the IWW cosponsored a bilingual conference on Alternative Forms of Worker Organizing in New York City, with the participation of 150 Wobblies, activists from immigrant workers' centers, rank-and-file unionists, and others. Participants exchanged information on a wide variety of grassroots campaigns working to build workers' power on the job and through community solidarity, noting the need for approaches that escape the legal/contractual straightjacket that has reduced the mainstream labor movement to an increasingly marginalized shell. A Brooklyn-based workers center, Make the Road By Walking, that participated in that conference also sent a delegation to the IWW's June 2005 centenary conference in Chicago, discussing alternative organizing strategies with nearly 400 IWW members and other rank-and-file activists.

Today, the IWW faces a much more promising future than it did when the first two editions of this history were published. The IWW has established job control in several public service units on both coasts; recycling workers in the San Francisco Bay Area have enjoyed more than 15 years of IWW representation, and the union maintains job control in several workplaces including a satellite television network, a number of print shops, retail outlets, social service organizations, and computer software and support workers. More importantly, the union has major organizing campaigns underway under municipal transport workers in Chicago, short-haul truckers, and retail and restaurant workers in San Francisco, Madison, Ohio and Philadelphia. Spirits among the nearly 400 people who participated in the IWW's centenary conference in Chicago were high. The U.S. labor movement may be in crisis, but the IWW is on the move – looking forward to its next 100 years, and to fulfilling the promise spelled out in the Preamble to its constitution.

Notes:

1. Judi Bari, *Timber Wars* (Common Courage, 1984). The Redwood Summer Justice Project maintains a rich collection of materials on this campaign at www.judibari.org/ FBI agent Richard Held headed the Judi Bari "investigation." Earlier, he was involved in the murders of Panthers in Los Angeles; the creation of the Secret Army Organization, which was directly involved in the terrorism against the IWW in San Diego, including the shooting of one Wobbly; and the stand-off at Pine Ridge that resulted in the frame-up of American Indian Movement activist Leonard Peltier.

2. Staughton Lynd's *Lucasville: The Untold Story of a Prison Uprising* (Temple, 2004) tells the story of the tragic consequences of the failure at this and other attempts by these prisoners to redress the inhuman conditions under which they were held.

3. Twelve years later, in November 2005, the manager of the bingo parlor approached the IWW looking for help with a Hazelton, Penn., construction job he had been fired from after raising a safety beef; faced with an employer in the process of firing most of his long-term crew, the Philadelphia General Membership Branch put nine workers in touch with a labor attorney who

filed suit on their behalf for unpaid overtime and other damages.

4. The Philadelphia General Membership Branch compiled a resource guide on this campaign, *Are You Furious? Boycott Borders information packet* (1997). I discuss the solidarity campaign at greater length in "Taking on Borders," *Anarcho-Syndicalist Review* 42/43, 2005, pages 53-55.

5. The *To*Gather* newsletter and *Industrial Worker* offered extensive coverage of this campaign. A compilation of newsletters and other documents was issued by IWW headquarters in connection with national actions against ACORN in March and April 2001.

6. The term is borrowed from a book of that name by Staughton Lynd, who has generously shared his thinking on the subject with Wobblies through presentations (many reprinted in the *Industrial Worker*) and discussions at conferences and an IWW General Assembly.

7. As this volume heads to press, Scottish Wobblies are pressing Scotland's Parliament to withdraw its decision to withhold one month's pay for 14 staff employed by the Scottish Socialist Party delegation and jointly represented by the IWW and the National Union of Journalists. The pay was withheld in an attempt to punish the SSP for a Parliament-floor demonstration; the IWW is challenging it through public pressure as well as legal action.

General Sources:

Based upon accounts in the *Industrial Worker* and *General Organization Bulletin*, correspondence and conversations with participants, and oral histories in John Silvano's *Nothing in Common*.

Edinburgh Wobblies leafleting in solidarity with New York Starbucks workers, January 8, 2005.

Bibliography & Sources for IWW History

In 1955, when this book was first published, there was little reading material on the IWW readily available. The books by Brissenden, Dowell and Gambs cited in it were out of print. Growing interest in the IWW since then has led to their being reprinted (in 1957, 1970 and 1971 respectively) and to the publication of most of the articles, dissertations and books listed in the bibliographic notes that now follow the original chapter notes. The IWW's recoverable records have also been carefully archived at Wayne State University, and many of its publications preserved on microfilm. Several general accounts of the IWW have now been published, many with extensive bibliographies and documentation that this volume does not seek to duplicate. In addition, several biographies and accounts of particular strikes or IWW efforts in particular areas or industries (or with particular immigrant groups) have been published in the past 25 years, many of which greatly enrich our understanding of the union.

An annotated bibliography of books on the IWW (including general histories with substantial treatment of the IWW, biographies, and poetry and other IWW writings) compiled by Steve Kellerman in 2005 is available from the IWW. The major general English-language histories (besides this volume, in its three editions) of the IWW include:

Rebel Voices: An IWW Anthology, by Joyce L. Kornbluh. University of Michigan Press, 1964. It has been republished several times, and is currently available in an expanded 1988 paperback edition from Charles H. Kerr. It includes photos, cartoons, poems and articles from six decades of IWW periodicals, each chapter opening with an historical essay and including information on the authors quoted.

Red November, Black November: Culture and Community in the IWW, by Salvatore Salerno. State University of New York Press, 1989. This history focuses on the culture of the union, approaching its subject from the point of view of the rank and file.

The IWW: A Study of American Syndicalism, by Paul Brissenden. Columbia University Press, 1919. Reissued by Russell & Russell in 1957. Long considered the standard historical work on the IWW, taking the story up to World War I.

The Decline of the IWW, by John Gambs. Columbia University Press, 1932. Attempts to bring Brissenden's work up to 1932. Not as good or as sympathetic as Brissenden, but still useful.

Rebels of the Woods, by Robert L. Tyler. University of Oregon Press, 1967. The focus is on the northwest lumber industry to the mid-twenties, but includes general background. The book develops the author's 1953 dissertation and later articles. It is out of print, but the text is available online (see www.iww.org for links to this and other historical material).

The Industrial Workers of the World, by Philip Foner, Volume 4 of his multi-volume *History of the Labor Movement in USA.* International Publishers, 1966. Covers the period 1905-1916, making extensive use of local, labor and socialist press and of AFL correspondence regarding the IWW. There is reference to IWW activity in many later volumes of the *History* as well.

We Shall Be All, by Melvyn Dubofsky. Quadrangle Books, 1969. Reissued in a 1974 paperback edition that corrects some errors, and by University of Illinois Press (2003) in an edition abridged by Joseph McCartin that preserves all chapter headings while trimming a third of the text. The book covers the period to 1924, omitting Philadelphia, drawing heavily on material in the National Archives and from lumber company and AFL correspondence. Fred Thompson's highly critical review of the first edition appeared in the November 1969 *Industrial Worker.*

The Wobblies, by Patrick Renshaw. Doubleday, 1967. A later paperback edition includes some corrections, and was translated into Italian and Japanese. A 1999 paperback edition (Ivan R. Dee) includes a new preface, some corrections, and a somewhat more extensive bibliography. The focus is on the IWW as part of the world syndicalist movement, and it has more coverage than other histories of the IWW's trans-national activities.

Solidarity Forever: An Oral History of the IWW, by Stewart Bird, Dan Georgakas and Deborah Shaffer. Lake View Press, 1985. Transcripts of the interviews from which the film "The Wobblies" was made, containing much material left out of the film but marred by many errors in transcription.

At the Point of Production: The Local History of the IWW, edited by Joseph R. Conlin. Greenwood Press, 1981. A collection of essays on ten local IWW organizing efforts from 1912 through the 1930s.

Nothing in Common: An Oral History of IWW Strikes, 1971-1992, by John Silvano. Cedar Publishing, 1999. A short survey of IWW orga-

The Sand Point, Idaho, IWW hall was one base for the 1917 timber drive. November 26, 1916

nizing activities in the 1970s and 1980s and eight accounts of IWW strikes by the organizers who worked on them.

Paul Buhle and Nicole Schulman's *Wobblies! A Graphic History of the Industrial Workers of the World* (Verso, 2005) contains some stunning images, but can not be relied upon.

Other sources: Dione Miles' *Something in Common: An IWW Bibliography* (Wayne State Univ. Press, 1986) is an exhaustive and well-indexed bibliography of books, articles, dissertations, documents, fiction and other material on the IWW through the mid-1980s. Subsequently published material can be found through finding aids such as Dissertation Abstracts International, America: History and Life, Alternative Press Index, etc. The *Industrial Worker* publishes historical features including an overview of new work published on the union every November.

Steve Kellerman's *Annotated Bibliography of Books on the Industrial Workers of the World* (IWW, 2005) includes general histories of the union, biographical works, books including substantial treatment of the IWW, Wobbly writings, and a list of English-language novels in which the IWW plays a prominent role.

Archives: The chief earlier archives of IWW materials were those built up at the Wisconsin Historical Society and in the Labadie Collection at the University of Michigan, Ann Arbor. Most records seized by the federal government in 1917 were burned July 13, 1925, following an earlier federal court order. Cornell University has five boxes of IWW correspondence from the 1920s. There is an extensive, largely regional collection at the university library at Thunder Bay, Ontario, and the Ministry of Labour at Ottawa has extensive microfilm and printed materials. The University of Washington in Seattle has an extensive collection of documents and printed materials and the Mark Lichtman papers, some of which are on the 1933 Yakima strike. The Mary Gallagher papers at Bancroft Library, University of California Berkeley, have materials on San Pedro, 1923-1924, and on the Colorado strike, 1927-1928. At the Immigration History Research Center in Duluth are files of *Il Proletario* (1899-1946) and an extensive Finnish-language collection including *Industrialisti* and other IWW publications and the records of Work Peoples College. Dirk Hoerder's (ed.) *The Immigrant Labor Press in North America, 1840s - 1970s: An Annotated Bibliography* (Greenwood Press, 1987, three volumes) includes information on publication runs, editors and holdings for several IWW publications.

In 1965 the IWW made the Archives of Labor and Urban History at Wayne State University, Detroit, its official depository. Records from 1930 on were placed there and what could be found of earlier records, including a transcript of the big Chicago trial, in 1918, and an extensive collection of printed materials. Subsequent deposits have kept these archives up to date. Other holders of such material have been encouraged to make this collection as complete as possible, and many unpublished manuscripts and related IWW materials are held there. Since much of the material at Wayne State exists in one copy only, access is restricted under archival rules to persons with serious scholarly interest. This includes non-academic researchers, but all prospective users should contact the archives in advance.

At the National Archives there is extensive material cited by William Preston in his *Aliens and Dissenters* and by Joan Jensen in her *Price of Vigilance,* though some of this material was later withdrawn by the FBI from public accessibility. Data on disputes is mostly in conciliation files, arranged geographically. Considerable material gathered for the Commission on Industrial Relations before World War I on migratory workers but not published is available. In general, government files are to be made public within 25 years, but in 1974 when the

IWW sought access to Department of Justice papers possibly explaining why it had been put on the subversive list in 1949, it was told that this information would not be released until 2024.

The International IWW

The only general history of the IWW to devote significant attention to the IWW's international presence is Patrick Renshaw's *The Wobblies*, which devotes an 18-page postscript to a brief survey of IWW organizing in Australia, Britain, Canada, Chile, Mexico, Norway and Peru. The IWW also had administrations and branches in Argentina, Germany, Guam, New Zealand, Puerto Rico, South Africa, Sweden and Uruguay at various periods, few of which have drawn attention from historians.

There is a growing literature on the IWW in Australia, but the definitive work is Verity Burgmann, *Revolutionary Industrial Unionism: The Industrial Workers of the World in Australia* (Cambridge, 1995). Also useful are Frank Cain, *The Wobblies At War* (Spectrum, 1994), which focuses on IWW opposition to conscription and the subsequent government repression, and Ian Turner's *Sydney's Burning* (Alpha, 1967), which focuses on the frame-up trials. Monty Millers' *Eureka and Beyond* (Lone Hand, 1988) is a collection of autobiographical writings about the "Grand Old Man of Australian Labour," taking his story from the 1854 Eureka Stockade to the show trial of IWW leaders in 1916 in which FW Miller, at age 85, was a principal defendant. E.C. Fry, ed., *Tom Barker and the IWW* (Australian Society for the Study of Labour History, 1965) is an oral history focusing on his Australian years.

Lucian van der Walt's "A History of the IWW in South Africa" (part of a larger study available at www.anarchist-studies.org/article/author/view/18; also see his "The Influence of the IWW in Southern Africa," *Anarcho-Syndicalist Review* #42-43, Winter 2005-2006) sees the IWW as central to the story of South African labor; John Phillips, "The South African Wobblies: The Origins of Industrial Unions in South Africa" (*Ufahuma* 8[3], 1976) is an earlier account focusing on the IWW's effort to build a multi-racial union under colonial occupation.

Norman Caulfield's *Mexican Workers and the State: From the Porfiriato to NAFTA* (Texas Christian University Press, 1998) offers the most comprehensive treatment of IWW organizing in Mexico available in English. See also, Troy Fuller, "Our Cause is Your Cause: The Relationship Between the I.W.W. and the Partido Liberal Mexicano

Australian IWW leader Viola Wilkins speaking at a mass meeting in Perth, August or September 1939.

(M.A. Thesis, University of Calgary, 1997); and Dan LaBotz, "Slackers: American War Resisters and Communists in Mexico" (Ph.D. Dissertation, University of Cincinnati, 1998).

Peter DeShazo's *Urban Workers and Labor Unions in Chile 1902-1927* (Univ. of Wisconsin Press, 1983) in its many scattered references offers the most extensive discussion of the IWW's Chilean administration available in English. IWW organizing in Argentina is touched upon in Goffroy de Laforcade, "A Laboratory of Argentine Labor Movements: Dockworkers, Mariners and the Contours of Class Identity in the Port of Buenos Aires (Yale Univ., Ph.D. Dissertation, 2001).

Many histories treat the Canadian IWW as part of their broader discussion. Book-length treatments include Mark Leier's *Where the Fraser River Flows* (New Star, 1990) and Jack Scott's *Plunderbund and Proletariat* (New Star, 1975). In 1975, the IWW published a short survey by Gary Jewel, *The IWW in Canada*.

Wayne Thorpe reviews the IWW's international relations in "The IWW and the Search for an International Policy, 1905-1935," *Anarcho-Syndicalist Review* #42-43, Winter 2005.

Index

The Walsenburg, Colorado, IWW hall after it was shot up by state police, 1928.

Also available from the IWW

The IWW distributes a wide variety of literature and other material about IWW history and the history of the labor movement more generally, an annual labor history calendar, IWW decals for hard hats, t-shirts and baseball caps, and IWW music. A catalog is available on request, many items are listed at www.iww.org/en/store, and the *Industrial Worker* regularly publishes notices of newly available titles.

Little Red Songbook: New edition of the IWW's classic songbook, containing classic and modern labor songs suitable for singing on a picket line near you. $7.

1923 IWW Songbook: Reprint of 1923 edition of Little Red Songbook. $5.

Arguments for a 4-Hour Day: Jon Bekken's pamphlet reviews statistics showing that shorter hours are both practical and urgently necessary. 16 pages, $2.50.

Whatever Happened to the 8-Hour Day? Arthur J. Miller's hour-by-hour chronicle of the effect of forced overtime on our bodies and our planet. 16 pages, $2.50.

Rebel Voices: An IWW Anthology edited by Joyce Kornbluh. Excerpts Wobbly poems, pamphlets, cartoons, stories and songs. 446 pages, $24.

Joe Hill: The IWW & the Making of a Revolutionary Workingclass Counterculture by Franklin Rosemont. A journey into Wobbly culture. 639 pp., $20.

Starving Amidst Too Much and Other IWW Writings on the Food Industry edited by Peter Rachleff. Four classic IWW texts. 128 pages, $12.

Oil, Wheat & Wobblies: The IWW in Oklahoma 1905-1930 by Nigel Sellars. One of the best local histories of the IWW, 320 pages, $12, hardcover.

Bread & Roses by Bruce Watson. New history of Lawrence strike. $12, hard.

Slaughter in Serene: The Columbine Coal Strike Reader, $19.05, paper.

Big Trouble by J. Anthony Lukas. Monumental history of the Haywood-Moyer-Pettibone frame-up trial and the struggles that led to it. 873 pages, $12, hardcover.

Industrial Worker: Subscriptions to the IWW's monthly paper are $15 a year.

IWW Patch: A 3" embroidered patch in black, red, white and gold. $3.50.

IWW Baseball Cap: Black cap with embroidered IWW logo. $15.

Rebel Voices: 20 IWW songs by Wobbly musicians. CD, $15.

We Have Fed You All for a Thousand Years: IWW songs, Utah Phillips. $15.

To Fan the Flames of Discontent: Jack Herranen & the Ninth Ward Conspiracy's soulful celebration of IWW song with a New Orleans flavor. CD, $12.

IWW Posters: Pyramid of Capitalist System, Don't Scab, $9.50 each. Ben Fletcher, Joe Hill, Lucy Parsons posters by Carlos Cortez, Frank Little poster, $7.50 each.

IWW Solidarity Forever Calendar. Annual labor history wall calendar, $10.

Add $2 for first item ($3 to Canada; $4 overseas) for shipping, and 50 cents for each additional item. IWW Literature Dept., PO Box 42777, Philadelphia PA 19101.